W9-COL-696

The
Competitive
Archer

The
Competitive
Archer

Simon Needham

THE CROWOOD PRESS

First published in 2013 by
The Crowood Press Ltd
Ramsbury, Marlborough
Wiltshire SN8 2HR

www.crowood.com

British Library Cataloguing-in-Publication Data
A catalogue record for this book is available from the British Library.

ISBN 978 1 84797 482 2

Typeset by Jean Cussons Typesetting, Diss, Norfolk

Printed and bound in India by Replika Press Pvt Ltd

CONTENTS

INTRODUCTION

Since the publication of *Archery – The Art of Repetition*, many archers have been complimentary about the book but have then asked a question such as 'How do you get the best bracing height?' It then transpires that they have not read it all, but skipped over some vital portions. I would recommend reading the entire book: once you know the available content you will be able to reference it fully as and when required.

The other odd question that seems to crop up is 'Is there a better way of doing it?' There may be other ways of achieving comparable results, but the information given is the way I approach the problem and is the best I can give from the experience I have gained over the years.

Archery – The Art of Repetition was written to help non-archers become archers and to help archers become better archers. I believe it was successful in this but still the question keeps arising: 'How do I get better still? I want to represent my country at the Olympics.' When The Crowood Press asked if there might be enough material for another book for those wanting more from their archery, I put together a proposal for *The Competitive Archer*.

This book should be seen as the competition supplement to *Archery – The Art of Repetition* and should be used as such. It particularly covers how to go about succeeding in archery, but the methods of achieving success are the same for every activity and should be used in everything you do to help achieve your goals.

CHAPTER 1

CRITICAL POINTS

There will be certain points in your life that lead you to where you are today. At the time they may have seemed innocuous but nonetheless they are enough to change the direction of your life. This chapter gives a brief outline of how I arrived at this point in my archery and some of the critical turning points that led me here.

I am now fifty-two years old. I left school at eighteen and joined the Royal Marine Commandos, with whom I served for twenty-two years and rose to the rank of Colour Sergeant. I then became a full-time lottery-funded athlete for four years. From 2004 I was employed as a technician at Montrose Academy, working ten hours a week, and worked full-time from September 2010.

I have been shooting since I was seven or eight as archery was offered as a weekend activity at Mount House School, the boarding school I attended. When I was twelve the 11th Gosport Scout group started doing archery and I had another go as I had shot before. This time I bought my own bow, a 36lb recurve fibreglass bow with victory arrows. With

Archery practise at Ballykelly airfield, Northern Ireland, in 1979.

Glamis Castle shoot, 2012.

Critical point 1. Success at the Banchory shoot was really down to the years of shooting I had done prior to it, but it was important in that it convinced me that I was good at this sport. Your first experience with anything you try is important: initial success leads to a perception that you can do it. I have always had a sense that I am 'lucky', although I am not certain where this initially came from. By looking for luck I think I have become luckier because of it, and respond to comments such as 'You're lucky, you shoot well' by replying 'The more I practise the luckier I get'. Starting every new venture with good planning ensures that the initial impression is good and this increases the chances of success. With a new bow, for example, take time to set it up properly, with a good initial arrow position, stabilized and balanced properly prior to shooting. The first arrow shot out of it will then give a lasting impression that the bow is great. When I received my BMG I shot 359 at 30m within two hours of shooting the first arrow out of it, but be aware it takes a lot of practice to be able to set up a bow properly in two hours.

my friend James Downing I made my first archery training presentation with a slide and tape sequence to help new archers in the Scouts. In 1979, during a year-long tour of duty in Northern Ireland with 40 Commando Royal Marines, I bought a Border bow, a Forest Knight, and shot on the airfield in Ballykelly. After the Falklands in 1982, I had saved enough money to buy a Yamaha YTSL II with all the Yamaha accessories. I shot with Alton Archers and then when I moved to Plymouth, shot with 'Bowmen of the Tors'. For me this was a good social activity and enabled me to meet people that were not military. I think I shot one outdoor competition over this period. I did make the Devon 'B' team for the indoor league, which I was very pleased with at the time.

When I was drafted to RM Condor, Arbroath, Scotland in 1982 I joined the Lochside bowmen in Forfar, which was a good club, keen on competitions. At that time, however, I was still looking at archery as a social pastime and stopped shooting for a few years apart from getting the bow out occasionally to shoot on the airfield at the base.

In 1988 45 Commando RM was on spearhead duties, which meant that we had to be on four hours'

notice to go anywhere in the world. This in effect meant that we could not go far from the camp. Over the years I had enquired about an archery club in Arbroath, but there did not seem to be one. One of the workshops' store men, though, was interested in archery and had found Links Archers, a club in Montrose. It seemed a good idea to see what the club was like, so I turned up on a motorbike that promptly broke down when I got there. After joining in for the club session I then had to push the bike twelve miles back to Arbroath, but it seemed like a good friendly club and so I joined.

I was still shooting my YTSL II; it was a 70in bow and I had a 26in draw length (to the button). I had decided back in 1982 that a 70in bow would give me a smoother draw, which I suppose was true enough. Keith, the club coach, showed us how to make strings and this led on to the subject of nocking points. I then thought that if I lowered the nocking point slightly, the arrow would go further.

Up to this time I liked shooting but enjoyed the chat. It seemed that competitions would be good for more chatting and socializing with a picnic at lunch. I wrongly thought you had to pass some sort of shooting test to enter, but all I had to do was say that I wanted to go and pay the entry fee.

My first competition was an American round at Castle Fraser. I was not too surprised when I won as I was shooting reasonably well at the time. The next competition I entered was a FITA Star at Banchory. On the first day I shot around 850, mainly due to my billowing white shirt. It went much better after borrowing a chest guard and I shot 1113 on the

Critical point 2. Words make a difference. Mental reinforcement only works if the words are sincere and have an element of truth. Words work just as well in the negative as the positive. Words used by associates can make a huge difference to an athlete. An offhand comment by a 'friend' can eat negatively into someone's confidence, while an insincere false positive reinforcement can be just as bad. In thought, word and deed, comments should give strength and belief to the area that is being worked on, the thoughts of the individual (their 'self talk'). It is working on why you can do something that 'enables' you to realize those thoughts.

Sunday, so claiming my 1100 Star. (I never did get my 1000 Star.)

This was the first pivotal point in my shooting. I had been put on a target with some of the top archers in Scotland and held my own at 30m. I had not previously thought of myself as a sportsman and was surprised by the congratulations of the club archers at my second-day score. Something seemed to 'click' and I thought that I might be able to do well at this. Here was a sport that relied on the individual and their equipment. Any variation in score levels was down to the individual. This suited me as my past experience of football and other team games had not been too successful.

In 1989 I was still shooting the YTSL II and decided that I needed better arrows. I was using X7s, which I had bought the year before to upgrade from the XX75's that I had bought with the bow. I upgraded to Beman (carbon tube) arrows but had a lot of bother tuning them. I was going to quite a few

Simon Needham til topps i bueskyting

HT — Asbjørn Hjelvik

Engelskmannen Simom Needham vant lørdagens bueskytterstevne i Harstadhallen med 1107 poeng. Et absolutt bra resultat. Det var bare Kvæfjords Trond Reidar Andreassen som bød han skikkelig konkurranse, men måtte til slutt gi tapt med sju poeng.

— Jo jeg er fornøyd, men kan bedre enn dette, sier Needham som aldri tidligere har konkurrert over dobbelt program. Han har skutt 563 av 600 oppnåelige i enkelt program.

Trond Reidar ledet

Trond Reidar Andreassen ledet etter 60 piler med ti poeng på engelskmannen, men ga fra seg ledelsen i begynnelsen av andre runde og tapte jevnt mot slutten. 1100 poeng er slett ikke noe dårlig resultat selv om Kvæfjord-bueskytteren flere ganger har skutt mer.

Opp i A-klassen

Det beste resultatet sto nok 16 år gamle Tor Inge Bøe for ved å skyte 1086 poeng og dermed tpk han steget opp i A-klassen. For å gjøre det kreves 1070 poeng. Harstad-gutten Tor Inge sto forøvrig for litt av en prestasjon da han for 14 dager siden slo samtlige konkurrenter i Kiruna i forbindelse med en finaleskyting.

— Jo, dette er jeg meget godt fornøyd med, sier Tor Inge Bøe til Harstad Tidende. I Kiruna

Trond Reidar Andreassen, Kvæfjord (til venstre) og Tor Inge Bøe, Harstad måtte bare innse at engelskmannen Simon Needham ble for sterk i bueskytterstevnet i Harstadhallen.(Foto: Asbjørn Hjelvik)

skjøt han meget sterke 556 poeng på halvt program.

NM og NNM

Nær står store utfordringer for tur for bueskytterne. 17. mars går nordnorsk mesterskap i Bodø av stabelen og 14 dager senere, 31. mars , er det klart for NM i Stav.

anger. Her stilles det ikke minst forventninger til Tor Inge Bøe. Mange mener at han kan ta hjem medalje i sin årsklasse.

Fremgang

Det deltok 47 bueskyttere i Harstadhallen, noe eom er bedre

enn på lenge, men det er ennå et stykke til bueskyttersporten er tilbake der man var for noen år siden da det var vanlig med 80-90 deltakere. — Men det er positive tegn. Vi er i ferd med å få frem en del unge skyttere, sier det.

Winning shoot in Norway with YTSL II.

Critical point 3. Your approach to any situation that is not under your control defines your future. Control the controllables. As my hopes of promotion were curtailed and outside my control, I determined that I would focus on the sport in which I believed I could succeed. You can only change what is going to happen to you. What's done is done and there is no point in dwelling on the past. Learn from your experiences so that it can help you shape your future as you desire. You might not get it all, but it will help you get most of it.

competitions and would camp at the venues to save money. The first competition with my new Bemans was at Greenock, just outside Glasgow. I was on the target with George King and I told him that I was unhappy with the tuning. He suggested I tuned as I shot. I was so engrossed in adjusting the button that I was distracted from the scoring and ended up beating George, much to his chagrin. What I had not realized, being new to the competitive side of the sport, was that it was between the two of us as to who would take third place and represent Scotland later on in the month. On this occasion he ended up as reserve. Even after I shot a personal best at 30m of 330, it felt odd that this competition was the first

shoot for a year at which I had not won anything, apart from the place on the team. The other thing I took from this shoot was George's observation that I always shot the short metric very well, which was mainly because we were somewhat lazy at the club and did not put the bosses up much over 50m most of the time. His comment, though, has come to mind at many a shoot and bolstered my shooting of the short metric, serving as a good example of realistic positive re-enforcement.

Later in the year, at the Scottish championships at Haggs Road, we had to explain to Tiny Reniers, who had come over to shoot a York, the approximate metric equivalent of 100yds, 80yds and 60yds. He asked Alan Cook from our club what colour nocks was he using. We were surprised that he had three sets of arrows with him. In those days I would change nocks on my ten arrows: little did I think that in a few years' time I would be the one with three or four sets of arrows in my case.

Although shooting was going well, I was in the Marines and looking for promotion. I had completed my senior command course (for Sergeant) and in 1990 went on a six-month VM 1 (Vehicle Mechanic) course at SEME Bordon in Hampshire. After this I was hoping for promotion before moving on to an Artificers course that would lead to becoming a

Alison Rhodius taking a session with the Scottish squad.

Dr Alison Rhodius, 2012.

Warrant Officer. This seemed a good plan, but in the military you cannot start a course without an appropriate return of service, which for an Artificers course is six years. I knew that I would need promotion shortly after the course at Bordon if I were to become senior enough to do the Artificers course. Any delay would mean that I would not get the course or promotion to Warrant Officer. As luck would have it (a double-sided coin), the other three on the course were senior to me and there

Critical point 4. The opportunity offered to Alison Pope changed the direction of her life as well as mine. Perhaps a different student accompanying Dr Cripps would not have sparked my interest in psychology at this time. Almost certainly Dr Alison Rhodius would not be the expert she is in the field of archery.

Critical point 5. From my introduction to mental management, I came to realize that significant adjustments to ways of thinking would help me succeed in anything I tried. The key to mental management is the absolute belief and understanding that it works. Finding that belief opens the door to using the tools you have been given. Much of what holds you back lies in your way of thinking and this can be addressed. For me the door was opened by a short talk from Alf Davis and his enthusiasm, combined with Jay Barrs's video presentation of *The Mental Game*.

were only three spots for promotion coming up in the near future. Even though we all passed, this meant there would be no immediate promotion for me. Since the next due date for promotion was in two years' time, I would not be a sergeant long enough to get the course and have return of service for Warrant Officer. It was a big disappointment, so I decided to make the best of my options and put my efforts into archery instead of a career. I requested a draft back to Scotland so I could continue shooting and compete for a place in the Scottish team again. Before then, though, a six-month draft to Plymouth included a three-month deployment to Gul, Norway, for winter training. I had been contemplating buying a Yamaha EX, but instead waited for the Eolla to come out and bought a red and purple one with the ceramic limbs. I figured that if I was going to work at archery I would give myself the best equipment to work with.

I now knew a bit more about tuning and bow selection and bought a 68in bow, with long riser medium limbs. I also bought my own string jig and changed from making strings from Kevlar string material, which required a new string for every 1,000 arrows shot, to using Fastflight. At this time I had to make a new string every month.

I moved back to Scotland in 1991 to take up duties with 3 Advanced Workshop Detachment Commando Logistic Regiment. I decided that I would give it a year of working hard at the shooting. If I was better, I would give it another year. If not, well, I was sure I would find something else to do.

At the end of the season I had made the top ten in Scotland and won an invitation to the Scottish

In front of the Olympic Stadium, Sydney, with Alison and Team.

squad, which was run on a new training format by Peter Willerton. He determined that the top archers in Scotland collectively knew a reasonable amount about the sport and wanted to give us the 'other' things that would help us compete: physical fitness, mental tools and nutrition for sport. For the mental side he brought in Dr Barry Cripps, who introduced us to Dr Alison Rhodius (then Alison Pope). Alison was great to work with on the mental game. I found this aspect of the squads especially interesting and realized that this was the key to success.

Despite not being an archer or coach, Alison has become one of the world's leading experts in the mental side of archery and is a Professor in Sport Psychology at John F. Kennedy University in California:

I started out in archery by chance. I didn't set out to work in this amazing sport. Dr Barry Cripps made a presentation at the British Psychological Society annual conference in 1992 and then asked if anyone would like to get some experience in an internship with the British archery team. I, of course, jumped at the chance. I worked closely with Barry Cripps for the next few years. I attended all the training events at Lilleshall training centre in Shropshire, sat in on all individual and team sessions and learned a lot from Barry. I also travelled up to Scotland for a few years to work with the Scottish squad in Largs. I had a great time up there and loved the camaraderie that the squad embodied.

After a few years, Barry retired from the sport and I took over as the Sport Psychologist for the GB squads (juniors and seniors). Those years working with the elite archers were fantastic. I learned so much from everyone and I was grateful for the opportunity. It was hard to stop the work with this group, but I took a lot from our interactions and still keep in contact with many of the British archers today (Simon being one of those!).

In 2000 I finished my PhD in Sport Psychology and within days had emigrated to California with my English husband, Virgil. Since then I have become a professor in Sport Psychology at

Critical point 6. By the time I made the British squad I felt I had made advances in setting up and tuning my bow. At the squad I accepted the offer of having my bow tuned. After some fiddling I was informed that it was now better, even though my arrow group size was bigger and my bow appeared to be pointing at the next target. On the long drive home I thought over all the aspects of bow tuning and set-up from a mechanical point of view. Halfway I stopped off for a quick coffee with Jim Buchanan and began to regale him with my findings. Three hours later I left to continue my deliberations on the rest of the drive. This greatly improved my understanding of bow set-up and the dynamics of the shot, which led me to revisit bow tuning and enabled me to set up and tune my bow better.

Critical point 7. No matter how good you are or what your shooting potential may be, everything depends on the support you receive. Are you able to get the equipment you need and still have the funds to get to competitions? This does not have to be the newest equipment, but it does have to be of a sufficient quality to allow you to compete. Especially with youngsters, it is the support of parents and family that determines the level they will achieve in their endeavours. Quicks Archery has supported me for the last twenty years. The Marines allowed me the time to go to events and the money for travel within the UK, which meant I could get to all the competitions I needed to. WO1 Nigel Barrett made sure that for the final run-up to the Olympics I could train full-time and ensured I had a six-month extension so that during the Games I was not concerned about future employment. Lottery funding enabled me to afford extra equipment so that I could trial and test it while identifying what was best for my shooting. It bought my first set of X10s, which allowed me to judge whether they would raise my scores at 70m (and they did).

Critical point 8. Training time is critical for performance. Ray Criche once told me that he could hold his own in the rankings over the year, but he fell behind in shoot-offs. Later he found out that the other archers took time out from work to increase training time prior to selection. For me the run-up to the Olympics was two-and-a-half years of balancing work and training with just the last nine months shooting full-time. This is where planning comes in, enabling you to achieve a good groundwork of shot execution within compressed training times. This helps you peak for your chosen events. Barring injuries, shooting five or six days a week, with one rest day, and an average count of 1,000 arrows, or equivalent, per week is the minimum you need for success.

JFK University in the San Francisco Bay Area and am currently the Interim Chair of the department. Despite a busy academic life, my work in archery continued once I got to the US because of good connections I had made. Alison Williamson, my longest-term client, introduced me to Don Rabska who recommended me to the US team. I worked with them for a few years and went with them to the 2004 Olympic Games in Athens. That same year, I worked with the team from India and travelled out there to work with them twice. One of the most interesting trips was when my services were combined with USA, India and Alison Williamson in a tournament in Italy. During the Games itself, I worked solely with the US teams and Alison, not the team from India.

Since the Games I have continued to do some work in archery, directly with some archers and run workshops for coaches. This past January [2012] I took one of my students, Fernando Lopez, to present with me to archery coaches at the USOC in Colorado Springs. They loved his work and he is now working with members of the US women's archery squad. I really feel like I have come full circle and am grateful for all the opportunities that came from the sport of archery.

For the 1992 squads Richard Priestman was asked to give advice on performance. He brought in Alf Davis, who had just started a course on neuro-linguistic programming (NLP), to give us an introduction to the fascinating subject and demonstrate how the mental tools used for sport could be employed in everyday life, empowering you to succeed. In simple terms, NLP provides a means of examining the very best in a given profession and seeing how these traits can be copied elsewhere.

It was at these squads and summer shoots that I came to know Jim Buchanan, a great mentor in the sport, and John Low, who also took a deep interest in Alf's talk. John was also keen on competing, so we decided to venture over the border to events in England.

In Scotland we were both usually towards the top of the leader boards at competitions. Going south of the border had two immediate results: we found ourselves lower down the leader board and wanted to be higher, and because we were shooting with or near more experienced archers we could take advantage of the knowledge that was gener-ally freely given at events. One time, for example, I overheard Jon Shales, a top British archer I then knew only by reputation, talking about why he had put a weight on the bottom of the riser to stop it jumping around. Thanks, it worked for me.

Although I was competing against others, for me it was all about improving my shooting. I had no thoughts of the British team or the Olympics: that seemed to be for others and did not concern me. Over the next few years my average scores went up from 1200 to 1220, and then to 1245. When I was offered promotion to Sergeant in 1993 I asked for it to be delayed as the first two drafts were to

With Alan Wills, Larry Godfrey and Roy Nash, winning the team silver medal at the 2004 European Championships.

the south of England. This was frowned upon, but I knew that a draft was coming up in Scotland and if I could get this it would ensure that I could stay and shoot in Scotland. Not only would this enable me to compete for my adopted country, but the shooting ground for Links Archers was available twenty-four hours a day and this would be a key point in training for competitions.

I was picked for the British squad for winter training in 1996. This led to being selected for a European Grand Prix in Turkey, a great introduction to international competition. Even at this point I was still not thinking about the Olympics, but the Marines were now helping with my travel expenses within the UK. I was also selected for Scottish Lottery funding. Early in 1998 I had an inkling that, with a concerted training regime, I might have a chance at the Sydney Olympics in just over two years' time. From then on all my spare time was spent training, which meant that my work in running the workshops of 45 Commando had to be efficient to ensure there was time to train. From November 1999 the Marines allocated me to the 'Sergeants' mess', enabling me to train full-time for nine months up to the Olympics.

Although I was due to leave the Marines in July 2000 after twenty-two years of service, I was kept on for an extra six months, so I was still a serving member during the Olympics in August 2000. For me the Olympics went well: I came ninth in the seeding round, which at the time was during the event, and seventeenth overall. My pass was the third highest on the board for that round and was a personal best, a good place to have one. Although disappointed at being knocked out, I had shot better than I had ever done in competition before. The extra six months in the services would have given me time to go on educational vocational training courses towards another career after the services, but I decided that my world ranking gave me a chance of making the top twenty in the world. Instead of taking time out to do the courses I carried on training.

Second place in an event in Cuba gave me enough points to make a top twenty ranking and led to UK lottery funding that allowed me to train full-time. By the end of 2001 I had secured seventh place at the world championships in China and twelfth in the world rankings. Although I was one of the silver medal-winning team at the 2004 European championships, with Roy Nash, Larry Godfrey and Alan Wills, funding ceased as I did not secure an Olympic place for that year. I chose to work ten hours a week as a technician at Montrose Academy to supplement my forces pension. This provided enough money to get by and still give me plenty of time to train as far as the 2010 Commonwealth Games in Delhi.

Between 1996 and October 2010 I trained at least five days a week. The diary I kept of all my shooting activities for every day in that period, in numerous forms, shows that I shot on average more than 1,000 arrows a week (780,000 arrows). The longest spell without shooting or training was three consecutive weeks after the Olympics. All holidays were taken for shooting events. I have represented Great Britain on fifty-four occasions and Scotland on sixty-two: my mantra for this was 'Archery First'.

You will find that getting what you want from life sometimes means having to take a calculated risk. Taking delayed promotion could have gone against me, as could turning down the opportunity to retrain for a civilian job. My friends Nick and Isobel Evans are examples of how a risk can pay off. They run a bed and breakfast in the south of France, canoe in the canal outside, are keen cyclists and spend the winters as ski instructors in Andorra. Isobel tells their story:

> In the early 1990s we were both working in London. We loved skiing but couldn't afford enough ski holidays. Nick's job with the police allowed for an unpaid career break, holding all pension and seniority rights. We decided to take a break of two-and-a-half years to 'get it out of the system' rather than wait until we retired, when we had no idea how fit we would be.
>
> Initially we planned to return after three winter seasons of running chalets and looking after campsites in the summer. We decided that we would like to continue with this way of life and considered buying an Alpine property, but very quickly realized we didn't have enough capital. Spending all our time in France, we looked into buying something to provide a business for the summer season so we could continue skiing in the winter. At no point did we feel we wanted to run away from the UK. We moved away because

there was something more exciting we wanted to do – and who knows, we may yet return.

In 2000, after selling our house in Sevenoaks, we purchased Les Volets Bleus in Sallèles d'Aude, near Narbonne, in partnership with Nick's brother, and set up a successful bed and breakfast business. Nick and I continue to work winter seasons as ski instructors in Andorra.

The plus factor is that you are working for yourself; the minus factor is that you are working for yourself. There is no holiday pay, sick pay or other corporate benefits. But it does mean that, if you are brave enough, you can just say 'We're closed today'.

It has been exciting and scary creating a business from scratch. My administrative background in accountancy and office skills has obviously been very useful, as has our mixture of people skills, fluent French, wine knowledge and practical experience. The downside is marketing and publicity, which we find challenging. And the French authorities are every bit as difficult to deal with as everyone says – but then even the French agree.

What does the future hold? A long haul to retirement and bits and pieces of a pension from the UK, France and Andorra, but at the moment we feel we'd rather be poor in the south of France.

Good things: living in the south of France; climate; lovely food (great fruit and veg) and affordable wine. Great cycling. Skiing all winter. Friendly social life in Andorra. Staying fit. Meeting lots of nice people, summer and winter.

Bad things: being too busy to get out and do things; not having much of a social life in France (we work too many evenings), plus everything closes down for the summer, which is when we are here. The worry of being ill or injured and not being able to work. The uncertainty of the tourist trade.

The purpose of this book is to give you as much information as I can to allow you to make the best of your time and help plan the way forward in your archery. I have travelled the world with this sport and made many friends. If just one line here helps towards putting you on the world stage of archery and winning a medal at any event, then I will be pleased that all the time devoted to it has been worthwhile.

CHAPTER 2

DETERMINING YOUR GOALS

The setting of 'great' goals is the key to being successful in everything that you undertake:

> Many people fail in life, not for lack of ability or brains or even courage, but simply because they have never organized their energies around a goal.
> Elbert Hubbard

I find that setting goals, and planning to achieve them, is fairly easy for me. With the right motivation, setting out to do something is easy to plan. I do most of the planning in my head and find that this, for me, requires little or no written lists.

In 1983 I was asked if I wanted to run a marathon. I wasn't keen. My then boss pointed out that I was reasonably fast on the regular Wednesday afternoon run, but there was a good reason: we started the run at 3pm and when we finished we could go home. The faster you ran, the sooner you were finished for the day. After a few drinks, however, I was eventually persuaded to take part. We had six weeks to train. We ran most afternoons, anything from four to thirteen miles, working up to six-minute miles, finishing for the day when we had completed the running. I ended up completing the marathon in 3 hours 46 minutes, although walking was a bit tricky for a couple of days afterwards.

I thought I would like to maintain that level of fitness and went for a run a few days later. About halfway around the 3-mile course I decided to walk back. I just didn't have the motivation.

For archery it was easy: I liked shooting and I wanted to shoot better. At Scottish and, later, British squads I pieced together good practice methods for training by talking and listening to both British and foreign athletes, and incorporated them into my training plans. These were recorded in my diaries. When asked by various squads to submit plans for the forthcoming month it was easy as I had already planned everything in my head. I plotted on a year planner the competitions that I wanted to enter, starting with the ones that would lead to qualifying for events. I pencilled in the events that I hoped to be selected for and the shoot-offs to get to those events. These would include major events in the coming years, such as the Olympics, four years ahead, and World and European championships every second year. This was about all I would commit to paper.

Working with people over the years I have found that the amount of paperwork required differs from person to person. Some need a detailed plan for every hour of every day, with alternatives planned to cover changes in the weather and venues. Others require very little written down and the rest can be anywhere in between. How your mind processes information will determine the level of paperwork necessary to achieve your goals and therefore dictate your progress.

To start with it is better to make a detailed plan of your goals and how you are going to achieve them. Once you have established a good training routine you may find that you are able to reduce the amount of written planning and still progress towards your goals. Finding the right balance between time spent planning to ensure you do the training and doing the actual training will take some effort.

Outlined below is a plan for setting your goals and planning how to achieve them, based on the thought processes I use. In this book the goal setting is orientated towards achieving in archery, although it will naturally take in other aspects of your life. The same techniques can be used for achieving anything you set your mind to.

Setting Goals

The three determining factors for the outcome of achieving those goals are:

- Setting an ultimate goal for all your endeavours, providing a path to the very top of all you are trying to achieve.
- Setting the priority now in your life to achieve those goals.
- Time available.

It is the priority you give to each of these that will help determine how far you get. As time passes so will the priority you have given to each. They may well change, as will the list of your goals.

Many of you may have come across the acronym SMART in goal setting. Various words have been applied to the concept, such as:

S specific, significant, stretching
M measurable, meaningful, motivational
A agreed upon, attainable, achievable, acceptable, action-orientated
R realistic, relevant, reasonable, rewarding, results-orientated
T time-based, timely, tangible, trackable

The acronym can be used well as part of your goals-setting programme, but if you are not careful it can negate your dream. Are the Olympics, for example, a realistic goal to an archer who is now trying out for an area team?

Goal setting must include the dream for all your desires. The priority you give to all your different desires will determine which you will follow towards the top. The limiting factors will then only be your own potential in each chosen area of endeavour and the amount of time you can, or want, to allocate to it.

This chapter will supply a template to work from to help you get to the top of your game in your shooting, increasing the number of arrows you shoot into the middle. For this we will describe the 'Sport goal' of Olympic archery as the subject for the setting of this goal. Once you understand a method for setting a goal and prioritizing it, it becomes quicker and easier to work out steps to your dreams and aspirations in every aspect of your life.

Olympic Goal

Most of you will have started archery as a hobby or a pastime. You may well have had a go at a 'come and try' or participated at a holiday venue. However

you started archery, it is unlikely you did so with the idea that the outcome would be to represent your country.

It tends to be on the lines of: start shooting; enjoy shooting; and then being persuaded to go to competitions or go to them because you want something to do at the weekends.

There will come a point when you feel you want more from shooting. It might be that you want to make your club or county team, or you find you are getting close to selection for your country and need more than your club can offer.

The issue will be that until this point you will have been participating in archery as a hobby. Some will never make the transition from hobby archer to athlete on their own. This is not because they don't want to, but because they do not have a method of determining a path to success.

In considering what you want to achieve from your shooting, you should lay out the steps to be used to help with the transition to sportsman or woman. Success in anything is determined by goal setting: with a good structure of goal setting in place all the other requirements necessary for success will fall into place. Goal setting is not enough on its own, though, as it requires two other main ingredients: priority of desire for your goals and time allocation.

Goal = What do you want from life?
Priority of desire = How much do you want it?
Time allocation = How much time are you prepared to give towards it?

Goals – What Do You Want from Life?

'Goal' seems to be a widely used word that some people use consciously without fully thinking about what it means to them, while using it exclusively in the context of their sport or a single activity. Others want good things in life and will strive towards them but do not think of them as goals. My interpretation of goals is that they determine what you really want. These pertain to all aspects of my life, not only to sport.

[Archers] need to have clear goals set and ask themselves what is their reason for wanting to be a top competitive archer. Some archers are doing it for the wrong reason. They can't realistically achieve the goals, either with the amount of time to train or their ability to travel.

Matthew Gray

When managing multiple desires, I need to rationalize them and ensure that I allocate a priority and time to the separate areas: work, money, holidays, friends, activities, sports, house, clothes, happiness, possessions and so on. Analysing the priority allocated to the different desires ensures that what I most want to happen is given the highest priority. This gives it a better chance of occurring. It goes hand in hand with how much time I have and am willing to put into it. When my funding finished as soon as I did not make the 2004 Olympics at the European qualifying shoot-off, I decided that I wanted to keep archery as my highest priority. I knew that to have a chance at the 2008 Olympics I would need most of my time for training. To that end I took a part-time job in a local school for ten hours a week to supplement my pension from the Royal Marines. That still left me with sufficient time for the training necessary if I were to have a chance of rejoining the Olympic team in four years' time.

As I have suggested, goal setting can be used in all aspects of your life. As a means of understanding this method of setting goals, the construction of

a goal-setting pyramid will help you to realize the priorities in your life and allow you to make the most of it with fewer regrets.

The goal setting for this book, of course, relates to archery. It is a model that can be used for anything you wish to achieve.

The best way to start requires a friend, a pen and a pad of Post-its. As you think of goals and the steps towards them, you can put each on an individual Post-it, making it easier to arrange your thoughts and the order of your goals. If possible you should sit down with someone who knows you well, someone you trust and can chat with comfortably about your goals. The person need not be from your sport. Talking to someone from outside the sport ensures that they are not biased by what they have seen within it and can view your aspirations more clearly. Discussing your dreams and hopes with them can help as a check and balance on what you think you want to achieve. Verbalizing a hope to someone else opens up the opportunity of it coming true because it changes from a thought to a deed. Once it is written down it enters into the reality of it possibly happening. This is partly due to the fact that hearing, writing and seeing what you have written uses more areas of your brain, providing a better insight of what you are trying to achieve.

Making a Goal Pyramid

An ideal model for determining what you want is a Goal Pyramid. The boxes on the left of the pyramid show the steps to your ultimate goal, the blocks across the bottom indicate the amount of time you are willing to spend on trying to achieve those goals.

The first step is to determine what will be your ultimate goal. If this is to be world champion, an Olympic gold medallist or the best in the world, it may seem so far from your present ability as to be just a fantasy or it may indeed be close to your current hopes and aspirations. It is very important at this point to come up with an ultimate goal that will be the pinnacle of what you are trying to achieve. In my opinion, you should choose aspiring to be the 'best in the world'. If your ambition is simply to win an Olympic gold medal you will not necessarily be the best in the world and there will be other competitions that you may not win.

Put your goals in order, adding other scores and goals to give attainable steps. KAREN HENDERSON

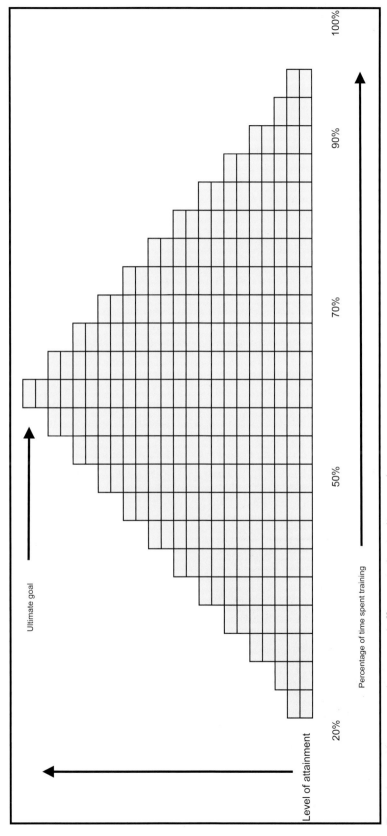

Level of attainment

Ultimate goal

20%   50%   70%   90%   100%

Percentage of time spent training

The goal pyramid represents the steps and effort required to reach your goals.

The ultimate goal you choose will be placed on top of your pyramid. Discussing this helps to ensure that you have found the right goal at the top.

> I had been to the talks, read the books, watched the movie and worked out by myself that my goal was to be a 'world-class athlete', which I then became. The error with my goal was that I had become a world-class athlete, but not really winning anything! I had not chosen the correct ultimate goal, so I changed it to a goal of 'Being the best archer in the world.'
>
> Simon Needham, 1999

It is true I did not achieve this, but it did not hamper me from being the best I could be, achieving 7th at the 2001 world championships and 12th in the world rankings. It also allowed me to attain results above those of a world-class athlete. At this point in life your ultimate goal may seem to be an out and out dream. You might only want to make the area team, a valid aspiration, but this is your opportunity to fantasize about what could be.

Next is to determine the steps (short- and medium-term goals) leading from your present status to your ultimate goal. These Post-its should be placed under the ultimate goal on the left side of the pyramid. With your ultimate goal in place, this becomes easier to work out. The Post-it at the bottom left of the pyramid stands for where you are now in the sport. Above this place others indicating reasonable steps of attainment. It is entirely up to you how many steps you include, but the transition between goals needs to be realistic.

One suggestion is to construct an initial pyramid with just scores down the left-hand side. If you are scoring 1224 for a FITA, for example, it would be unrealistic to put 1300 as your next step. Moving up to 1250 points, an increment of just 26 points, on the other hand, is a realistic challenge as when you break it down it is only an increase of 6 or 7 points per distance, or an extra point per end.

The pyramid can easily be started by using scores to give you the steps to success. You will notice that as the scores get higher the score increments in the pyramid will get less. A 1200 shooter may well put 30 points on their average score, but a 1320 shooter is less likely to improve with a step of 30 points. Although using scores will provide a fairly good structure to your pyramid, leaving them in the primary position on the left side of the pyramid will tend to channel you into concentrating just on scores, which can be detrimental to your progress.

One suggestion is to work the FITA Star awards system into your steps. On its own, however, this is not really enough because it would give you steps of 100 points and you will need to add achievements inbetween. Many countries have achievement levels. In the UK we have Bowman, Master Bowman and Grand Master Bowman. These can also be included in the construction of your pyramid and it is sometimes better to work on achievement rather than a score, for example making your club, county, area or country team.

This will be an organic pyramid to which layers can be added as you get used to working with it. You will also find that when using a combination of goal varieties some of them will coincide. If placed on the same level, these can be used as markers that can be ticked off as you achieve them. This will fill the levels of the pyramid, giving more depth and purpose to your goals.

The realization of these goals will, to a greater extent, be determined by the amount of time you are willing or able to dedicate to your goals and desires. The base of the pyramid contains a scale of the time and effort you are willing to commit, starting at the left and increasing to a level determined by the base of your pyramid. The highest number indicates that 100 per cent of your time is to be available to spend on archery; it does not mean you spend twenty-four hours a day on archery.

With this example you can see the steps that are required to get to your ultimate goal. How far you climb the steps to success will depend on how much time you are willing or able to commit.

Use the Post-its to lay out the basis of your pyramid. If you are a club archer wanting to make the area team, you only need to construct the pyramid from where you are now to your immediate goal, and perhaps allow the next couple of steps above that. You do not have to construct all the levels leading up to the top. You still put your dream/ultimate goal in place and then add to your pyramid as you approach the immediate goal of area team. This means you can keep adding to the levels as you go along.

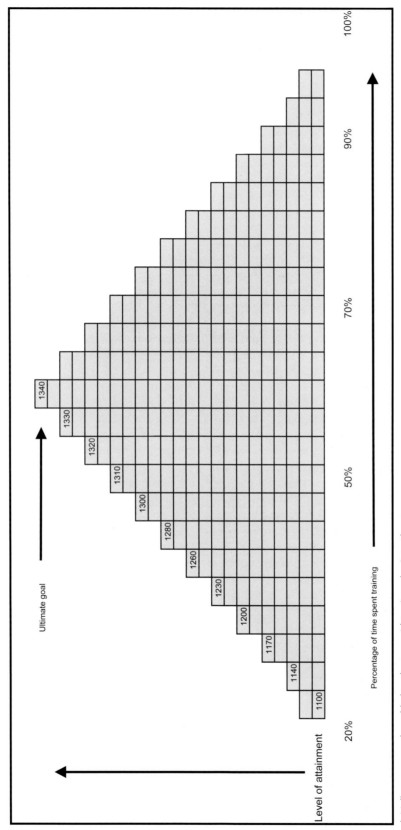

Level of attainment

Ultimate goal

1340
1330
1320
1310
1300
1280
1260
1230
1200
1170
1140
1100

20%   50%   70%   90%   100%

Percentage of time spent training

Initially scores can be added to the pyramid to give a basis to the steps.

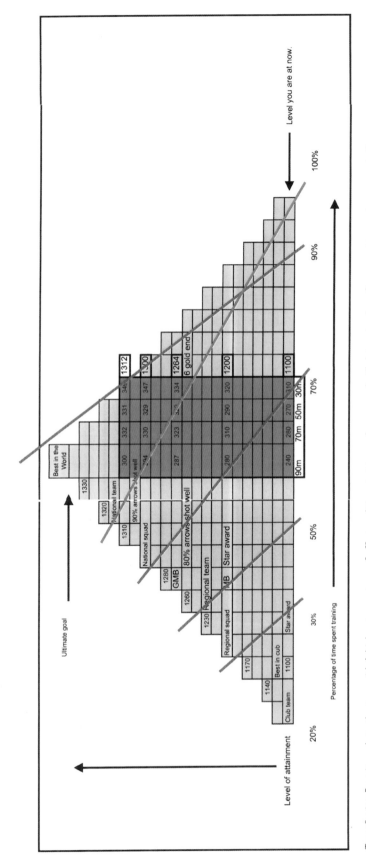

Transferring Post-it goals to the pyramid. A higher percentage of effort and time put towards your goal will determine how far you get towards your goals. Be aware that 100 per cent effort does not always lead to you achieving 100 per cent of your goals.

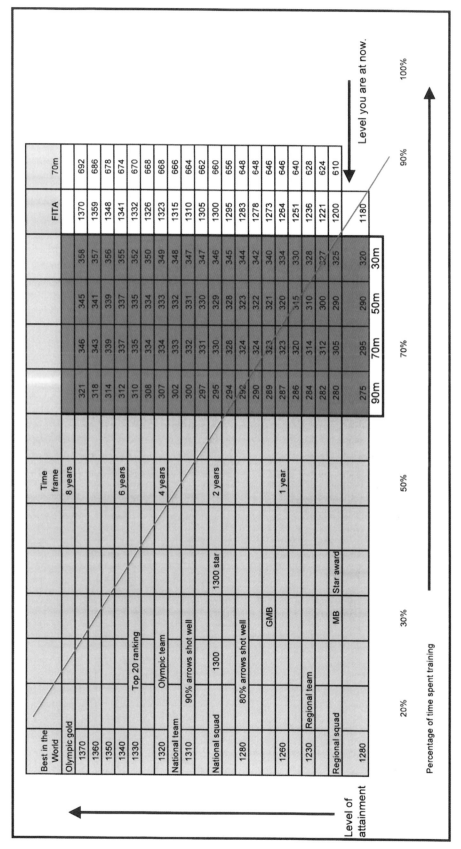

With your ultimate goal in place, initially you only need to fill a couple of layers above where you are now. The levels above become more apparent as you work up the pyramid.

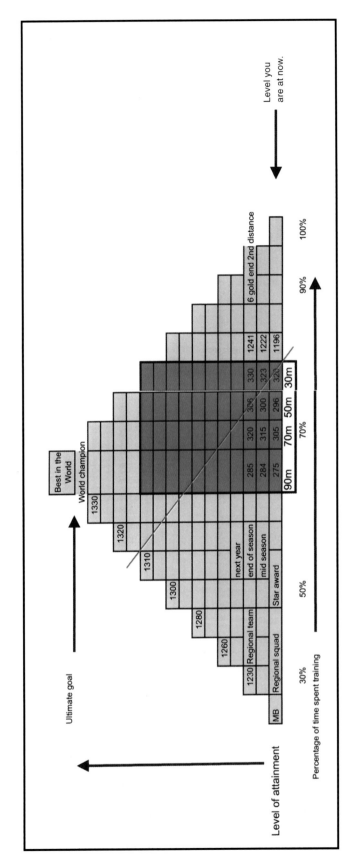

In reality the pyramid is a list of levels on a spreadsheet, although I still perceive it as an actual pyramid.

Once you have your basic pyramid plan laid out, you can either turn it into a poster to put on the wall or transfer the information to a spreadsheet and print it out. Putting your goal pyramid on a wall where you can easily see it helps to remind you what you are trying to achieve. Tick off your achievements as you start to climb the steps, keeping track of all your goals from when you start. This ensures that you have a visible account of your successes. The act of ticking off your achievements is a tangible positive reinforcement and gives you the satisfaction of recounting how you are progressing.

Life Goals

Setting sport goals does not take into account the other aspects of your life, such as work, housing, food, family, holidays and transport. Goals should be set in the same way for every aspect of your life. This will enable you to apportion time in such a way that you can achieve a level sufficient to support you in your shooting. To achieve the goal of archery you will need money, transport and somewhere to live.

Deciding Your Priorities

No matter how much you plan for your goal, it is the significance that you place on it that will help determine your willingness to work towards it.

Many archers have said, 'You are so lucky to have gone to the Olympics. I would love to do that.' They genuinely seem to think that luck has a lot to do with it. It appears, however, that they do not want to put more time towards their shooting. So many other things are stopping them from doing any more than possibly two sessions a week at the club: resting after work, going to the pub, playing with the kids, lunch with the in-laws – the list is endless.

If you wish to achieve more from your shooting you need to strengthen your determination to succeed by determining which of all your goals in life and sport have the highest priority.

For some the order will be family first, job second and archery third. By deciding what you want from life you will be better placed to apportion your time and effort. If you want to make the Olympics, your family will need to be kept informed of your intentions, as will your work, which pays the bills to

Stick your goal pyramid on the wall or a pin board so that you can see where you are, ticking off the achievements as you reach them.

allow you to compete. This is where time becomes a factor. To reach the top you will need to apportion most of your time to shooting. As a rule of thumb, to be the best in the world the minimum you will need to shoot is one thousand arrows a week. It takes approximately one hour to shoot fifty arrows, so that means twenty hours a week. Do not get too caught up in the number of hours required, however, as Chapter 3 is all about making the best of your time.

If family and work do not allow sufficient time at the moment, you can still strive towards your potential with the time you currently have available. As time passes you may well be able to apportion more time towards you goals.

Having decided that sport is to take priority, you may need to increase your desire to work towards that goal above all else. In the days when I was improving from 110th in the UK rankings to 15th, I enjoyed competing and wanted to see how far I could go with it. When I realized that I was close to making the British team I started to change the way I thought. 'Archery First' became the first consideration in all that I did. If there were a choice between shooting or going to the pub, going to a party, going on holiday or watching television, shooting won every time.

To help give emotional weight to your desires, you need to put together a list of what attracts you to your ultimate goal. This will enable you to put into perspective how much you want this and the weight of desire needed to reach your goal.

I would suggest that winning the gold medal is not enough on its own. International athletes have suggested many attractions that go with the commitment to shooting better:

- Shopping around the world
- Appearing on television
- Travelling the world
- Free clothing from the Olympics
- Wanting to be the best
- Having a good party after the events
- The kudos it brings
- Flying on different airlines
- Meeting friends at events
- Beating other archers
- Enjoying shooting arrows
- Perfecting the shot
- Competing on the world stage at major events
- Breaking records

Making a list of what attracts you will help highlight why you practise every day, driving you to do better. Lanny Bassham, author of *With Winning in Mind: The Mental Management System* (3rd edition, 2011), labels this 'Pay Value'. The more it means to you personally, the more likely you are to do something about it.

Allocating Time

As you work through setting goals and deciding their individual priorities within the time you have available, it will be much easier for you to decide how much time you have for working towards your goals. This will give you a

Putting together a chart that enables you to plot all the hours of the day gives you something to work from.

	0:30	1:00	1:30	2:00	2:30	3:00	3:30	4:00	4:30	5:00	5:30	6:00	6:30	7:00	7:30	8:00	8:30	9:00	9:30	10:00	10:30	11:00	11:30
Monday																							
Tuesday																							
Wednesday																							
Thursday																							
Friday																							
Saturday																							
Sunday																							

	12:30	13:00	13:30	14:00	14:30	15:00	15:30	16:00	16:30	17:00	17:30	18:00	18:30	19:00	19:30	20:00	20:30	21:00	21:30	22:00	22:30	23:00	23:30
Monday																							
Tuesday																							
Wednesday																							
Thursday																							
Friday																							
Saturday																							
Sunday																							

Time allocated to sleep

Time allocated for work

By blocking in the time that you have to allocate for work and sleep, you can then fit a training schedule into what remains.

good idea of how far you will get towards them.

Once you have considered all your goals in life and decided their relative importance, you can now apportion time to them. The easiest way is to make a weekly chart on a spreadsheet, dividing each day into forty-eight segments of half an hour.

First block in what you have to do on each of the days. If you have to go to work, you should allow for travel there and back. Most people will count their hours from the start to the finish of the working day. Lunch and breaks, though, can be your time and are free for you to use.

When looked at this way it can be surprising how much time you have available. It is up to you to decide the propor- tion of this you want to allocate towards your shooting. The next step is to block in the time you currently spend shooting, then see where you can fit in further training.

When I was in the Royal Marines, I usually worked my lunch hours to make sure I was on top of my work and did not have to stay late. I also kept a bow at work that I could use to do reversals or, if I had made time, I might go for a run in my lunch hour. I would get home from work, make a sandwich, go to the field and shoot until it grew dark, go home, cook something to eat, then go to bed.

Chapter 3 details ways of making the best of the free time you have available. It is for you to decide how much of your spare time you wish to apportion to your sport.

Week 1	Morning	Lunch	Evening		
Monday	Run 40 min	Reversals 30 min	70m 10 arrow ends (approx 250 Arrows)		
Tuesday	Cycle 10 miles		90m 70m 10 arrow ends (approx 200 arrows)		
Wednesday	Run 40 min	Reversals 30 min	30m 50m double face 12 arrow ends (approx 300)		
Thursday	Cycle 10 miles	Reversals 30 min	70m double face 6 and 4 scoring the 6 arrows (approx 200)		
Friday	Run 40 min	Check fletches	50m double face 4 and 6 scoring the 6 arrows (approx 250)	1500 arrows	
Saturday	Fita star Banchory		Travel home		
Sunday	Fita star Banchory		Travel home		300 scoring

Week 2	Morning	Lunch	Evening	
Monday	Run 40 min	Reversals 30 min	90m 10 arrow ends (180 arrows)	
Tuesday	Cycle 10 miles	Reversals 30 min	70m 10 arrow ends eyes closed for first half (150 arrows)	
Wednesday	Run 40 min		50m 12 arrow ends double face 6 at each score 2nd six (200 arrows)	
Thursday	Cycle 10 miles		30m check tune - 6 arrow ends scoring (150)	
Friday	Run 40 min		evening off	
Saturday	Lie in		70m practice 9 arrow ends scoring total every 4 ends. (200 arrows)	
Sunday	Lie in		Hill walking - Equipment maintainance make strings	1100 arrows

Week 3	Morning	Lunch	Evening		
Monday	Run 40 min		Long metric practice 9 arrow ends (200)		
Tuesday	Cycle 10 miles		Short metric practice 9 arrow ends (250)		
Wednesday	Run 40 min	Check fletches	All distances, 9 arrow end at each distance and move - check record sight positions (150 arrows)		
Thursday	Cycle 10 miles	Check fletches	Practice at distance that needs polishing finish at 90m leave sight set (150 arrows)		
Friday		Pack car	Travel to Glasgow	750 arrows	
Saturday	Scottish champs				
Sunday	Scottish champs				300 scoring

The three-week training plot is a rolling outline of training to cover the next three weeks. During week l you will be projecting what you will be doing in week 4, three weeks away.

Achieving Your Goals

It does not matter what goals you put in place, achieving them requires detailed planning and a system to do so. Be like Baldrick from 'Blackadder'. Always have a cunning plan. This should cover not only how you are going to achieve your goals, but how to tackle situations that may distract you from reaching them.

With the steps of your goals laid out and a fair idea of what time you have available, it is easier to make plans as a logical sequence of achievable steps becomes apparent. Breaking the steps down into single plans is too simple a way of looking at it. The plans you put in place will overlap both in their depth and their reach. The depth is the variation of tasks you undertake in your planning. The reach of the various tasks you plan to carry out will also vary. Both will be dependent on how much time you have available. More time will allow you to carry out more tasks on a daily basis and for longer. Picking the right tasks and allotting them the right amount of time is the key to successful results.

Selecting an 'Aim'

To start with you need to come up with an 'Aim' for what you are trying to achieve. This will serve as an underlying theme that you can remember and use to reinforce your endeavours throughout all your future training, no matter what level you reach. This needs to be a short phrase that reminds you of what your planning is trying to achieve through the steps or goals laid out on your pyramid. 'My aim is to improve the consistency of my shooting, both physically and mentally' is a bit of a mouthful, but the idea is on the right lines. I settled for 'Improve the percentage of good shots executed during all my shooting'.

Having a good aim gives purpose and direction to your training. You should ensure that the tasks you choose to carry out are consistent with your aim and that their performance ensures focus on that session.

Keeping a good aim in mind while working on all areas of your archery will help you to improve without limiting you. As you carry out your planning,

thinking about your aim helps clarify the direction and value of the plan.

Planning

Planning involves considering all aspects of your life and adjusting them for the better. Neuro-linguistic Programming (NLP) indicates three steps to successful planning:

1. Come up with a plan
2. Carry out your plan
3. Evaluate your plan. Carry on with it if it works, adding any improvements. If it is not working, change the plan.

Planning involves deciding what tasks need to be done to improve your shooting and how much of your available time will be spent on those tasks.

Each task, such as shooting, needs to have a purpose that works towards your aim and your current goals. Going to shoot four times a week for three hours gives you your location and the amount of time spent there. What you plan to do there is the vital piece that some archers fail to realize. This detailed task is the key point that gives the improvement you are looking for. Your detailed planning should cover at least three weeks ahead. A three-week running plan enables you to ensure that all the planned tasks complement each other and together build towards your goal. The detailed planning for the next 'third' week should be completed at the end of your first week, ensuring that you always have a clear idea of what you are going to be doing for the next three weeks.

By plotting your competitions on a year planner you can determine which events are most important to the advancement of your shooting. Some will be there because you have to be a member of a team; others will be because it is a good venue with a higher probability of getting a score that advances you up your goal pyramid. With this in mind, set your three-week cycles to culminate on the high-priority competitions.

Your planning needs to include:

• Increasing practice times and frequency
• Making the best of those practice times

- Planning what you will do at each practice, and a possible alternative
- Fitness
- Nutrition

Earlier, when discussing laying out a goal pyramid, I gave the example of increasing your score from averaging 1224 to more than 1250. Start by breaking down the total score to distances (90m – 280; 70m – 310; 50m – 304; 30m – 330), then down to dozens and finally to individual ends. Although it seems that you only need to add one point to each end over all the distances, greater improvements in overall score levels are significantly increased by working on improving your scores for the longer distances.

Looking at the score pattern I would suggest mainly working on 90m and 50m. The scores for 70m and 50m should be comparable, with 50m being a little lower this time, and I would want to see an improvement in this area. In mainly working at 90m and 50m in your training, 70m and 30m will also show some improvement but will still need some work.

Shooting around 1,000 arrows a week is central to my planning. Practising over longer distances means more walking and less shooting. This means that during the weeks I am working on the longer distances my shooting time will need to be increased. In order to keep the arrow count up to the intended level it may be necessary to do less cardio training that week, substituting short-range 3m shooting.

Increasing your scores at the longest distances may not be just about shooting and improving consistency. It may also require adjustments to your equipment. This would mean adjusting fletches, position, angle, size and manufacturer, and plotting the differences to identify improvements. Time will also need to be set aside for these changes.

Looking down the main range of the Links Archers indoor facility.

I was once asked by Martin Eubank, the British squad psychologist, how often I thought about archery each day. It was easier to tell him when I did not think about archery. It's a sign of a good film if it can distract me from thinking about archery.

When I woke in the morning, I would be thinking about what I would be doing for the day. Opening the curtains and seeing the weather would enable me to think about the shoot training for the day. I found that running in the morning gave me a better feel for what the weather would bring and whether I would have to modify my training accordingly. I would always have alternative plans.

If I had planned to go to the indoor shooting range (up to 70m) to shoot 50m, ten arrow ends, first twenty arrow warm-ups, then scoring each end out of 100, for 250 arrows, I might find other archers there practising shooting six arrow ends. The alternative would be to shoot 70m at their pace, then when they finish carry on at ten arrow ends at 50m.

Most of the time I would be thinking about future events and how past events went, selecting the best bits and rehearsing how I was going to shoot, and looking at where I could improve my consistency. It was like searching out the best path for improvement, constantly thinking about what I would be doing for the next three weeks. As shoots finished I would revisit the best moments and look at where improvements could be made.

At any time in your training, if you are asked what you are doing, you should be able to give a clear account of that session and what you are planning to do for the rest of the session. Plans can be modified and changed during a session to make the most of what you are doing. It might be that as you are shooting you feel the bow is not shooting well. Stop and check the tuning. There is no point in sticking to a plan just because it is what you started with. At the same time, though, if you plan to score ten arrow ends and it is not going well, dig in and make it as best you can. If you can do that in practice you have a better chance in competitions.

How Much Writing Is Required?

I would suggest that the best way of finding how much written work you really need to do for setting goals, priorities, time allocation and planning is to start with everything. Once you have constructed an hour chart for your standard week, you will probably not need to do it again, but it will set you up for fitting in the tasks to improve your archery. Many archers will not want to go into such detail, but those who do will tend to advance quicker and further. As you get used to the thought process of planning and reaching goals, you may find that less needs to be put on paper. If you are unable to give a clear account of what you are doing over the next three weeks, you are not writing enough.

> My favourite quote is 'If you don't know where you are going, any road will take you there'. It comes from a book by Al Henderson. To me it means that, without goals to direct you, it does not matter what you do, you will still wander aimlessly and be unable to realize your dreams.
>
> Jon Shales

MAKING THE BEST OF YOUR TIME

Everyone's circumstances are different and so are the demands on their time. This chapter is about making the best of the time that you have available during the day and the week. It is not just about using the waking hours when you are not working, but exploiting the whole day to your best advantage in order to give yourself the opportunity for success. Making the best of your time falls into two categories: apportioning all the time you have during the day most effectively; and using that available time for the most effective training.

On a Royal Marines base we worked a fairly normal daily routine much like any job, although when the workload permitted we were able to use Wednesday afternoons for sport. On deployment abroad or exercises at home, I was able to adopt training plans that ranged from shooting in the workshops, once the work was done for the day, to reversals every day for two months on my knees, as the cabin roof was too low to allow me to carry them out standing up. Moving into a position running 45 Commando workshops brought more responsibility but with fewer deployments, which left weekends free to compete. By being more efficient and carrying out all of my duties in 'work' time, I was better able to regulate my free time for practice and competitions.

Once I became a full-time athlete, I did not have to work. This left every day for training and competing. For five years I had to ensure that I kept focused on training and had a good practice structure in place, otherwise it would be too easy to leave things to later the same day or the next. This was a great time, as I was able to spend as much time as I wanted trying out different training regimes and tuning methods.

I then took part-time employment, working to provide enough money to get to competitions, but ensuring that I had plenty of training time.

Apportioning Time

In Chapter 2 I suggested putting together a table showing all the hours available to you in your week. If you are determined to succeed you will need to fill this in now. However much you feel this is a mundane exercise, it will give you a far better insight into your available time. This model will only have to be carried out once or until your circumstances change, for example with a new job. It apportions your time into two areas. 'Fixed' time applies to when you have to be doing certain things, like sleeping and working. 'Flexible' time describes what you have left to carry out your training.

Fixed Time

Sleep is the main area you can block out on the chart to start with. However little sleep you can get by with in everyday life, to compete at the highest level you need to have sufficient sleep to keep you at your best. One or two early nights prior to an event to try and catch up on sleep are not enough. Sleep is a peculiar thing. It's not like eating: eat too much and you get fat. Tiredness can be likened to a glass of water: while awake the level of water in the glass drops, when you sleep it fills back up again. What you are doing during the day will have an effect on how much the level drops. Without enough sleep the glass is not refilled fully, so by the end of the day the glass has less in it than the day before. As nights go by with insufficient sleep the level in the glass drops further and it takes more than one good night's sleep to refill the glass fully. It is better to keep the glass filled by the end of every night. Trying to sleep longer than you need does not make you fitter. Once you have filled your glass, extra sleep just makes it overflow; it does not fill the glass further. Sleep cannot be saved up and

The level of sleep deficit increases as the week progresses.
FRANCES KEATS

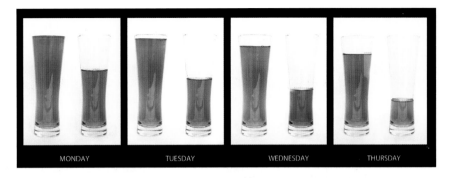

After going out on Friday night and having a lie-in on Saturday, and additional sleep on Saturday and Sunday nights, you can still start the following week with a deficit of sleep.
FRANCES KEATS

banked for later. If during the week you are half an hour short of sleep every night, by Friday you could be two-and-a-half hours short. Two extra hours of sleep over the weekend still leaves you half an hour short at the start of the next week. In the long term you are better off making sure you have that extra half an hour every day.

Good sleep patterns can also make it easier to sleep in strange surroundings and being fully rested before travelling through time zones can make the transition easier. Making a routine prior to sleep every day at home can act as a trigger to help induce sleep when you are away, giving you a better chance of sleeping and getting the rest you require. This might involve putting a scent such as lavender on your pillow or taking a shower with a lavender-scented body wash every night. You can listen to music tracks conducive to relaxing as you go to sleep. This can also help if you are troubled by noise when you are away, as it will help to mask it. Reading is a favourite with many as a prelude to sleep, as is sex, given the right company.

Working out the amount of sleep you require will take some trials before you get it right. Some years before I started competing I found that nine hours was about right for me. A general recom-mendation is that 97 per cent of adults need between seven-and-a-half and nine hours of sleep a night. Sleep follows patterns and rhythms that generally follow a ninety-minute cycle. Waking at the end of a cycle can leave you better rested than waking halfway through it. At the end of a cycle you will be close to waking, whereas half-way through you will be coming out of deeper sleep. So waking after seven-and-a half hours can leave you better rested than after eight-and-a-half hours.

You may be sleep deprived if you:

- Need an alarm clock in order to wake up on time
- Rely on the snooze button
- Have a hard time getting out of bed in the morn-ing
- Feel sluggish in the afternoon
- Get sleepy in meetings, lectures, or warm rooms
- Get drowsy after heavy meals or when driving
- Need to nap to get through the day
- Fall asleep while watching TV or relaxing in the evening
- Feel the need to sleep in on weekends
- Fall asleep within five minutes of going to bed

While it may seem like losing sleep is not going to affect you much and you can get by with it, sleep deprivation has a wide range of negative effects that go way beyond daytime drowsiness:

- Fatigue, lethargy, and lack of motivation
- Moodiness and irritability
- Reduced creativity and problem-solving skills
- Inability to cope with stress
- Concentration and memory problems
- Impaired motor skills and increased risk of accidents
- Difficulty making decisions

A further list of negative effects are due to chronic lack of sleep:

- Reduced immunity; frequent colds and infections
- Weight gain
- Increased risk of diabetes, heart disease and other health problems

These effects will become more apparent the more deprived you are of sleep. None of them, at any level, is conducive to sport at the highest level.

Having a regulated sleep pattern helps ensure that you are always at your best. The other quirk with sleep, or the lack of it, is that its effects seem to skip a day. A poor night's sleep on Friday night will have more of an effect on Sunday, even though you sleep well on Saturday night. Knowing more about sleep patterns will help with planning travel so that you are at your peak for the key elements of the event, either getting there early so you can be rested beforehand or coming in at the last minute and performing before you are affected.

This is why sleep should be the first consideration in planning your week.

Work/Time You Have to Take

If you need to work you should block in the times spent working and travelling there and back. For those able to shoot full-time, there may be appointments you have to keep with physiotherapists, coaches or funding bodies. This sets out the time that you have to use. Most of those working should have a lunch hour that could be used in various ways towards improving your shooting, such as going out

for a walk or carrying out reversals. You may be able to use the time to refletch arrows, so ensuring that time after work can be used for shooting and not for maintenance. If you are working on flexitime you may be able to extend your lunch to allow time to swim, run or go to the gym. Taking an extra half-hour for lunch will reduce the time you have in the evenings, but your time may well be better spent with this adjustment. Others, due to their workload or type of work, may find it beneficial to work on, lunching as you go. I did this while in the Marines, making sure that my work was done during the day. This meant taking 'working' coffee and lunch breaks to ensure that everything was completed during the time allocated for work, leaving the evenings free. Becoming more proficient at work ensures that overtime is kept to a minimum. A responsible work ethic can make it easier to approach your firm for additional time off for major events so it does not interfere with your training and practice times.

Flexible Time

Having marked out the fixed time that you need to use during the week, what remains is 'flexible' time for you to use for training as you see fit.

Shooting Time

My first consideration is always for shooting time. I will set aside enough time to be able to shoot 1,000 to 1,500 arrows a week or the equivalent. Having shot for many years and talked to many top archers, this is the quantity you should consider shooting. It takes approximately one month or 1,000 arrows to incorporate changes into your technique. If you can incorporate 1,000 arrows a week into your training plan you will progress four times quicker than an individual relying on time-based training to incorporate changes into their technique. Ideally having all day, every day to pursue your archery would be the very best for your shooting. You would then always have enough time to shoot the required quantity of arrows at whatever distances you felt would benefit you the most, while taking as long as you wanted to carry it out.

Unfortunately this will not be possible for many of you owing to the limited time you have available, either through work or education. It is the detailed planning of what you want to achieve in your training that will determine the routines you need to plan.

It is at your longer distances that you will probably need to put in the most work to give you the highest increases in score levels, but practising the longer distances will always require more time than the shorter distances – maybe more time than you have available – to shoot the same quantity of arrows and maintain your arrow count.

Limited Time, Maximum Arrows

To maintain your weekly arrow count and give yourself enough time to practise at longer distances, you need to adopt training practices that enable you to sustain your arrow count during the limited time you have available. The shortest practice that gives maximum benefit for recurve shooters would be to carry out reversals every day: 30 minutes of reversals at 30 seconds up, 30 seconds down, at approximately 2lb over your normal draw weight, is equivalent to shooting 180 arrows. Over a week this would give you the equivalent of shooting 1,260 within just three-and-a-half hours. Reversals are a good supplement for limited shooting time, but there is no substitute for shooting arrows. Reversals can also be made use of by compounds, although they would have to get hold of a recurve to carry them out. The most impressive advocate of this is Chris Marsh, who spent a year working in the USA, carrying out reversals every day, and still shot 1260 when he returned to the UK.

Short-distance shooting (3–5m) is the next best way to keep your arrow count up. Setting up a short range within the house or garage enables you to make better use of limited time as none is wasted travelling to a shooting venue. I have an 80cm boss set up in the house so I am able to shoot whenever I am unable or do not have the time to get to the club. An 80cm boss will last longer as you can spread your groups around more than on a smaller one and you can easily shoot the centre out of a smaller boss. Neil Wakelin (Great Britain Compound Team, 1995–2008) set up a permanent short range in his garage that allowed him to practise all the angles for distances, with additional smaller bosses for practising more extreme angles. To compensate for the short distance, he produced scaled-down faces to ensure that he could practise with the correct sight picture. If it is not possible to set up a range at home, short-range practice at your club will still enable you to maintain a reasonable arrow count. When the club is busy you need to be able to set up a boss where you can shoot and collect at your own pace. Obviously shooting the shorter competing distances and higher volume ends (8–15 arrow ends) will enable you to shoot more arrows in the time available, as you have to allow for walking further when shooting the longer distances. Compressing some of your shooting time will provide more quality time for the longer distances. Getting the balance of time allocation to the various training distances will enable you to give quality time to every part of

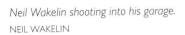
Neil Wakelin shooting into his garage.
NEIL WAKELIN

Even with limited space a boss can be set up in the house.
KAREN HENDERSON

are best for this, running for about forty minutes or cycling for a bit of variety. This equates to four miles running and ten miles on the bike. I prefer running as it requires no extra gear and running the streets and beaches in my area is free and quicker to complete. Going to a gym or sports centre can take longer and you may well find that the equipment you want to use is already in use. Running from home, including showering, you can be finished within an hour; at a gym this could take half an hour longer. A benefit of running in the morning is that you get a feel for what the weather is doing. This helps you to rehearse what you are going to do in the evening's shooting session. Another benefit is that you have the rest of the day to recuperate prior to a shooting session. When I was a full-time athlete I would run in the mornings during the summer months. In the winter, though, I had the time to go to the local gym when it was quiet. That left me the rest of the morning to sort out my equipment and ensure I had a reasonable recovery time before shooting all afternoon.

Once you have plotted out and accustomed yourself to a working and training routine, it becomes far easier to take part in activities outside archery. You will be able to adjust your training venues and durations to take time out for social events on your calendar. You may not always catch up on missed training times, but it is usually possible to adjust your training to ensure that you carry out the arrow count you have set for the week.

> I use a timetable to manage my time for family, work, training and social.
>
> Matthew Gray

Although you have now put together an average week, changes can be made depending on the events you have planned to go to and the distances you want to prioritize in your practices. You may need to do more work, and plan for a little less sleep, a month before a major event in order to ensure that the three-week run up to the event has the right amount of training time and sleep to give you the best opportunity to perform well. In working out your training plan, you will also find it easier to allow an evening or day off to work out where you will make up the arrows missed during that training week.

your training. Although the quantities of arrows shot are used to monitor your practice and training, you must ensure that these are quality arrows. It can be easy to fall into the quantity mindset and just thrash out numbers of arrows.

With your shooting time blocked in you can see what time is left for other activities.

Other Activities

Although time will have to be allowed for kit maintenance, some of this can be carried out at the field between ends.

Activities that help to enhance performance and health can be a matter of individual choice. After shooting itself, I found that cardiovascular activity came next on my list of things to help my shooting. This can take many forms. Running provides the maximum gain for the time taken, as long as you are fit enough and it can be fitted into your day when you have the time. I have found that the mornings

	0:30	1:00	1:30	2:00	2:30	3:00	3:30	4:00	4:30	5:00	5:30	6:00	6:30	7:00	7:30	8:00	8:30	9:00	9:30	10:00	10:30	11:00	11:30	12:00
Monday														Run	40 min									
Tuesday															Cycle	10 miles								
Wednesday														Run	40 min									
Thursday															Cycle	10 miles								
Friday														Run	40 min									
Saturday																								
Sunday																								

	12:30	13:00	13:30	14:00	14:30	15:00	15:30	16:00	16:30	17:00	17:30	18:00	18:30	19:00	19:30	20:00	20:30	21:00	21:30	22:00	22:30	23:00	23:30	0:00
Monday		reversals										70m 10 arrow ends (approx 250 Arrows)												
Tuesday												90m 70m 10 arrow ends (approx 200 arrows)												
Wednesday		reversals										30m 50m double face 12 arrow ends (approx 300)												
Thursday		reversals										70m double face 6 and 4 scoring the 6 arrows (approx 200)												
Friday												50m double face 4 and 6 scoring the 6 arrows (approx 250)												
Saturday																								
Sunday																								

Time allocated to sleep

Time allocated for work

Training time   This training week would give you 1500 arrows.

Competition

Travel time

Use your time chart to factor in all the training for each week. Archers who are able to train full-time need to ensure they have structure to their week's training. It is too easy to delay training to later.

CHAPTER 4

TRAINING PRACTICES AT HOME

Now you have made an outline plan of the time available and have an idea of how you are going to spend it, you must make sure that what you carry out in training is relevant and part of a package that will lead to improvement in your shooting, and therefore in groups and scores. This is not only about carrying out the different tasks but also ensuring that there is enough interest to keep you focused on the task in hand. Every arrow shot needs to be the best you can shoot. It is not about shooting 200 arrows, but shooting 200 arrows the best you can. While shooting I give every arrow shot a mental mark out of ten. At the end of the session or competition I work out a percentage of good arrows shot. To help maintain the focus on shooting well, it is necessary to have a range of tasks that can be carried out.

This chapter will offer ideas and details of the various aspects of time-limited training that can be carried out at home. The next chapter will cover training at full-length shooting venues. The suggestions are not comprehensive but will give you a good basis to work from.

Reversals

Reversals are carried out using a recurve bow, a Formaster elbow sling and a cord to attach the sling to the string of the bow around the nocking point.

The time you need to set aside for a full set of reversals is only 30 minutes. This makes it the shortest of your time-allocated training sessions but it offers the biggest increase in shooting strength for an archer wishing to make a good start towards the world stage.

Although reversals are used primarily for recurve archers, they can be very useful for compound archers looking to build up strength and get a good feel for line within their shooting.

As well as quickly building up shooting strength, reversals provide the easiest way to maintain form when you are away from home and unable to shoot. In Chapter 3 I mentioned how Chris Marsh carried out reversals every day for a year as he was unable to shoot while staying in the USA and was able to put in great scores when he came back. Even when you are able to train full-time they can also be used as a strength check to ensure that you are maintaining your shooting strength. Coaches can also use them to assess the shooting strength of the archers they are coaching. It is as a quick and easy way to monitor their initial strength and then while observing their progress through the training they have been set.

Formaster attached to the string for reversals.
KAREN HENDERSON

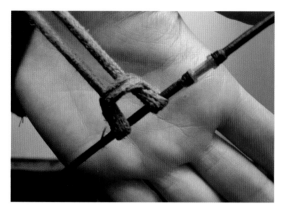

The reversal cord is only looped on to the string so it can easily be removed.

Setting Up the Formaster

It can take a little time to set up the Formaster correctly in order to get the greatest benefit from it, but it will make a huge difference to your progress when training. It is best to make up a bow string specifically for reversals, as the cord attached to the nocking point can damage the serving and move the nocking point. I made up a bow string with extra strands to ensure that it would last, as I did not want the bow string parting company at full draw in the house. How do you explain to the insurance company how your bow limb ended up in the TV screen?

It is important that the length of the cord is set so that the first joint of your middle finger is in line with the string.

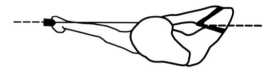

Having the sling at the correct length, as in the top figure, ensures that the elbow is in the correct position.

It is important that the length of the cord tying the sling to the bow string is set to a length so that at full draw the elbow is in the same position in the reversal as it would be at full draw when you are shooting. The easiest way of measuring this is by ensuring that, when you draw the elbow back, the first joint of your middle finger is in line with the bow string. If you make the cord too long the elbow will come back too far. Although you will find it far easier to maintain the reversal, because the weight is carried on your skeletal structure more than on your muscles, you will not be exercising the muscles at the correct optimum length. You should be aware that training with it wearing different thicknesses of clothing can make slight changes to the position of your elbow. If it pinches a bit, it is best to wear a thin sleeved garment to make the exercise more comfortable. If you wear a thick long-sleeved top the material will bunch up in the elbow and alter your position.

It is very important that at full draw with the reversal sling you are in the correct position. It is a good idea, especially when you start, to use a mirror to check your position. The bow should be drawn back in the same manner you normally draw your

To ensure that the draw elbow is in the best position, putting your index finger between the cord and your chin will give the same relative position as when you are at full draw with your tab.

Archer at full draw with the line of force in a similar position as when drawing up with the Formaster.

bow. At full draw the string should be in contact with your face in the normal position with your index finger between the cord and your chin. This will help to place the elbow in the correct position. Once your arms and shoulders are in position you should turn your head away from the normal shooting alignment, which also helps to keep your neck relaxed. This is an exercise to work the muscles required for the draw and is not a practice for holding the bow at the full draw position. As there is a tendency not only in this exercise but in shooting to build unwanted tension in the neck, turning and relaxing the head when using the Formaster sling enables you to prac- tise control and feeling the relaxation of the neck muscles will ensure that you are training only the muscles required to draw the bow.

The Exercise

This is primarily a 30-minute exercise. Your plan will be to work up to drawing your bow with the Formaster for 30 seconds, then relaxing for 30 seconds. This should be carried out continuously for 30 minutes with a bow set up to be 2lb heavier than your normal shooting set-up. Compounds can set up a bow for this practice at a draw weight of about 32–36lb.

When you first start this exercise it would be best to start with a lower weight bow than your own draw weight, drawing the bow for 20 seconds and then resting for 40 seconds. Base the exercise around a sequence of 60 seconds. Initially as you tire you may need to reduce the draw time to 15 seconds. This is an exercise to improve strength, not to damage yourself, so however keen you are, take it easy until you get used to it. Record each session to start with and try to do the same or a little more each session. Six weeks should be enough time to get to your draw weight for the full 30 minutes of 30 seconds up and 30 seconds down. This training is for one session of 30 minutes, not 30 minutes over a day. I would expect you to carry out this training as a supplement to your normal shooting regime three or four times a week in the build-up stage. Once you have reached the full 30 minutes for all your training sessions you need to start moving the bow weight up until it matches your bow weight and continue until you can carry it out reasonable easily. After this you can raise your bow weight until it exceeds your draw weight by 2lb. As you gain strength you will probably find that you need to increase your bow weight to match your strength. It is vitally impor- tant that when carrying out reversals the shoulder muscles engaged in the draw are kept in a state of stretch even when the draw elbow stops moving. I always use the analogy of a tug of war; when both teams are pulling, but are equal, the rope is static. Your muscles need to be in the same state. Lock- ing the muscles to maintain the position should be avoided at all times.

Initially just carrying out the exercise will keep you engaged in the task. I found it helpful to use a clock with only a second hand for timing the revers- als and a timer set for 30 minutes out of view to let me know when I had completed the session. If you can see the time passing on an ordinary clock, you will work to the time and not to your strength. You may find that you do a little less on some sessions during your strength build-up period. Once up to the 30-minute session I found that watching television during the session ensured that I kept the conscious mind occupied and completed the task. It is better if you can have a bow set up permanently for carrying out reversals. Leaving it in a prominent position in the house will induce you to carry out the exercise. It is all very well having it tidily away in a cupboard, but you will be more inclined to use it if it is staring at you in your living room. During the summer season, when the evenings are longer and you are able to put in more shooting time and arrows, you can still carry out reversals from time to time to monitor strength levels or to augment training when the arrow count is low, for example when practising long distances.

Further Tasks

Once you can accomplish the full session you can incorporate other movements to make the exercise more interesting. When carried out in conjunction with a mirror you can use the exercise to practise the shooting positions of elevated and depressed shots. This is useful for both field archers and target archers as tilting of the hips gives the correct angle for the distance but also maintains the correct position of the arms in relation to the shoulders.

It is important to maintain the position of the bow arm and shoulder but additional movements can be made with the drawing arm and shoulder. Relax the draw arm and shoulder by about 1in and then draw back to full draw position in a one-second

rhythm, fifteen times for thirty seconds. Alternatively, while facing ahead out of the way, you can increase the draw length slightly with the same sort of rhythm as in the previous exercise. By keeping your head facing forward, you are exercising and strengthening the muscles for shooting at the same time, ensuring you are not interfering with your shooting draw length.

From time to time, it helps to see how many full reversals you can do; more than an hour is quite good going. Ian Crowther was introduced to reversals when he was a junior. A couple of months later his parents rang up the squad coaches and asked, 'Is an hour and a half of reversals enough?'

Checking Shooting Muscles

The Formaster can be also used for illustrating the use of the correct muscles when you shoot. To do this you will need to rig up a second loop on your elbow sling approximately 4–5cm longer than the first. This is secured to the string just under the nocking point, ensuring that you can still put your arrow on the nocking point as you will need to be able to shoot it.

With the elbow sling fitted and the cord secured, take up your shooting position in front of a target. Come up and shoot your arrow as normal. If you are using the correct muscles and following through with the shot, the bow string will be restrained by the cord and elbow sling. The cord should end up just touching your neck and you will find that the

To shoot with the reversal sling, the cord needs to be lengthened.

Ready to shoot with the lengthened reversal sling.

Once the string has been released the cord should end up against the neck, provided the back tension and the subsequent follow-through are correct.

arrow will not travel too far. If you are not maintaining the follow-through, the string and cord will pull the elbow forward. This exercise should not be practised excessively as the chest and arms are compressed after the shot instead of being released. I have had problems with my bow shoulder when using this technique too much. It can be best utilized when you are working to maintain your follow-through. With the cord attached, shoot three or four arrows, remove the cord and sling and then shoot a few more arrows, maintaining the feeling of when the cord was attached. You can then alternate with the cord on and off to improve on your follow-through.

The Formaster also comes with an extra rubber band attachment designed to allow you to shoot the bow with an arrow, when you have a soft target to slow the arrow down, or without an arrow so you can train when there is no target available. I find that this, too, has the downside that the shoulders and arms are compressed after the shot, which is unrealistic, and this can lead to joint discomfort and irritation if carried out too frequently. Normally the joints are unloaded on release after the initial loading. This rubber band attachment works in a similar fashion to the rigid longer string but is a lot easier on the release.

Scorten Exercet Trainer

If you are able to take a riser with you, one of the best trainers you can use to help practise your release, as an addition to reversals, is the Exercet-type trainer, which bolts on to the front of your bow using the long rod and button bushings. The clicker incorporated in it allows you to shoot your bow without damage to you or your equipment. If you have your sight fitted you can put miniature targets on the wall to practise aiming and shooting.

The Exercet trainer can be used when you need to shoot but there is no provision for a boss. KAREN HENDERSON

Although you will not have to collect your arrows, the training time with this exercise will take longer than doing 30 minutes of reversals to carry out the same amount of work.

The above practices can easily be carried out at home or in accommodation where actual shooting is not possible. This ensures that you are able to keep up your training wherever you are.

Limited Distance Training

Although reversals are good for strength training and for when you have limited time, shooting is better. When shooting at home, if you have an arrow in the bow, make sure you have a boss in front of you. It is unbelievable how many archers have holes around the house. Fortunately I have not heard of any lethal accidents. I don't have any holes in the house, but I did shoot a hole in a workshop once. I was testing a home-made back stopnet at the time; it didn't seem to slow it down but it looked good. A short range can be set up at home, either within the house or the garage. Having a target set up permanently at home, no time is wasted travelling or setting up the boss or equipment and shooting can be carried out when you have time available. You should be able to shoot fifty good arrows in about thirty minutes; shooting 150 arrows will take about one-and-a-half hours. Shooting before breakfast for half an hour enables you to start the day with shooting feelings and thoughts that you will carry with you through the day. Another session of an hour to an hour and a half in the evening will help keep shooting uppermost in your mind.

In setting up a boss at home you need a distance of only 3m. Obviously it needs to be where others cannot get between you and the target. If a barrier is required to restrict an area it is best to make sure it is a physical one like a child's stair gate, so that no one can walk in on your shooting accidentally. An 80cm foam boss allows you to get the best use from the boss. With a small boss you will tend to use only the centre section and it will wear out much more quickly. As long as you spread your shooting around you should get a year or more from an 80cm boss. When using it in the house it is best to stand a board behind it to protect the wall when the boss starts to get soft, otherwise you will end up with

Practising at the top of the stairs. NEIL WAKELIN

Even with limited room, it is possible to set up a short range at home. BRIAN STRACHAN

arrow wormholes in the wall. The garage is also a great place to set up a short range. It is better if you can set it up so that it can be used with the doors closed, when it is wet and cold, or open when the weather is better and you want to shoot at a slightly longer distance.

When shooting at these short distances it can be very easy to damage your arrows, especially if you are shooting a quiverful at a time. I tend to shoot between ten and fifteen arrows an end. As I have quite a short draw length, I have a collection of old arrows donated by longer-limbed friends, which have damage to the ends of the shafts. I cut them down from either end so that they are all the same length and shoot them without fletches.

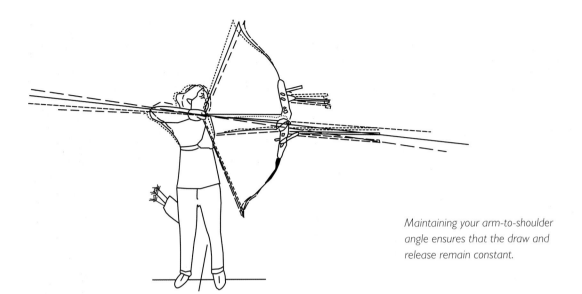

Maintaining your arm-to-shoulder angle ensures that the draw and release remain constant.

When shooting at short distances, vertical shooting patterns are a good way to start as your feet can stay in one position and, with a slight change in the angle at the waist, you can maintain the shooting geometry of your arms and shoulders. When shooting horizontal patterns, realignment of the feet will be required to maintain the vertical relationship of shoulders and feet. Owing to the closeness of the boss, body shooting angles change dramatically with what appears to be a small change in the point of aim. Unless you are aware of this phenomenon it can be very easy to fall into the trap of shooting every arrow with a different body position, which is not recommended. You need to make sure that the vertical and shoulder-arm relationship is constantly maintained. Every shot needs to be the best you can shoot. Although counting the number of arrows shot or their equivalent helps to keep track of all your training, numbers can become the task and not the shooting of good consistent shots. You need to ensure that your focus is on shooting at short distances, especially if time is short. It is easy to fall into the trap of thrashing out 150 arrows for the arrow count, instead of 100 arrows shot well.

Shooting Tasks

Many tasks can be carried out shooting at the back of a target face, as this gives a clear blank sheet to see the sight against.

A simple shooting task is to adjust your sight low, shoot one arrow at the boss, then aim at the first arrow's nock, then at the second and so on. Adjust the sight so that the impacts of the arrows are about 2cm apart. This will save your arrows from damage and give you a shooting task that focuses on aim and consistency as the task is to produce a line of arrows that are equidistant. If you repeat the exercise you will be able to cut the face along the line of aim. Using this task you can shoot up or down the face by tipping at the hips. Vertical lines or dots can be drawn on the back of the face with a felt-tip pen to provide points of aim. Horizontal nock shooting or marks can also be used, but because a turn is required to shoot a horizontal you must ensure that you move your feet by the same amount of twist as the aim point moves across the target in order to maintain your body alignment.

You can combine the two practices by marking out a square of dots to aim at or shoot at a target face by aiming at the divide of the colours but spacing the arrows by shooting around the clock: 12 o'clock, then 6 o'clock, 3 o'clock, then 9 o'clock and so on. You can then work on cutting that ring from the target face.

Closed Eyes Release
Closed eyes release is a shooting task that can be carried out at all distances, although it is best to make a start at 3m.

Carry out your shot sequence as normal with

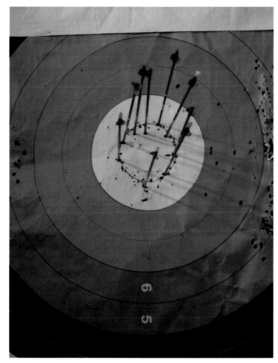

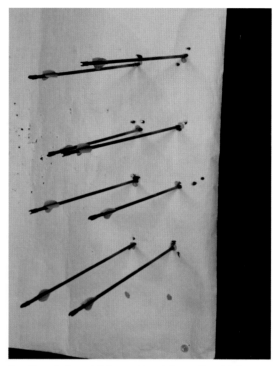

Shooting at the line at short distances ensures that a degree of focus on the aim is maintained, combined with minimal damage to arrows and fletchings.

Shooting at spaced dots on a target face will maintain focus but keep the arrows apart.

your eyes open right up until the point where you have aimed the bow. Then close your eyes and complete the shot. It is the feel of the shot that is most important. When you close your eyes, though, maintain the image of your sight on the target throughout the rest of the shot. Keep it there and improve the image in your mind. The sight should be imagined steady and clear, just as it would be on your best shot. As the shot is executed you should visualize the arrow scoring a ten. For some archers doing this, even at 3m, initially aiming at the centre of an 80cm boss can be slightly unnerving, although you will quickly find that you can carry this out quite comfortably. You can then use it at longer distances and with practice you should be able to carry out this task at all your shooting distances. This is one of the best shooting tasks that you can use in any of your training, because it is the feel of the shot that makes the shot. When you consider what you can actually see when you shoot, your eyes are only useful for pointing the bow in the right direction. The main part of the shot is the feel of the draw

and the release. Closing your eyes allows you to focus and remember the feel of the shot. Once you have become comfortable training using this practice, when you are shooting like this at 70m in calm conditions you should be able to maintain the group in the red and 100 per cent on the target; at 90m it should be 98 per cent on the target.

If you can do this with your eyes closed, it should be easier with them open. To translate the timing and feel of the shot with your eyes closed to shooting with your eyes open, the best way is to prepare ten arrows: eight with green nocks and two with red nocks. Place them randomly in your quiver. If you pick up an arrow with a green nock you close your eyes to release; when a red nock is taken up shoot with your eyes open. The practice is to maintain the feeling of the shot whether your eyes are open or closed. As you are better able to maintain the feelings the ratio of coloured nocks can be adjusted to give more or fewer arrows in the quiver, so varying the percentage of open and closed eye shooting.

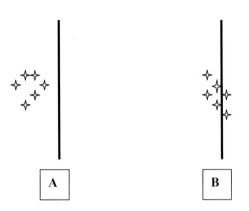

When your horizontal body alignment is correct the arrows will continue to impact on the line even with your eyes closed.

Horizontal Body Alignment

Short-distance shooting is a great way to find a good horizontal body alignment. This needs some experience and practice in shooting with your eyes closed and you should be reasonably comfortable with shooting like this. Once you can do this you can check and adjust your body alignment. To carry this out, draw a vertical line down the centre of the back of a target face and pin it to your boss. Carry out closed eyes release, aiming at the vertical line before closing your eyes. When you have good alignment, the arrows will usually impact on the line. For a right-handed shooter, if the group is to the left of the vertical line on the target, closing your stance should bring it to centre; if grouped to the right, open your stance a little. This is a useful trick to learn for both indoor and outdoor shooting. The correct body alignment ensures that even when you are tired the bow will remain centred on the target, keeping the group in the centre of the target. It can also be utilized for making slight

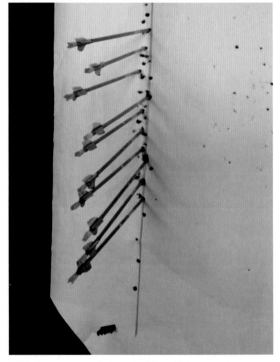

With the correct adjustment of the sight, each subsequent arrow can be aimed at the previous one and will impact either above or below. This will help to ensure that damage to arrows is kept to a minimum.

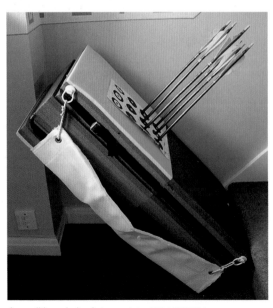

A small boss helps bring variety. NEIL WAKELIN

adjustments to group positions without moving the sight. If at 18m the group is a little to the left in the ten, adjusting your front foot a little to the right will tend to centre the group. It can also be used when shooting outdoors in a breeze, as turning the foot position slightly into the wind will help in maintaining groups centrally. It can also be used when shooting across a slope.

Distance Shooting at 3m

With an 80cm boss you should be able to practise all your distances for target shooting. The boss should be set on a high stand with a target face marked at 1.3m from the ground. Start with your 30m sight mark. The boss needs to be adjusted so that the arrows will impact towards the bottom. You should then be able to shoot using all your sight marks, but make any necessary adjustments as you get towards your longest distances or you might find the arrows in the wall behind instead of on the boss. You can use more than one boss if you have the room. I like shooting in the house because I can listen to music and adjust the temperature: when practising for India I was able to turn the heating up high to check the issues of shooting in the heat and how it affected my grip.

A small solid foam boss is a very useful addition for field shooters who live in a house with stairs, as you can practise more extreme elevations of shooting.

Garage Set-up

A garage set-up may be a better solution for some and has the advantage of usually being a more enclosed space that is easier to control entry to. You should also have more room and you may probably be more inclined to build a stand into it. The downside of shooting in your garage in colder climates is that going out there in winter can be discouraging, but when the weather is good or dry you should have the advantage of shooting longer distances.

Some of you may have the opportunity to shoot outdoors at home, possibly up to full shooting distances. If you can do this you have the advantage of not having any travelling time, but you still need to practise with other archers.

Summary

There is much you can do at home to maximize your available time. Even if you have low ceilings, you can always sit on a chair or kneel down to shoot to help keep your arrow count up. Although it seems that you can do so much at home, you should still shoot at full distances when you have the opportunity. The ideal would be to have all day to shoot the arrows and train, but as this is not always possible the exercises given above are some of the ways you can augment your training.

Neil Wakelin's garage set up. NEIL WAKELIN

CHAPTER 5

SHOOTING PRACTICES

As you may well be new to setting up training and shooting at home, you should be able to start all these practices with few or no preconceptions. Most of you wanting to progress will undoubtedly have shot both indoor and outdoor in practice and competition. In stepping up your training, different training patterns will need to be adopted to get the most out of the venues you currently use and make use of other venues close at hand. Those who have somewhere to practise whenever they have time have the best opportunity to progress. Having set up training at home you are able to fill in the bits where venues or the time available preclude you from shooting at standard distances. When you are at your normal venues you will need to make changes to your training. Changing from what you used to do to what you need to do takes a deliberate plan to ensure you are getting both the quantity of arrows and the quality to help you improve. At club sessions you will need the support of the club archers to deploy these changes. Unfortunately some clubs do not see the benefit of an archer stepping up their training to improve; they only see the increased damage to 'their' bosses and target faces. The real benefit to them is in supporting your aspirations and reaping the benefit of the insights into shooting that you can pass on to all club members. With goodwill from them and your use of sensible training practices that reduce damage to the equipment, both usually benefit.

Good planning will lead to you making the most of the training time available. When other members of the club are in and you have to shoot to their shooting pattern, make the most of the time by shooting more arrows in the time per end. Tuning and variable distance training will have to be done when you have the range to yourself or your own private range.

Some archers I know have been able to get permission from a landowner to use a secluded venue on private land for practising.

Indoor Short-Distance Practices

I am well aware that some archers around the world can shoot outside all year round. For some, though, that is not possible; it's a little chilly in winter in Scotland, for example. Elsewhere summers might be too hot and archers have to shoot indoors to keep cool. It is always about making the best of what you have available.

At the Club

Although most clubs will have 18m for the minimum shooting distances, some may not and have to make do with a shorter distance. For a number of years on a Saturday morning our club was able to shoot a distance of only 12m. The one great benefit with this is that you are closer to the target. When you shoot at a 40cm target you get more tens. When shooting and scoring at the shorter distance, scores increase with the face size, raising expectations for when you shoot at the full distance of 18m and helping to increase your score levels. If you have the equipment you can print smaller faces so that the size is relative to the distance you are able to shoot. Another way of getting round shooting a shorter distance, without printing new faces, is to shoot a regular 40cm face but shoot negative line cutters. It is usual in archery to score positive line cutters. At 12m on a 40cm face you can score negative line cutters, so if it touches the line you get the lower score. This is a good exercise in itself as it improves your focus of shooting at the centre of the ten, instead of just at the ten. This helps to improve group size and consistency. At 12m scoring negative line cutters gives a comparable score to shooting positive line cutters at 18m.

Especially at the shorter distances it is best to shoot single arrows at multiple faces. At 18m you can put up three or four vertical three-spot faces, Vegas or Field targets. These faces will ensure that you do not damage your arrows by shooting them into each other. Practising multiple faces ensures that you have a plan concerning the order in which you will shoot the faces, as you are practising not only the shot itself but the sequence of shooting. Personally I shoot from top to bottom, or in number order. I have seen archers practise shooting vertical faces from top to bottom, and then at a shoot decide to shoot from bottom to top. The result is inevitable, shooting bottom, middle, bottom as the practice shot sequence kicks in and just two arrows are scored for that end. Everything you do needs a plan, then you need a plan of anything that might happen.

What you do at the club is dependent on where you are with your training. If your arrow count is up from home or other venues then you can carry on at the normal rate of shooting.

Club sessions will generally give you good shooting conditions, decent light and a reasonable

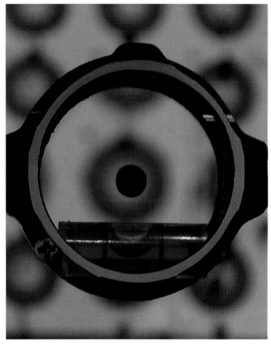

Scale-sized faces can be reproduced so that even when practising at 3m the correct view of the sight picture can be maintained. NEIL WAKELIN

Links Archers.

temperature, so it may be possible to take advantage of these to carry out 'check scoring' to see what affects your scores. Some archers do not enjoy short-distance shooting, but it is an opportunity to perfect the precision of your shooting. As indoor shooting conditions create little or no external variation in your shooting, they offer scope for testing yourself and your equipment, since you can judge by score and group size the effects of any external influences. You should use any shooting sessions where the conditions are reasonable for checking group size, not only to practise your shot but as an opportunity to test clothing, footwear, drinks and the effects of exercise and sleep patterns. You can experiment by running or exercising in other ways before the session to see if it alters your scores and group size. In varying the time between exercise and shooting you will be able to adjust your training plan to find the best time for exercise. Some will find that two hours or more before shooting enhances their scores, while for others cardio exercise carried out after shooting training for the day works best. Try different types of drinks to see if any help you perform better. I found that drinks containing multidextrins seemed to maintain energy levels and did not adversely affect scores, but the downside is that some of them contain a lot of calories.

Competition clothing and footwear should also be tested at these sessions. This especially applies to tops, as badly fitting ones will restrict movement

If you are trying to compete with a tight top it requires a little stretching.

or catch if too big. The clothing I was given at the airport for one indoor event was at least two sizes too small. There was no way I could shoot comfortably as it so restricted my movement. All the work I had put in before the event was wasted, and still I was asked at the end, 'Why do you think you didn't shoot so well?'

Competition footwear is often overlooked, not only in archery but in other standing sports where balance and consistency is required. I have talked to Olympic skeet shooters who have practised in old shoes and done well, but have then worn good footwear for competitions and not done so well. The footwear you practise in should be what you compete in. It is unbelievable how many archers practise in comfortable old trainers and get out their 'Special' footwear for competitions. Even if you have two identical pairs bought at the same time, using one pair for practice and the other for competition, the more used practice pair will change as the sole compresses and may well give better support, leading to more consistency.

Shooting Practices

At a normal two-hour club session you may be able to shoot sixty arrows if you stick to three arrow ends. In putting two faces up you will be able to shoot twice the number within the same shooting time. This will ensure that you shoot more quickly. The trick is to get a rhythmic balance of good but not hasty shooting. Start off with shooting four arrow ends and work up to shooting ends of six or more arrows per end. Depending on how your club shoots, you may be able to do more arrows per end.

Another practice you can adopt is to arrive at the club, set up to shoot the customary six sighters and then score thirty arrows at the normal end rate scoring. Finish off the remainder of the club session shooting six arrow ends, maintaining your form and rhythm. At the next club session, start the session shooting a higher volume of arrows, then finish the session scoring thirty arrows. With good record-keeping in your diary, you need to look at the scores, group placement, size and so on. The differences in patterns and scores can be analysed in an electronic plotting program such as Target Plot or on prepared paper plot sheets. For checking group sizes and group patterns scoring is not the best way of judging. You need to be able to plot the position of your arrows and this can be done on paper or electronically. Paper will give you a good visual representation of your fall of shot, but electronic plotting is much quicker for putting it into a best score for group size. Whichever method you choose it is important to plot the position of the arrow accurately. Poor plotting will lead to inaccurate results. Plotting group patterns can also pick up anomalies in your shooting, such as groups that are generally good but with the odd arrow low and left. This provides information for you to work on keeping all the arrows in the group. Field shooters can set up two or three bosses at different distances and possibly at a lower height. You can then practise moving the bosses at every end until you become used to the different angle and face size. Although very little sight adjustment will be needed for the shorter distances, the change of distance practice and view will help to improve your scoring in conjunction with distance changes. Shooting well is about having a good idea about how to enhance your shooting and then

At the end of competition or training check the position and consistency of the groups on all the faces.

actually trying it out. It is the extra effort in setting up and trying different target set-ups that maintains your focus on good shooting and doing more than you have before. Just shooting a set distance is easy. Again, plotting groups between distances will enable you to work on ensuring that the first shot at any distance goes into the middle.

Shooting at the range on your own allows you to shoot your chosen quantity of arrows at your own speed, dependent only on the time available. You should be able to work up to nine arrow ends using three three-spot vertical faces. For the same number of visits to the target as three arrow ends for a 60-arrow round you will be shooting a set of 180 arrows, a good half practice session. The faces can all be set at the same or at varying heights, and each face can be scored and plotted either vertically or horizontally. If using new or stick-on replacement centres there is no real need to plot, as at the end of the session you will be able to see the fall of shot and you can take photos with your mobile phone as a record. Ensure that as you change vertical faces you also move your foot position to maintain your body alignment. Vertical scoring across faces at the same height will just give you scores for each face. Note the scores for each face in turn, as the differences between the first and last target score will give you some indication of your shooting fitness. You are looking for comparable scores across the three faces.

By having the three faces set at different heights, with one each above and below normal height, you are able to work on maintaining your shoulder position for all your shots and getting the shooting angle by bending at the waist. This is a good exercise for both field shooters and target shooters. Field shooters can also add in distance changes. By setting the targets above and below your normal position for shooting the three-spot faces, you can work with an exaggerated bend in the waist girdle, emphasizing the position of the waist on each shot. Many archers find that the arrow position on vertical faces differs from top to bottom faces, but tends to

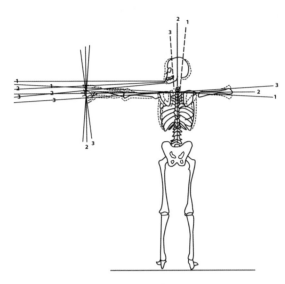

Provided the vertical alignment of the body is made by the waist and hips, the alignment of the arms and shoulders remains constant.

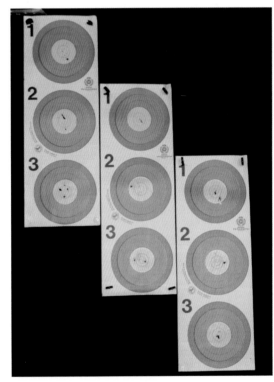

Placing the target faces higher and lower than you would normally shoot ensures that you can practise maintaining the correct shoulder alignment at augmented angles to reinforce the tilting at the waist.

follow a pattern for each face, for example top high, middle centre, bottom low and left. This is generally because the archer changes the angle of the shot by changing the angle of the arms to the shoulders instead of bending at the waist. If the angle change is accomplished by altering the angle of the arms to shoulders, each of the shots will be released differently as different muscles will be used in the draw. It is best to learn one shot from the chest up and alter the angle of the shot by bending at the waist. Shooting at targets either higher or lower than is normal for target archers will help to ensure that the waist position is worked on. This is relevant to all distances, although it can be much harder to maintain the arm to shoulder position fully for extreme field shots. The giveaway is how hard or easy it is to get it through the clicker, or not to use one at all.

When shooting at three-spot vertical faces set at the same height you can score and plot across the faces. Shoot the faces from top to bottom, or in the order you have decided to shoot them (for example, strip 1, strip 2, strip 3), then score across the faces, adding together the total score from the top faces, and then the centre and bottom. This exercise provides another way to help you judge the consistency of your shoulder and arm position. In theory when the body position is correct the score pattern

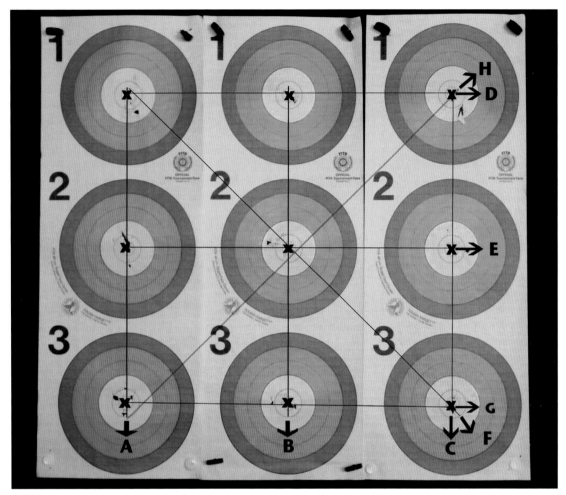

When your shooting is consistent, the vertical and horizontal scores will also be consistent. FRANCES KEATS

and group pattern down or across the target face should be the same.

Closed Eyes Release

The closed eyes release (see Chapter 4) really comes into its own at 18m. At this distance you are able to work seriously on body alignment. Early on in my shooting I found that foot markers helped maintain my body alignment; I left a lot of target pins in fields at the end of shoots, but it did help keep the group at the same place on the boss during the distance. After working on alignment with closed eyes release, however, I no longer required foot markers. I found that for me the optimum position was with my front foot in 2.5cm open alignment

and the heel of the front foot slightly angled back towards the shooting line.

Closed eyes release is not just about letting go of the string with your eyes shut. It is about the feel of the shot. Since there is very little you can actually see when you shoot, it is most important that you feel the shot. The draw is carried out as normal up to the point where you start the aim; you then close your eyes but see the sight steady on the target in your mind's eye for the rest of the shot. Some archers have trouble getting used to the feeling of the shot. A simple exercise you can try to replicate that inward feeling of body awareness is to practise thinking about breathing by just moving your diaphragm and keeping your rib cage still. Close your eyes and put one hand on your navel and the other on the side of your chest. When breathing using your diaphragm, the navel moves in as you breathe out and moves out as you breathe in. At the same time the hand on your chest should remain still. As you get used to it you can move the hand on your belly onto the rib cage to monitor that your ribs are still as you continue breathing. In practising this you will feel yourself focusing on the movement of your body parts: the only movement should be the stomach moving in and out. A similar exercise is to hold your arm out to your side, keeping the hand still, and rotate your elbow while keeping the arm straight. This sort of exercise can be carried out on various body parts, for example moving a single toe or tensing a single muscle. As you carry out these exercises you should start to sense the internalizing required to 'feel' the shot.

If you have already started working on closed eyes release at home you will probably be able to carry on with this at 18m. Those who are new to the practice should bring a target forward to 4m so that right from the start you may be confident that the arrow will land on the boss. For extra security you can ask a companion to 'spot' to ensure that your arrow is kept aligned with the boss. You will quickly find that it is very easy to maintain the bow in the correct position to hit the target and the boss can be moved back in steps to 18m. It is important to feel secure that the arrow will hit the boss. If you start at a distance at which you are not comfortable, it will be detrimental to your shooting.

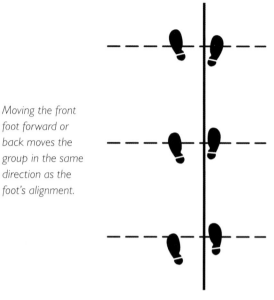

Moving the front foot forward or back moves the group in the same direction as the foot's alignment.

If you practise this you should be able to maintain your group size even with your eyes closed. At 18m you will be able to work on the ideal foot position to maintain the group in the centre of the target. If the group is to the left of centre, move your front foot to the right. Conversely, if the groups are to the right of centre, move the front foot left.

Closed eyes release can be used at the same pattern of targets that you have been shooting at this distance, for example three vertical three-spot faces, but now closing your eyes on the release. Once you have the feeling of the shot and smoothness, this will take at least 1,000 arrows of continuous training.

The feeling of the shot is when you can shoot the arrow without any doubt that it will hit the target you were aiming at before you closed your eyes. That comes from focusing on each area of the body and how it is working during the shot until you have built up a holistic feel to your shot. It is the feeling of there being a line that goes along the arrow between your eye and the target. As you are directly behind the arrow, on release it can go nowhere but into the target you are looking at in your mind's eye. This needs to be the same feeling that you have when your eyes are open. To integrate this into your shot, do the same as you did at home and start by shooting some arrows with your eyes open. Using nine arrows, change two of your nocks to a

The normal placement for my feet on the shooting line.

different colour and place the arrows randomly in your quiver. When these come out shoot them with your eyes open, but with the same feeling and shot time as when your eyes are closed. The number of odd nocks can be increased or decreased as your shot becomes consistent.

This is very much like refined blank boss shooting as it enables you to work on a fluidity of shooting, while maintaining an image of the sight picture for every shot, whether your eyes are open or closed. I am not keen on shooting blank boss as I consider it is too easy for an archer to thrash out arrows while failing to maintain a consistent image of hitting a ten on every shot. I also think that, once a target face is presented, the initial rhythm may be maintained for a short period but the shot tends to degrade as the archer starts to over-aim, becoming anxious over the care of the shot. By blank boss shooting with a target face in place, I am always used to having a target of some sort on the other side of my sight pin. All your shots – at whatever distance or size of target, whether competition or practice, with eyes open or closed – should be the same shot. Shooting blank boss with a target face is the same feeling as shooting with your eyes closed. Internalize the shot and direction without the concern of where the arrow will fall on the target. The group size is the result of the consistency of the shot. Putting your sight in the correct place will lead to the group falling in the centre of the target face. The resulting score is directly related to how well and consistently you execute all of your shots. Too many archers try to get a good score by shooting tens, whereas it actually comes from focusing on executing good shots. The exercises of closed eyes release and blank boss with a face will help enable you to achieve and improve that consistency.

Continuously practising more than 1,000 shots for every aspect of your training is a key aspect to significantly improving your shooting and helping you progress faster. If you feel that you need to work on relaxing your bow hand in your grip, you should make that the focus of your training for 1,000 shots. It is not enough to work on it for 20 minutes and then move on to something else. Remember that it takes a month or doing something 1,000 times to get into the habit without thinking. This may be as simple as deciding to wear your watch on the other wrist. Even then you will sometimes revert

to what you did before. Practising an action 1,000 times enables you to shorten the time until you can do it without thinking. By shooting 1,000 arrows a week you can fit four months of changes into one and speed up your progress.

Field shooters are used to altering the target height and distance. Target shooters will find that setting the targets overly high or low exaggerates the angle required to shoot multiple target faces. Doing this with closed eyes release helps to identify the muscles involved in maintaining the shooting position of arms and shoulders with the change of angle. The NFAA World Archery Festival at Las Vegas, for example, is an 18m competition where the target face is a three-spot 'Vegas' face set in a triangle instead of a vertical configuration. For this you have to take into account the change in vertical height as well as the angle left and right. This adds another dimension to the shot, needing slight adjustments to your foot position to allow for the changes of angle to either side, together with the vertical of the centre target face. The bosses are lower to the ground than for normal target rounds and the bottom target faces need to be practised.

Outdoor Practice

All the practices described above can be used for full-distance training. At distances of up to 50m it is best to put up twin faces so that you shoot no more than six arrows into a face in order to reduce arrow damage. Having two faces on the boss keeps the centres of the targets away from the middle of the boss. This makes you use more of the whole boss and it therefore lasts longer. When shooting more than 1,000 arrows every week, you would otherwise find that the centre of the boss soon becomes too soft to be any use. The other advantage of moving the faces out to the edge of the boss is that it helps to build confidence that the only area of the target you will hit is behind the centre of the face. Even at 70m I will put two faces on the boss, one full and one folded. This helps to spread out the use of the boss and reduces damage to your arrows. Although in a target competition with four archers shooting you would have twenty-four arrows in a boss, they are likely to be of differing standards and group position. Therefore I would want to limit nine arrows to each

Targets at Las Vegas are lower than you will be used to shooting at. DEAN ALBERGA

target face; by putting up two faces you can shoot nine arrows at one face and six at the other. This increases shooting time and reduces walking time. Shooting fifteen arrow ends helps to build stamina. By changing the order that you shoot, you can shoot nine practice arrows and then six scoring arrows, or the other way around, scoring the first six. Comparing the scores shot by the different orders, or their consistency, will also give you an indication of how shooting fit you are. It can be difficult to simulate the excitement of competition when you are in the field practising shooting multiple arrow ends. If you shoot a 200-arrow practice of fifteen arrow ends, then shoot the nine and six sequence. Scoring the six arrows after the nine, given slight fatigue after the initial part of the 200 practice, will help to simulate the condition of your body at a competition.

At 90m I will shoot at a single face as the whole face is part of my sight picture, whereas at 70m in calm conditions I only use out to the red.

At all distances you can practise closed eyes release. In calm conditions I would expect the group to stay within the red at all distances. As when training indoors, at club sessions you will have to adapt your training to what the other archers are doing. Generally you will be shooting more arrows per end than the rest of the club. While it can be onerous shooting with a mixed bag of archers, it is well worth continuing to shoot with others of mixed abilities as it gives you an opportunity to work on strategies for dealing with varying standards of archers at competitions. Even at world-class events you can find yourself shooting with inexperienced archers who struggle to hit the target. This was the case even at the Olympics in 2000. Shooting at the club ensures that you are used to shooting with others around you, giving you the opportunity to work on focusing on the shot. Some archers who continually practise on their own are totally thrown at competition because

RIGHT: *Using two faces reduces damage to arrows. The occluded face can be used for the practice arrows and the full face for the scoring arrows.*

BELOW: *On ten arrow ends, you can shoot four for practice and six scoring.*

they are not used to shooting with distractions around them.

In order to maintain the focus of shooting well you need to invent shooting games and routines that keep you focused right up to the very end of your practice sessions.

- Shoot nine arrow ends, maintaining a score out of 90 points.
- Finish the session by shooting every arrow in the ten. Once an arrow has hit a ten, put it away in the box. Carry on until all the arrows are in the box, even if it means shooting the last arrow in one arrow end at 70m.
- Shoot an end score over your average to finish.

- Score a distance at the beginning of your practice; beat that score at the end of the practice.
- When testing equipment you must work towards shooting consistently. Carrying out test scoring at the beginning and end of sessions on alternate days will help identify the best equipment and/or settings. This should be carried out every day for at least a week.
- Set up two bosses, one at 30m and one at 70m, and shoot single ends at each distance. Then move back 20m and shoot single ends at 50m and 90m. With a two-boss set-up and moving shooting lines, you can practise varying distances and adjusting sight changes for all your distances. Field shooters can put up two faces per target.

Compression Shooting

This shooting exercise has many values. I first tried it primarily as a way of seeing if Korean claims that they were shooting 1,000 arrows per day were viable. Initially I thought this was one-upmanship as the archers they were claiming were doing this were still at school. Providing the students were in a school geared up for shooting, they could follow the following practice session format:

2 hours in the morning before school
2 hours at lunch
2 hours directly after school
1 hour later after supper

This would seem a reasonable amount of time that could be used for shooting in a day with studies included. So how many arrows can reasonably be shot in a two-hour session at 60m? I picked 60m as it is a distance that can be shot at our club's indoor venue and ten arrow ends are easy to count.

The practice is to shoot all ten arrows in three minutes; that includes compounds. Shoot all ten arrows quickly and smoothly without pause, put the bow down and walk quickly to the target, withdraw your arrows, walk back and repeat for two hours. Shooting in this fashion you will be able to shoot between 280 and 300 arrows in a two-hour session. This showed that the claim that students were shooting 1,000 arrows a day could be true. More arrows could be shot if the target were closer but there would be more likelihood of damaging arrows. You could put on twin target faces, but it would split the consistency of the ten arrow practice.

When I first tried this I thought that I would tire quickly and the group size would suffer. After an initial wobble of group sizes as I became used to the practice, the groups tightened up and stayed tight throughout. To carry out the full two-hour session you do need to be shooting fit, making it a good exercise for coaches to use for assessing the fitness of their archers, not all of whom may be wholly honest in carrying out all the training asked of them. This exercise can be cut to an hour as a stepping stone to the full two-hour session. It also makes for a good group session, with a countdown timer visible for all the participants to see. At the end of three minutes, for example, shooting ceases and everyone collects however many arrows they have shot. This ensures that archers of different strengths can all participate.

The benefits of compression shooting are that:

- With a timer visible, archers can pace themselves to shoot their arrows at the same pace as the team round.
- Due to the frequency of the shot rhythm, idiosyncrasies that have no benefit and slow down the shot sequence are eliminated or at least identified.
- It enables archers to fit a good number of arrows into a limited time period.
- It is similar to blank boss shooting with a target.
- It allows coaches to assess fitness.
- It builds confidence in shooting quickly and accurately when short of time, either due to weather constraints in competition or to the time left in team rounds.

The quantity of arrows shot during the week means that you will be able to use the shooting time to carry out tuning tasks (see Chapter 8). When allocating shooting time in your weekly plan you need to work out the content of the time spent at home or at the club. You always need to have alternatives to take into account the weather or other users of your shooting facilities. At our club shooting sessions the frequency and distance of a practice is generally governed by the first person at the venue for the session. If I am shooting ten arrow ends, those who arrive later will ask how many I am shooting and what I plan to shoot for the session, and then will fit in with that. If necessary I will modify what I am doing to help out other archers requiring alternatives, as next time they will be obliging and change their plans to help me out. It is far better to work with other archers and with the club in general rather than against them. If you are too rigid about carrying out your plans you will often be disappointed and the resulting frustration will not help your shooting. Having alternatives available means that you will always be able to achieve something and it is this that brings progress.

CHAPTER 6

REPEATING THE SHOT

Consistency of shooting is the key to improving your groups. The shot starts by putting the arrow into the bow and finishes when the arrow hits the target. Spending a lot of time shooting does not necessarily mean that you will produce a consistent shot. The underlying theme to your shot is repeatability. This applies not only to the physical movements of your body during the shot but also to the thoughts behind it. Ask yourself in all that you do, 'Can I repeat this?'

Once you have released the string, at the front end, the arrow shaft remains in contact with the rest/plunger/launcher for only 5cm (2in) of its forward movement. After this it should not be in contact with the bow at all. At the back end the arrow remains attached to the string until the string hits the bottom of its stroke, the brace height, at which point the nock parts company from the string. The critical period is while the arrow is still attached

After moving about 5cm (2in) the front of the arrow is no longer in contact with the bow.

After 5cm (2in) the arrow is still attached to the string.

The arrow continues forward. At this stage the only contact with the archer is at the nocking point.

The brace height determines the detachment point of the arrow.

Once the nock has detached from the string the arrow should then be in free flight towards the target.

I had two 6 ten ends over the weekend at the Euro Nations event.

to the string. Any extraneous movement imparted to the bow or string will affect the arrow's trajectory.

The consistent release of the string from your fingers is dependent on the consistency of your draw. As you draw the bow back, you load up your muscles. How you release the string is directly proportional to the load placed on those muscles during the draw. Muscles are not like simple elastic bands that, once they are stretched to a length, will release the same every time. There is far more interaction between them if you load them differently. Even though you might get the string and tab back to the same position at anchor, by loading the muscles differently for each shot they will then unload differently, giving you bigger groups. The more consistently you can load up the muscles during the draw, the more consistent will be the release and the better the groups.

String Clearance

No matter how consistent you are with your shot, if the string is distorted against your chest at full draw or hits your arm/bracer before the arrow is released from the string, it will make it incredibly difficult to maintain good groups. Try as hard as you like, until you have ensured that you have full clearance on all your shots it will be incredibly difficult to achieve repeat consistency. The two main factors of the effect of poor string clearance are that:

- It will affect the path of the string and the arrow attached to it.
- Any interference with the string will also alter the position of the riser in the hand, either during or after the release.

It is remarkable how many archers who get reasonably good scores do not consistently have clearance for every shot.

Chest Clearance
At full draw your string will be connected to the limb tips of your bow either around the wheels or directly to the tip of each limb. The arrow should be fitted to your nocking point and the string held back with either your release aid or the tab. There

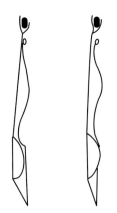

Contact with the chest will affect the path taken by the string.

should only be contact between the string and your chin (and possibly your nose) – nothing else. At full draw, from the tip of your limbs to the tab or release aid, the string will be in a direct straight line with no deflections. The string should not make any other contact with your body. However hard you try, it is unlikely that you will be able to deflect the line of the upper string as it contacts your nose. The lower string must clear your chest so that the line from limb tip to hand is not deflected. Any deflection or bending of the lower string will lead to inconsistencies in the path the string takes from release to when the nock is released from the string, leading to inconsistent groups. Also, if the string is resting against your chest as it is attached to the limbs, it will torque the riser. On release not only will this interfere with the path of the string but the riser will try to realign, causing a bigger error in the path of the string.

Archers using compounds and low poundage recurve bows are more prone to deflect the string position with their chests as there is less tension on the string, making it easier to deflect. As the poundage held on the fingers increases, so the pressure to deflect the string will be less apparent but it is still there. With recurves, resting the string on your chest will tend to make the arrow drop on the target in the direction of your bow arm. For right-handed archers, for example, the groups will tend to go low and left. Although you may have clearance at one distance, it is quite possible that, as the distances change, some archers will not be able to achieve clearance. This indicates that you are not changing the angle of the shot by tipping at the hips but by moving the angle of the arms to shoulders. If you are not strong enough, you will tend to rest

As the string's first movement is towards the chest, adequate clearance ensures that there is no interference to the string at this point.

the string on their chests to steady the shot and relieve the muscles slightly. This is indicated when the start of the competition goes well but consistency drops off towards the end. Keep your attention on maintaining string clearance on the chest at all distances and angles. The other factor that needs to be considered for recurves when ensuring you have good chest clearance is that as you release the string, as well as the string moving towards the bow, it also moves towards your chest. Although you may be clear of your chest at full draw, on release the string may still hit your chest. If this occurs it will affect the path of the string and give inconsistencies to the groups. Compounds, however, do not have this issue as the string should be moving directly towards the riser.

Chest Guard

Your chest guard is there to help keep clothing and your chest out of the way. If your chest guard is too thick you will not be able to tell if the string is touching your chest, so use either a thin chest guard or

shoot in a tight T-shirt. This way you will be able to tell if your string is resting on your chest.

Arm Clearance

If the string hits the front arm before the nock has left the string it will alter the trajectory, leading to bigger groups. From a technical viewpoint the groups would be consistent if you could get the

If the string hits the arm before the arrow detaches from the string, the path taken by the arrow will be variable, giving bigger groups.

Shooting without a bracer enables an archer to monitor changes to equipment or form, since string impact on the arm tends to focus an archer's attention.

string to hit the arm consistently, but the likelihood of hitting your arm in the same way every time is very low, however hard you practise. There are a number of reasons for the string hitting your arm. The front arm and shoulder may not be in position for clearance, or poor tuning or a recent change may increase the horizontal amplitude of the string, making it harder to get clearance. String material and weight will also have some bearing on the horizontal amplitude of the string. I was getting great

results from using BCY450. When they brought out BCY452x I switched to this, however, and found that I was not able to get clearance on my arm. I ended up switching back to BCY450.

At a competition in Norway I was shooting an 18m FITA. I kept getting the odd arrow in the 6 at 9 o'clock, always in the same place. I also noticed that I was getting cuts in my centre serving below the nocking point. At the time I was using a leather bracer with steel rods for rigidity. It became apparent that the string was hitting the bracer, sometimes before the nock had left the string, and this is what was giving me the 6s. The leather on the bracer had worn through and the end of the steel rod was protruding, cutting the serving. After I removed the bracer I found that the string was hitting my arm quite hard. Although the consistency of the groups increased, I was bruising my arm. The medics gave me some sticky corrugated bandage for my arm, ensuring that I was able to feel when the string hit my arm but it did not bruise it. Using this bandage I was able to adjust my body position over a few months until, combined with a little retuning of the bow, I could shoot without the bandage. At this point I realized how close the string came to my arm, as I could feel it brush by the hairs on my arm as it passed. I also noticed that if my brace height dropped the string would start hitting my arm. This gave me an early warning of changes to the set-up. When the brace height dropped the groups would get bigger, the difference between more than 580 at 18m and a 565. In shooting without a bracer I was able to get a warning to reset my brace height, ensuring I kept my score high. You should be able to shoot without a bracer. If you are unable to manage without you are having an issue with clearance. No matter how hard you try there will be a limit to the top scores of which you are capable.

Bracer

A bracer is good for keeping clothing out of the way, as having your arms covered does help with keeping warm in colder climates. If the string hits your bracer, however, you will need to manage without by wearing a short-sleeved top or shortening one sleeve of a long-armed top.

Take a look at the thickness of your bracer and whether it is being hit by the string. If you are unable to see if the bracer is being hit, cover the bracer in lipstick and then start shooting. If you have clearance there will not be any marks left on the lipstick. Remember that different clothing has different thicknesses. Clothing you are considering shooting in should be tested to see if you are getting clearance all the time. Instead of just taking off your bracer and bruising your arm, try using a tubigrip support or an arm sock. Cut out a small section of a thin plastic bottle and slip this under the tubigrip. The tubigrip will keep the plastic in place and, as

The middle section of a drinks bottle will wrap around an archer's arm so that it is protected from string burn, but it can still be felt by the archer. KAREN HENDERSON

both are quite thin, there will be less interference to the string. Because you are using a very thin layer of plastic and material to protect your arm, you should be able to feel when the string strikes your arm, allowing you to make adjustments to both yourself and the bow to ensure you maintain clearance.

Contact with Equipment

There should be only two points of contact with your equipment at full draw: the bow grip and the string. The issues for the grip are similar for both compound and recurve bows. At the string end,

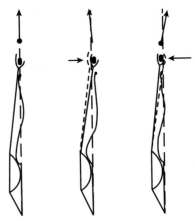

Any movement of the riser while the nock is still attached to the nocking point will be transmitted to the arrow, resulting in variable groups.

TOP LEFT: *Recurve limbs, showing their position at full draw and after the shot.* JAMIE CUTTS

TOP RIGHT: *The limbs and cams of compounds are drawn together.* JAMIE CUTTS

On release the movement of the limbs is more up and down. JAMIE CUTTS

compound archers have a distinct advantage as there is minimum contact with the string compared to recurves, which have more contact with the string. On release, the only contact between the archer and the equipment is the grip, but until the nock detaches from the string any movement of the riser will affect the path of that string. Torsional movement of the riser and any lateral movement will affect the horizontal path of the nock. Ensuring that the pressure is directly behind the bow will help maximize the consistency of the movement in the riser when you release.

Grip and Bow Arm

Despite a multitude of bows of all types, each with its own grip, the premise for ensuring consistency is the same. The pressure at full draw needs not

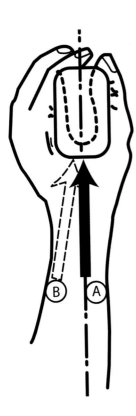

With hand pressure in the grip coming directly from behind, lateral movement is kept to a minimum during the shot.

ing). On release this will affect the vertical path of the string and nock. As you release, the pressure low in the grip causes the top of the riser to move back towards you faster than the bottom. This has a twofold effect: firstly the movement causes the nocking point to move downward; secondly, because the riser is moving back, the top limb is in effect weakened, slowing it down and causing further downward motion of the nocking point.

From these issues alone you can understand that keeping the front arm in place with pressure directly to the target is highly desirable when you are shooting. Keeping the bow arm directly behind the bow and finishing the shot will ensure that, once you have released the string, the bow has a stable and consistent platform to resist against while the string and nock are connected. As the string is released the riser moves towards the archer at a magnitude directly proportional to the mass moving in the opposite direction. On a compound bow most of the movement is vertical, up and down, with only minimal parts of the bow moving away from the archer. The main mass moving away will be the arrow, which is only a small proportion of the weight of the bow and stabilizers. For recurves, a larger proportion of the mass of the bow moves away from the archer on release, as this includes the limbs in addition to the mass of the arrow. Therefore there is more mass moving back towards the archer. With both bow types, however, ensuring that the bow arm is pressure loaded correctly will ensure that the bow has a consistent platform to resist against on every shot.

Grip and Hand Position

The pressure from your bow arm has to press forward through the centreline of the bow. The easiest way of determining how close you are keeping to the centreline is to take a photograph. Set up a camera behind and above the shooting line. The camera should be in a position where it can pick up the string and the long rod through the sight window, so it might take some time to set this up. You can ask someone to stand behind you and look at your alignment but this is very subjective. A photo can be easily enhanced to show the actual alignment and gives you a permanent record of what you are doing. With your bow supported, photograph it from behind so that you can see the align-

only to be consistently directly behind the bow but centred in the riser's axis ('A' on the diagram). Ideally your arm would be directly behind the bow, but if that were the case the string would have to run through the centre of your arm, so that is not possible. Your arm and shoulder are always to the arrow side of the riser ('B' on the diagram). In this position it is very easy for the pressure on the grip to come from that side and this will torque the riser. If you torque the riser at full draw, on release the bow will want to compensate against the turning pressure and the direct pressure (Newton's third law: for every action there is an equal and opposite reaction). The turning pressure on release allows the riser to realign, which in turn changes the horizontal path of the string and the nock attached to it. If the pressure is not directly behind the riser, as you release the riser will move in the opposite direction, again making additional variations to the horizontal path.

The other issue is the vertical pressure placed on the grip. It is difficult to put pressure high on the grip, so that is not usually an issue. It is more usual to put pressure too low down on the grip (heel-

ment of the long rod to the centreline. This is easily done with a recurve as the string centre of the limb and the long rod should be aligned. For compounds you will have to put a temporary marker on the top of the riser, as the string is set to one side of the long rod.

Foam bosses make a good platform from which to take photographs. JAMIE CUTTS

With the camera set up behind you, at full draw the long rod should be in the same alignment as when the bow was at rest. If the long rod is out of alignment you will easily see where a pressure change will bring it back to alignment.

The grip can be modified using a grip former or similar resin builder to change its profile, but the pressure point must remain in the centre of the riser. Some grips have a high side built into them or, if you build a pressure point to the side of the centre, on release you will build a torsional twist into the riser. The height and width of the grip can be modified. If the grip is raised it will tend to focus the pressure into the throat of the grip but this can lead to a less stable wrist. Lowering it can induce pressure too low on the riser. This is more prone to lead to an inconsistency in the pressure point on the grip. In both cases the length of the grip must protrude past the palm of the hand. If it is too short and finishes in the hand it will induce a double pressure point.

The grip can also be adjusted for width and shape. The wider and flatter the grip, the more prone it will be to torquing. If it is too narrow the bow will become uncomfortable in the hand at higher draw weights. Keeping the neck narrow adjacent to

Photographing from an elevated position offers a clear record of alignment at full draw. JAMIE CUTTS

Using a photograph to check the alignment of the string and long rod ensures that results are accurate. JAMIE CUTTS

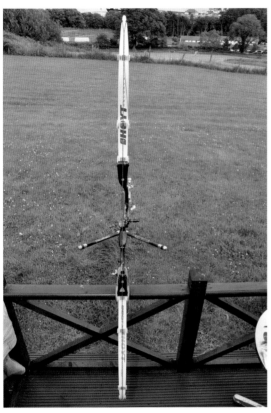

Bow alignment showing position of the string against the long rod. JAMIE CUTTS

Lining the string up with the centre of the launcher provides a reference when placing a marker on the top of the riser to check alignment at full draw.

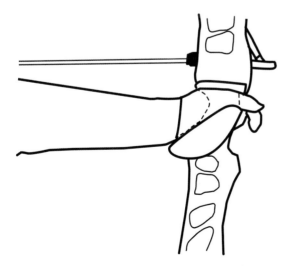

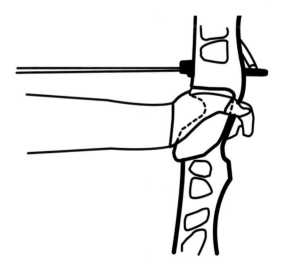

When modifying the grip, ensure that you maintain a full-length grip. This ensures that the pressure at full draw is kept in the throat of the grip.

If the modified grip ends within the palm of the bow hand, the pressure of the hand in the grip will be lowered, having an effect on the bow's performance.

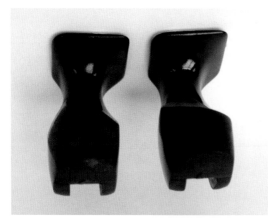

Jäger grips. The one on the left has been remodelled to maintain pressure down the centre of the grip.
FRANCES KEATS

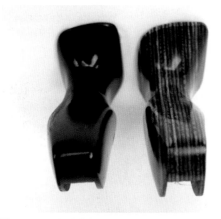

The grip on the left has had the high spot to the left of the throat removed to maintain centre pressure.
FRANCES KEATS

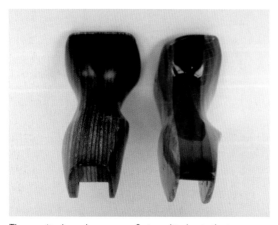

These grips have been manufactured to keep the pressure central and do not require modification. FRANCES KEATS

the pivot point, but wider as it extends, helps with locating it in the hand with the same pressure and alignment, but it also gives more cushioning lower down in the hand. The grip needs to be constructed so that it is easy for you to identify the feeling of where the pressure point should be, as this will aid with maintaining consistency. When you have the pressure behind the bow it will also help to keep the front shoulder in a good position as it induces the muscles in the front chest side of the shoulder to engage, strengthening the whole shoulder girdle.

Keeping your bow arm in position throughout the shot sequence ensures that the bow has a stable consistent platform to recoil against. It is the draw that loads all the muscles and joints in the body like a compressed spring. When the string is released any movement of the arms and equipment comes from the release of tension or unloading of the muscles joints that was built up during the draw. Remember that an increase in draw weight will induce more compression on the body. To maintain the correct draw length for recurve archers, the clicker will have to be moved forward; the opposite is true when moving to a lighter poundage.

Keeping the Front Arm Steady throughout the Shot

Technically the bow needs to have a stable hand to press against only until the nock has left the string. Once it has left the string any further movements to the bow will not affect the flight of the arrow.

The mind and body, however, are very good at anticipating the next step in a sequence of movements. Consequently, as soon as your mind has considered that the shot is finished, the body will start going through the motion of the next step of the sequence: lowering the bow, looking through the scope, reaching for the next arrow. In extreme cases archers can be seen leaning forward to look through their scope, reaching for the next arrow as part of the shot or lowering their bow as they shoot their arrow. The most common movement is lowering the arm. This can be due to the bow being far too heavy, but most of the time it is due to anticipation as the archer 'finishes' the shot on the release of the string while the arrow is still connected to it. Maintaining the bow arm's position throughout the shot ensures that the arrow is not affected as it exits the bow; any bow movement then can occur when

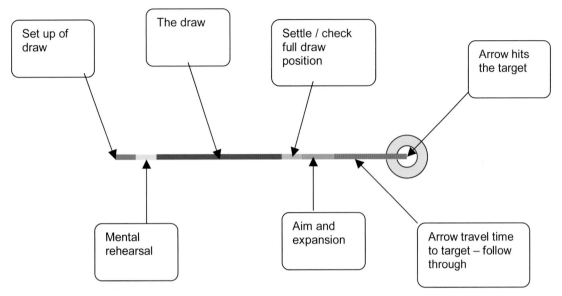

| Set up of draw | The draw | Settle / check full draw position | Arrow hits the target |

| Mental rehearsal | Aim and expansion | Arrow travel time to target – follow through |

The timing from release to impact should be the same for all distances.

The body remains stable as the bow and release hand moves. DEAN ALBERGA

The body remains stable as the bow and release hand moves. DEAN ALBERGA

The body remains stable as the bow and release hand moves. DEAN ALBERGA

The body remains stable as the bow and release hand moves.

the arrow is no longer connected. The usual advice to 'keep your arm up' is not what you need to be thinking about while shooting the arrow. 'Finish the shot' is a far better way of dealing with movement issues during the shot.

The only positive signal that the arrow has left the bow is when it hits the target. If your shot finishes when the arrow hits the target, then any anticipation will not affect the arrow leaving the bow. Not only does every shot sequence need to maintain the same

Thumb release. JAMIE CUTTS

Back tension. JAMIE CUTTS

Thumb release. JAMIE CUTTS

body position, but the length of time taken from when the string is released to the end of the shot should also be the same. To find the timing for this, shoot your arrows at your longest distance. The time from release of the string to the arrow impacting the target is the time period you should use for finishing the shot at all distances. It takes practice to focus on maintaining this timing period, especially at shorter distances, because the arrow impacts the target almost immediately after the release. This results in a tendency to finish the shot too quickly, even during the release, which affects the grouping. When moving from outdoor to indoor distances, you may initially find that you get good groups and scores as you maintain your timing from outdoor shooting. This can drop off, though, and without a determined effort to maintain your shot timing period after the arrow has impacted the target you may find that scores and groups drop off as anticipation movement degrades your shooting. Shooting at longer distances during the indoor season can be a good way to reinforce the focus on the shot timing period.

By developing a deliberate method of finishing your shot you can maintain your focus on the target for all of the shot sequence. All the movement of the arms and bow after the release of the string comes from the release of tension built up through-out the draw. Provided the front arm maintains its position, there is a stable platform for the riser to recoil against. This results in a minimum of anoma-lous movement vectors being imparted to the riser and therefore to the arrow while it is attached to the string, enabling you to shoot more consistent groups.

Release Aids

The only other contact with the equipment is at the string end. A varied choice of release aids is available for compound shooters, differing in the mechanics by which they operate. There are three main types: trigger to release; pull to release; and rotate to release (back tension). Having not shot compound for long, I am not qualified to comment on which type is best, but I do know what you are looking for as a result of the release aid being activated: the string on a compound should move directly towards the riser with the bend of the arrow being in a verti-cal plane, whereas a recurve needs the arrow to bend in the horizontal plane.

The horizontal bend in the recurve arrow can clearly be seen. DEAN ALBERGA

Carter evolution – pull to release. JAMIE CUTTS

Horizontal flex of arrow from Larry Godfrey's bow. DEAN ALBERGA

Although the arrow on a compound bends in the vertical plane, it is far less apparent than the bend in a recurve arrow.

Horizontal flex of arrow. DEAN ALBERGA

Release at 60 frames per second, taken with a high-speed camera.

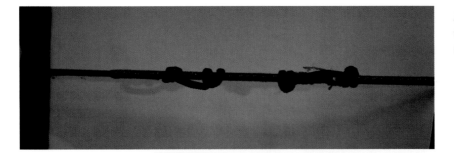

D loops tied on the string to show opposing angles.
KAREN HENDERSON

The D loop tied to the string to complement the angle at which the release aid will be attached.

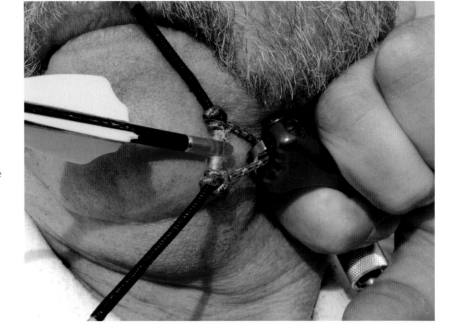

The release aid needs to be connected to the string so that on release it does not impart a sideways movement. The type of release aid used determines the amount of minor sideways movement imparted to the string. Whether the release aid is connected directly to the string or on a 'D' loop, the biggest variation that the archer can impart is the amount of twist/rotation delivered to the string at the connection point. Owing to the 'let off' on a compound at full draw, there is not a lot of tension on the string, so limiting the twist on it should be kept to a minimum. If you connect to the string directly, unless you have a swivel head fitted, care should be taken with keeping the jaws of the release aid at 90 degrees to the string. For a D loop shooter there is the initial conundrum of whether the loop knots should be tied on the same side or opposite each other. If the knots are tied on the same side, the D loop rotates towards the knot side. If the knots are tied opposite each other, which seems to be the preferred method, it imparts a slight twist over the nock. A slight twist imparted to the loop by the release aid, by arranging the knots of the loop in the opposite position, can cancel out both twists. If the twist caused by the position of the release aid is more severe, then increasing the length of the loop will help to ensure that the twist from the release aid is imparted more to the loop and less to the string.

Tabs

The tab not only protects your fingers, it also helps to position the vertical and horizontal alignment of the nock in relation to your eye.

As the string is released from the fingers it starts to move towards the bow. At the same time the string moves away from the fingertips, inducing a lateral bend into the shaft of the arrow. As it does so, the front of the arrow presses into the button. The path that the nock describes as it is connected to the string will determine the final path of the arrow to the target. Variations to the release will vary the path to the target, resulting in larger groups. In adjusting the finger position, alignment, tab and face material you can decrease the number of variables affecting the path of the string on release, improving group size. The draw weight will also have a bearing on how the string, fingers and tab interact. The higher the draw weight, the more it is ripped from the fingers on release. This makes it harder to interfere with the path that the string takes. The lighter the draw weight, the better the release needs to be, as it is easier to alter the string path.

The tab has a large contact area with the string. As a result it can induce a number of variables into the shot:

- Positioning of the fingers on the string
- Pressure of the fingers on the string
- Tab type
- Tab face material
- Vertical string displacement
- Use, size and position of a finger spacer.

The placement of the fingers on the string should be based around the position of the first joint of your middle finger at full draw, counting the thumb as a finger. This is because the middle finger should take the largest proportion of pressure as it is the strongest and has the best connection of tendons to maintain a consistent release. The length and position of the adjacent fingers' final joints will determine their

The tendon of the middle finger runs the straightest and is the most robust, hence the loading of 70 per cent on this finger.

The tab is as small as it can be while still protecting the fingers.

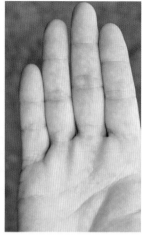

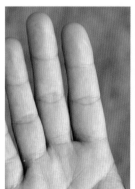

The alignment of an individual's finger joints will contribute to the fingers' positions on the string or release aid.

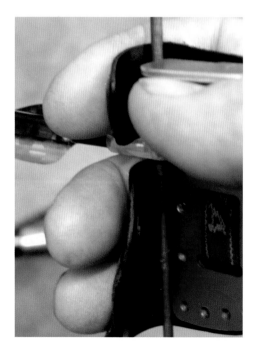

LEFT: The visual cue that my finger placement is correct prior to the draw is the position of the first joint as seen through the slot in the tab. As the string is drawn back it settles in the middle finger's first joint.

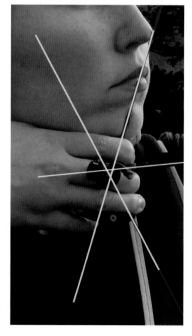

RIGHT: Displacement of the string by fingers and tab.

final positions on the string. If the middle finger joint can be placed in the same position every time, the other fingers can only go in the right place.

The best way of ensuring that the middle finger is properly positioned is to check the position of the finger against the tab and the string at the start of the draw. I start with the string in the area of the centre pad of the middle finger. The visual cue for this is to be able to see the crease of the first joint through the narrow split in the tab where the arrow fits. If I can see the joint it confirms that my finger is in the correct position to start the draw. Although there is a high sense of touch in the hands, a visual confirmation of the exact finger position helps to reinforce how it feels. The thickness of the tab face also has a bearing on how much you can feel the string: the thinner the face, the more you can feel the string but the less your fingers are protected. Since a thinner tab is less stiff, the angle from the nock will be less acute and it moves out of the way of the string on release. With a thicker tab your fingers will be better protected from the release, but you will be less able to feel the string position on

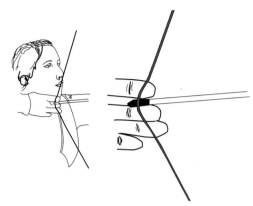

The dimensions of your fingers, combined with the construction of your tab, will determine the amount of vertical displacement of the string.

your fingers. This has the advantage, however, that slight variations in the pressure of your fingers will have less effect as it will be absorbed by the tab's thickness. The stiffer material increases the amount of horizontal movement to the string and it will be harder for the string to push it out of the way. It also increases the vertical displacement.

As a starting point, 70 per cent of the draw pressure is taken on the middle finger, with the remainder divided 10 per cent to the top finger and 20 per cent on the bottom finger. This means that the bulk of the draw weight is below the arrow towards the physical centre of the bow. It is best not to touch

LEFT: The tab is held aligned to the hand with the finger spacer and top plate.

BELOW: Elite and Saker tabs can both be shot without a spacer and are aligned to the string.

the arrow with the fingers as it tends to interfere with the release. If the middle finger presses against the arrow at full draw, it pushes the arrow up from the rest. Pressure down from the top finger is not so much of a problem as it presses the arrow down onto the rest, although any pressure should be kept to a minimum. If you need to use the clicker to keep the arrow on the rest at full draw, it is likely that the middle finger is pushing it off. The clicker is there to ensure that the arrow is drawn to the correct length, not to hold the arrow on the rest. To test this you should find that, when shooting without a clicker, the arrows should stay on the rest on every shot. In testing you will need to shoot at least 100 arrows.

Keeping the tab firmly in place on the fingers.
DEAN ALBERGA

The Soma tab plate is aligned with the string when used without a finger spacer. JAMIE CUTTS

With the hand held firmly against the jaw line, the pressure should be maintained while aiming.
DEAN ALBERGA

Every arrow should stay in place. If it comes off at any time it indicates that there is some element of variation in your finger position on the string and it will need to be worked on. The thickness of your fingers determines the vertical displacement of the string. Your plan should be to keep the vertical displacement as short as possible but without squeezing the nock. The further you spread your fingers away from the nock, the larger the vertical displacement. Once the fingers have been positioned on the string they should be kept there until you release. Many archers let their fingers relax (uncurl) at full draw. This makes it harder to get the arrow through the clicker because they are letting the arrow move forward while they are trying to draw it back. This also means that variations in the time at full draw will lead to variations in the position of the fingers at release, resulting in group variations. The best way of checking to see how well you are keeping your fingers in position on the string is to video your finger position. Moving the clicker back, so that the arrow does not come through the clicker, and then coming to full draw for an extended period will give you clearer information on how well you are maintaining your finger position.

There are basically two tab types or methods of using your tab. With the A&F type the tab is aligned using the hand and head, whereas the Cavalier Elite type of tab is aligned with the string. Using a tab with a finger spacer aligns the tab with the fingers and hand. If the spacer is too narrow, the tab's alignment with the fingers can vary. Spacers can be made out of all types of material, but it has to be semi-rigid since material that is too soft results in variations in its possible positions. You should always bear in mind that you will require at least one spare tab. When making any modifications to your equipment you will need to be able to reproduce them. You should be able to use either tab with little or no changes to the group's position or size. Plastic chopping boards provide a good material for making spacers. They are of uniform thickness and can be easily cut using a junior hacksaw and shaped with sandpaper. You can make quite a lot from one board.

With both types of tabs, the loop that your finger goes through should be made from a material that does not stretch. If elastic is used for the loop it will allow the tab's position to vary, depending on the tension put on it. With a cord, the position of the tab will remain more consistent. The gap between the platform and the spacer on an A&F needs to be adjusted so that your index finger is held firmly between the two to reduce the variation of angle between the tab and hand. If you are using an Elite type tab and aligning it with the string, the spacer should not be used. The front spine of the tab is placed against the string and this is what maintains the relative position of the hand and head. With

The slot in the tab needs to be made so that it does not pinch the arrow at full draw. If the slot is too big, however, it will lead to a vertical inconsistency in the position of the tab and fingers on the string. JAMIE CUTTS

both types of tabs, at full draw the hand needs to run along the jaw line. If the platform is too high it will lower the hand away from your face, making it harder to maintain a consistent hand position.

Not only does the thickness of the tab make a difference to how the string behaves, so does the type of material used in its construction and how the material in contact with the string behaves in combination with that used for the centre serving. Deciding on the contact area of the tab and string, and how much excess material protrudes past the fingers, is mainly about sorting out the best combination that works for you.

As you need to have at least two tabs, the materials used must be easily replaced and reproduced. It is better if the material is fairly hard-wearing so it does not have to be replaced too often. I would look for a material that lasts for a season. You have enough to do without shooting in and setting up a new tab face every month. For Elite tabs I use two cordovan faces with the second used as a backing. I have found that the original material used as a backing is too soft and is easily deformed. When this happens the backing for the index finger stretches and falls down, covering the gap where the arrow fits. It then interferes with the arrow on release, affecting the groups. By using two cordovan faces I have found that the one used as a backing is less prone to deforming. Even when using cordovan faces you need to make sure you are able to get the same thickness of face as there can be a lot of variation. Whenever I was at Quicks Archery I would ask to go through their stock of faces and select ones with the thickness I wanted. If you are going to cut and make tab faces from other materials, make sure that you have a good stock of similar material. Many leather goods producers have a selection of offcuts that can be bought at a reasonable price. I have a new spare face for my tab and use that as a template to mark out and cut new tabs. All you need for this is a good pair of scissors and a leather hole punch that removes the material as it makes the hole. Just puncturing the material moves it to the side and when you insert the screw to hold it in place it tends to pucker, causing an uneven face. This is especially so when making faces for the Elite tab. Because it is aligned with the string, you need to make sure that the gap for the nock is only just bigger than the nock itself. If the gap is too big you

can get vertical displacement on the string and the group height will increase. Too narrow a gap and it will catch on the nock again, giving bigger groups or errant arrows. When making tab faces from leather be aware that it has a grain; the hide of an animal will have less stretch when lined up with the spine than when across its spine. As you try to pull the leather in different directions you will see that it will stretch in one direction, across the line of the spine, but not so easily when it is aligned with the length of the back. The tab should be cut from the leather so that the line of the fingers is in the same direction as that of the leather that is more resistant to stretch, which was originally aligned with the spine. This will help to ensure that there is very little give in the leather as you draw the bow string.

With all tabs, excess material should be removed from the face of the tab as it interferes with the path of the string. This applies not only to the material extending past the ends of your fingers but also to the material above and below the fingers that affects the vertical displacement of the string. In order to see what parts of the tab are used, put talcum powder on your hand and then shoot the tab. This should show the areas of the tab that you are using. It is better to cut off a little bit of the tab at a time until you get it right. The tab face is there to protect your fingers and any extra just gets in the way.

Synthetic materials are especially good in countries where the weather conditions are variable. It is very useful to have a material that releases the string with no change of drag whether it is wet or dry. The Spigarelli Vulcolan face can easily be adapted to fit other tabs and works well in all conditions. Some shops can supply squares of the material from which to make faces. With a cordovan leather backing, this can make a very consistent hard-wearing face. All leather faces can be ruined by the wet. As the leather stretches it will remain deformed, so as far as possible you should try not to let them get too wet. This means keeping your tab in your quiver pouch all the time. This will help maintain the consistency of your shot routine and keep your equipment safe. At home competitions you may find that leaving your tab hooked over your sight does not cause any problems. Keeping your ancillary equipment in a pouch on your belt, however, will ensure that whatever the weather, and whatever you are wearing, you will be able to go to the same place to find your equipment, thus enabling you to carry out your shot routine. It will also ensure that it cannot be interfered with as you have your equipment on you at all times and you are less likely to misplace it.

Shooting Form

The above advice is all about anything mechanical that might interfere with the shot. Unless this is addressed first you may find you are just trying to chase form when there is actually a physical interference to your consistency.

To physically repeat the shot, the body needs to be in the same position for every shot and the muscles under the same tension. A consistent foot position gives a good base to work from. If you do not have a consistent position you can use target pins or tape for indoors. Working with a partner, you need to go through your whole shot sequence and record every aspect of your draw and release. You can use a video for this but you will still need to transcribe it after the session.

Record every aspect of the experience using one sense at a time – sight, touch, sound, smell – numbering them as you go. This needs to start from the point you walk on to the line. Starting with sight, record everything you see as you go through the draw:

1. I place my right foot close to the shooting line with the heel closer to the line than the toe.
2. I cross the line with my left foot and place it 1in behind the line of the right foot and with the heel pointed more towards the line.
3. I place the tip of my limb on the toe of my left foot.
4. I take the finger sling around the front of the bow and slip it onto my thumb.
5. Etc.

Once you have recorded all the visual aspects of the shots you can then record your kinaesthetic/touch associated feelings during the shot. You might need to go through the whole draw with your eyes closed in order to accurately record what you do. You can then do the same for sound and smell. Once this

has been completed you should have a list covering every aspect of your senses as experienced during your draw and shot. For many there will be very little to record for smell during the draw, except perhaps the smell of beeswax when you are at full draw.

You will then be able to combine all the senses for each step of the shot, which at full draw will culminate with:

1a. Visual – the blurry string, then the sight just to the left of it and the gold of the target in the centre of the sight.
1b. Feel – the pressure of the grip against the palm of my hand and the light touch of the finger sling on my index finger and thumb. The string against the centre of my chin and the tip of my nose. The pressure of the string through

First, position the fingers and tab on the string and tension the bow to keep the fingers in place. JAMIE CUTTS

Second, position the hand in the grip to align behind the bow. JAMIE CUTTS

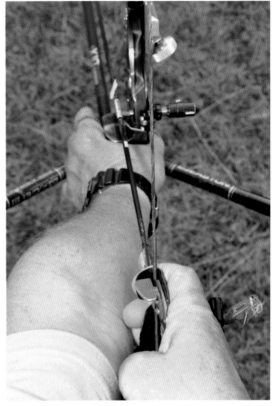

Third, position the fingers against the arm to align the body for the start of the draw. JAMIE CUTTS

the tab, mainly on my middle finger. The tab plate under my chin with the base of my thumb against my jaw line and throat. Pressure in my front shoulder pressing forward and the feeling of a line from my draw hand passing though my back elbow.

Ic. Listening for the sound of the wind to give an indication of strength.

Id. The smell of the string.

This records the senses, but you also need to record your thoughts while you carry out the shot. This helps to clarify what you are thinking about when shooting. The more you shoot, the better you will be able to put into words what you are thinking about as you shoot. When you are shooting your best at practice you should settle down and think about what was going through your mind as you were shooting. It will involve identifying a set of thoughts that gives your conscious mind something

positive to focus on that does not interfere with the shot. I would go through the checklist of the shot all the way up to full draw, making sure that all aspects of the draw felt right. When I am at full draw I keep my conscious mind focused on keeping the bow hand relaxed and let the subconscious shoot the arrow. This way my 'trying' is directed to relaxing an aspect of the shot. This ensures that the conscious mind is actively engaged and does not interfere with the movement of the shot. You may perhaps have noticed that the shooting went well on a breezy day because you were thinking of the wind and aiming off, but on a calm day it did not go so well. This could be because there were no mental distractions, so your conscious mind 'helped' with the shot. The trick is to find a mental sequence that will keep the mind occupied but not interfere with your shooting.

The reason for spending time making a list of all the mental and physical aspects of your shot

The string is initially placed against the jaw or chin.
DEAN ALBERGA

sequence is so that you have a detailed account of your shot. In cutting this into parts you will be able to study it and find areas that you can improve to make the shot sequence more consistent. As you make these changes, you can change your written sequence and keep it updated with your current shot sequence. This will also be used when you carry out mental rehearsals.

What you are looking for in improving your shot sequence are those parts of the set-up and draw that can be given visual positioning cues: the position of the fingers on the string, how the hand is set in the grip and the distance they are from your bow arm. It is quite easy to ensure that these are correct.

The final part of the draw is the anchor position. The only visual cue for this is the string or peep sight in front of your eye. The rest is about how it feels. The string needs to be drawn back so that it presses into the bone of the jaw; if it only touches the skin of the face it again can lead to variations in position. The string should then be placed on the centre of your nose as it is an easier place to feel than somewhere down the side of it. The key point of the draw is to place the string on the jaw first, then the nose. If you do this the other way around the nose can get squashed and the string is not placed firmly enough on the chin bone. A consistent hand posi-

The string is then settled into position on the nose.
DEAN ALBERGA

tion against the jaw can help ensure that there is minimum movement of the hand prior to the shot. If the hand is not against the jaw line and face it makes it very difficult to determine its position.

Although the anchor position needs to be consistent and easy to replicate, it is how you get there that gives consistency to the release that is more important. The two aspects that do this are the position of the shoulders at the beginning of the draw and the position they are in at full draw.

Even with your foot position consistent, the position of the shoulders can vary. In order to put the

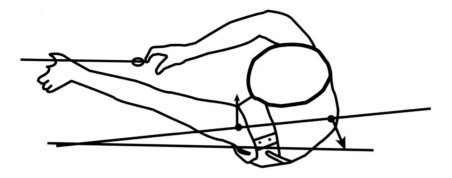

The back shoulder has to come forward at the start of the draw.

At the end of the draw the rear shoulder should have been returned back into the correct alignment.

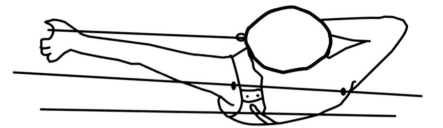

arrow into the bow you need to reach forward. This brings your shoulders squarer to the target at the beginning of the draw. The back shoulder is towards the target, opening your chest towards the boss. You need to ensure that the shoulders are brought back into line. This should be carried out during the first part of the draw so that any rotations on the joints are carried out when there is a lower load on them. If you carry out joint rotations later in your draw the joint will be under a greater load and there is more chance of injury.

The start position of your draw can easily be set visually. If the distance between the forearm of the bow arm and the draw hand is the same at the start of the draw, it will help to improve the probability that the draw will follow the same line, ensuring that the loading of the muscles is the same for every shot. Variations in this distance at the start of the draw will cause variations in the loading of your muscles and therefore variations in the release of those muscles. You can keep the string lined up on the riser as you draw and this will also help to keep

The back shoulder is moved towards the bow so that the hand can be placed on the string. DEAN ALBERGA

At full draw it has been rotated into the correct position. DEAN ALBERGA

Fourth alignment is the draw hand brushing the face to maintain a consistent draw. JAMIE CUTTS

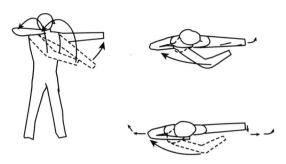

To get to full draw the various body parts travel in arcs. To execute the shot all movement needs to be towards and away from the target. After the shot the archer's limbs rotate again to absorb the release of the string.

the draw consistent. I prefer to keep my attention on the clicker during the draw, as this helps to keep my attention on what I am doing on the line. I then make the back of my hand brush past my face as an additional reference to help keep the draw as consistent as I can.

At Full Draw

Once you have brought the string back to your face you need to execute the shot while maintaining the sight on the target. At full draw there should not be

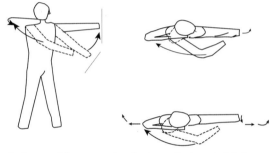

Both arms follow curved paths to get the bow to full draw.

The path of the arms to get the bow to full draw. Consistency in these paths ensures consistency on release. JAMIE CUTTS

perceptible movement to execute the shot. This is where there seems to be conflicting advice: some say pull, others say push or push and pull together. None of these descriptions are really much help. The ideal shot would be to start with the string/hand at the anchor central position and expand

At full draw only a minimum of the point should be under the clicker. DEAN ALBERGA

At full draw the clicker should be within 2 or 3mm of the end of the arrow.

With the clicker in this position on the arrow, linear expansion is possible.

around this point until you are at the position of full draw; for this, however, you would need telescopic arms. The draw brings the string and arm to anchor (the central position). In this movement the arrow moves towards your face. Once at the central position the arrow should remain motionless in relation to the head, body and ground. At this point the pressure for the shot is directed from the shoulders and chest, with the front shoulder towards the target and the back shoulder away from the target. If the string position is noted against the chest there should be no noticeable movement. Video of an archer shooting properly illustrates how the arrow remains stationary in relation to a fixed object in the background. From the start of the draw both arms move in arcs upwards and across the line of the target. In the act of executing the shot the pressure is directed along the line of the target. Once the arrow has been released the arms move in arcs across the target.

The movement is the same for both compound and recurve bows, but with recurve archers a movement is required to get the arrow through the clicker involving an extension from the centre forward, with a balanced pressure in the opposite direction. This is why the position of the clicker is critical. At full draw there should be only 2–3mm of arrow to get through the clicker as this is the amount of expansion available from the shoulders and chest. The only way to get more than 2–3mm through the clicker is to pull the arrow past centre or to overextend the arm forward. This is unwanted movement as it incorporates the movement of smaller muscles. When the movement is achieved by the shoulders, the expansion across them is more consistent as the muscles are bigger. If the clicker is too far back, making you overdraw when you are at full extension, the movement to come through the clicker has to come from an unwanted arc of movement. At the correct position for full draw you need to have 2–3mm of point left to come through the clicker, but you also need to have enough linear expansion left to execute the shot. This is why it is better to underdraw rather than overdraw. When under-drawing you are able to expand in line with the target. If you overdraw, the movement required to activate the clicker will have to come from an arced movement across the line of the target, which will lead to inconsistencies. This would be the same movement

View of the field of targets at the Commonwealth Games in Delhi, 2010. To the left are the practice targets.
DEAN ALBERGA

for compounds, although there is no clicker to come through at the point of full pressure. The pressure of draw expansion must be linear towards the target.

Point of Focus: Centre of Gaze

The point of focus is the size of the area that you can focus on at any given distance. Standing with the targets set out at 70m, as you look down the field you have a view of all the targets within your peripheral vision. Outside the centre of gaze you will be able to detect movement and direct your gaze to that movement. If you direct your gaze to one of the targets you will be able to see the whole target but you can then narrow down your gaze to smaller areas of the target. Even at 70m you can direct your gaze from one side of the gold to the other. The point of focus at 70m is roughly half the size of the gold. For every distance you shoot the size of the gold will be bigger, smaller or the same size as your point of focus. If the size of the gold is bigger than your point of focus, aiming at the gold will lead to inconsistencies in your group size as you can be aiming from one side of the gold to the other. If your group size is double that of your point of focus at 70m, you should find that if you are able to maintain your aim at the centre of the gold, all your arrows will then hit the gold. If you just aim at the area of the gold your overall group size will be within

the red, which makes a big difference in score for the same skill level.

A round shot in the UK, known as a Portsmouth, involves 60 arrows at 20 yards (ca. 18m) at a 60cm target face. If you compare the size of the groups shot at this size of face with groups shot at a 40cm face at the same distance, it is usually seen that the group size on the larger face is bigger. The reason for this is that when learning to shoot you are looking for your arrows to hit the gold, and that is what you aim at. As you progress you continue aiming at the gold. When aiming at a 40cm gold its size is only

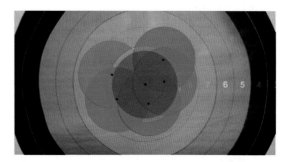

If you are shooting gold-sized groups and maintain a consistent aiming point, all your arrows will go on the gold. If you simply aim at the gold, however, even shooting the same sized groups will lead to arrows scoring in the red.
FRANCES KEATS

slightly larger than your point of focus, so good shots will go in the middle. The gold on a 60cm target face at the same distance, however, is twice the size of your point of focus. When aiming at the gold you can easily be aiming in the nine. The trick is to aim at the centre of the gold, as the ten ring is about the size of your point of focus.

When shooting target, the gold at 90m and 50m are about the same size as your point of focus, so if your arrows hit the centre of your point of focus you will get tens. At 70m and 30m, however, the gold is bigger than your point of focus and you need to have a plan. Aim at the centre of the gold or aim off at the divide between the gold and the red, adjusting the sight so that the arrow lands in the ten. This gives you a positive small area to aim at. Since this area is smaller than the point of focus, the size of the group will then depend on your skill and the weather conditions. Group sizes can be tested by either putting up smaller faces at the longer distances, for example 80cm at 70m, and then shooting and recording the size of your groups, or by putting a small black disc at the centre of the gold or using a felt-tip marker to black out the centre of the gold. You must be able to see the disc or target face clearly so you can focus on it. Shoot for score and see if there is any improvement in group size and score. If the score improves you need to work on refining your point

of aim. Poorer scores can come from simply aiming at an area and not at a point. Another way of achieving this is to put up a new 120cm face and place an 80cm face over the top of it, with the centre of the 80cm directly over the 120cm. Move to 70m and shoot at the 80cm face. When you have shot thirty-six arrows, remove the 80cm face and score the holes left in the 120cm target.

Sight Ring

Different sight rings suit different archers. There is no magic design. When selecting a sight ring you need to be aware of the factors that may help or hinder you.

A sight with a dot can be placed precisely on the target, but in trying to be precise it may lengthen the time you are at full draw. It will also appear to be a different size in relation to the gold at different distances. At some distances it may even hide the gold, which can lead to the archer moving the sight slightly before the shot in order to see the gold.

An open sight ring may at first seem to be less than precise but the brain is very good at lining up concentric rings. The size of the ring will also be a contributing factor: too small and you may start to over-aim, too large and you may end up looking away from the centre of the gold towards the edge of the ring, so drawing your attention and

Placing a smaller face over a larger one gives a point of aim instead of an area. This exercise can be carried out at all distances as a means of checking the aiming focus.

The gold is always visible when using a sight ring that cuts the gold but does not cover it.

If the sight ring is too thick it will obscure the gold, hiding it from view. This can affect some archers' aiming processes.

groups away from the gold. The thickness of the ring can also cause issues. If it is too thin you may struggle to see it in some light. If too thick it may block your view of the target on windy days. When you are focusing on the gold with a thick ring the gold will disappear for periods as the sight moves across the target face. I use an Arten pin sight with a plastic insert left in and the pin cut out. This makes the ring wall about 1.5mm thick. As this moves across the target face, at some distances it cuts through the gold but not obscure it; at others it may fully block the view of the gold, but only momentarily.

Magnification on compound scopes can also cause issues. At higher magnifications the gold looks closer or bigger, but they also increase the apparent movement of the sight.

Strings

The choice of strings for compounds is purely down to finding the best material and combination of strands for the string and cables that work for you and your bow. This in itself is a fair amount of work. The colour is a matter of choice as you will be using a peep sight and the colour does not make any difference visually. For recurves, however, you

need to find the material that works best for you, the number of twists, strands, centre serving material, loop end material and loop size. Colour also plays a big part in group size for recurves as the string picture is used to aim the bow. The colour of the string determines how the string looks to the archer at full draw. The brightness of the light has a great effect on the archer's perception of the string's width. Light-coloured strings look wider in a bright light, whereas dark strings look thinner. In poor light, lighter-coloured strings can be seen but darker ones can become indistinct. As your aim relies on the string picture, a thin but visible string enables you to have a more consistent aim. I tend to use darker-coloured strings outdoors and lighter ones indoors. It depends, however, on the location, time of year and weather conditions. The strength of the sun varies according to where you are in the world and the time of year. Early or late in the season the light can change according to sunrise and sunset times, as light levels increase from the start of shooting and drop off at the end of the day. Indoor shooting can have similar issues as some venues are totally enclosed and rely on artificial light of varying quality. Others have windows that let in natural light and again the sunrise and sunset times have to be taken

How well an archer can see the string while aligning the string picture depends on the ambient light and background conditions. In bright light strings can appear thicker. KAREN HENDERSON

In poor light conditions darker strings can 'disappear', making it harder to keep the string picture constant.

into account as they will radically change the levels within the venue. I found that red or purple are good all-rounders for outdoors and straw/yellow for indoor shooting. The other colours I like are black and blue, which also appear distinct in bright light. The serving material chosen not only has to give a good release from your tab material but needs to stay in place on the string. Some combinations of string and serving materials work well together and the serving stays in place. Others, though, can be very slick in conjunction with the tab but unfortunately may slide on the string, allowing the nocking point or D loop to move. Check-tuning will ensure that the nocking point has not moved, but a good combination of materials should give very little movement of the serving on the string and it is well tensioned. You cannot afford to have your nocking point move during a competition week: from start to finish it needs to stay where you set it.

Blank Boss and Closed Eyes Release

It is through blank boss shooting, with or without a target face, and closed eyes release that you can concentrate on working on aspects of repeating your shot. You can now understand why the initial part of the draw is carried out with your eyes open, using every visual cue to help ensure that the draw is consistent. At full draw the visual picture stays the same. This is when you can close your eyes, leaving the last image you saw held clearly in your mind while you to carry on with the shot, which allows you to focus on the feeling of finishing the shot.

There are many considerations to take into account when endeavouring to repeat your shot. It is not just your physical and mental condition that needs to be considered, but the environment in which you are practising and how that may differ from the one that you are preparing to compete in.

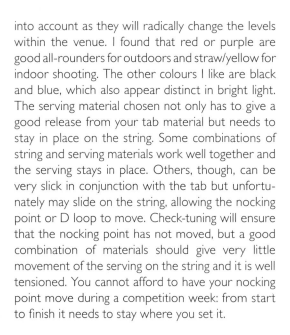

Closing the eyes on release enables the archer to feel the shot better. DEAN ALBERGA

CHAPTER 7

SHOOTING LOG: DEAR DIARY

When I first made the British squad in 1996 I was asked to keep a diary. I was under the understanding that it was for the benefit of the coaches so they could monitor my progress. I was very pleased at being on the squad, so I bought myself a diary and filled it in for them.

Until then I had not kept a diary or shooting log, which is what it really was. I would score my shoots in a score book but that was about it. I was somewhat surprised that very little attention was paid to the log I was keeping beyond a cursory look. As I found it a little tiresome to look back at the logs, I decided to put it on the computer as well using the following format, which evolved over the next few years. This allowed me to track the results easily and correlate them quickly to any changes to the equipment, training or tuning.

I used red to denote competitions and results and purple to indicate when I was shooting internationally. For the first year I kept a dual system, writing it in a diary and keeping it electronically. I later swapped to using only the computer, but I found that I needed to keep the diary daily, even when I was competing abroad, in order to make sure all the

		Activity	Arrows	Distance	Duration in hours	Remarks	arrow per week	Hours per week
24	Fri	drive to norwich						
25	Sat	norwich fita	170	1287				
26	sun	norwich fita	170	1318				
27	Mon	norwich head to head		70m		318,331. 151,162,107 out to Neil		
28	Tue	Travel to Scotland	185	70m	3	spacer on tab		
29	Wed	Cycle		18.5 miles		average 15.2		
		Montrose maltings	144		3			
30	Thu	indoor maltings	224	60/50m	8.5	fixed lights		
31	Fri	Montrose maltings	72	70m	2			
#####	Sat	bathgate fita		1278				
2	Sun	bathgate fita		1187		a bit of a gale	625	17
3	Mon	Cycle		10 miles	36'55"			
		indoor maltings	161	60,50,30	4	adjusted both bows		
4	Tue	Cycle		10 miles	33'54"			
		indoor maltings	173	60,50,30	3	TP		
5	Wed	Montrose maltings	203	70m	4	boy moved nocking point up.		
		Cycle		10 miles	32'25"			
6	Thu	Montrose maltings	142	70m	3	Girl good groups		
7	Fri	indoor maltings	258	60m50m	3			
8	Sat	Cycle		18.5 miles	1			
		indoor maltings	102	30m	3			
9	sun	travel to china			23		1039	24
10	Mon	arrive in China						
11	Tue	Climb the Great wall			1			
12	Wed	unofficial practice	132	30m,50m	6	girl		
13	Thu	run			0.5	run to park with Alison		
		unofficial practice	144	50,70,30	3			
14	Fri	unofficial practice	106	all	3	girl went well		

A simple spreadsheet enables you to track your training and scores without too much effort.

My paper diaries. FRANCES KEATS

key points were recorded. So I went back to keeping both a paper and a computer log.

Keeping a simple layout made it easier to keep track of any changes that I made. I would look at all the results and note the better results, taking into account the weather. From this I was able to start working out what training routines gave the best results. I could also see how scores changed with adjustments to equipment and tuning. These could be both positive and negative, as sometimes changes to tuning gave good results during practice but lower results during competition. Tuning is about making the bow as forgiving as possible but maintaining the groups. On a number of times I

was fortunate enough to shoot with Steve Hallard. I noticed that he always shot consistently, even if the groups were not always very tight, and this gave him a great score. Sébastien Flute won the gold medal in the men's individual competition at the 1992 Olympics by keeping his arrows in the gold. This was consistency under pressure. There are times when you are shooting well and the groups are superb, but if the shot is a little 'off' the arrows go wide. By backing away slightly from this point of tuning and bow set-up you will still get good groups, but if your shot is a little 'off' the arrow will still go close to the group, giving you a far better score overall. The key to this is good diary-keeping. The diary or training log is to help with your planning and to keep track of what you have been doing. When you spend most of your days shooting, either at competition or practice, you must have a comprehensive way of recording everything you do. I have lost count of the number of archers who claim to remember everything they do, but most are unable to remember what they had for lunch the day before.

Initial Diary

Although everyone aspiring to the top of their sport

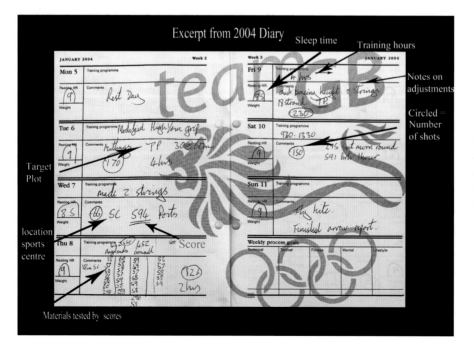

Sample page of diary with an explanation of notations. FRANCES KEATS

or profession will need different levels of information for their diaries to fully meet their needs, I believe that you should always start by covering everything. For the first year, at least, you should keep both full paper and electronic diaries.

Paper Diary

Select an A5-sized diary that shows a week for every spread. This ensures that you can see what you have done for the entire week and that each day is printed in the same place on every page. This enables you to follow your progress in subsequent weeks. The paper diary should be the main repository for your information.

Your diary should contain anything that might affect your shooting:

- The number of arrows shot
- Time at practice
- Practice distance and target size
- Focus of your practice
- Competition scores
- Positive key statements as a reminder
- Equipment changes and adjustments
- Strings made
- Other activities that may affect your performance
- Future events
- Reminders for future training
- Shooting venue
- Sleep patterns
- Diet changes or anomalies
- Check-tune
- Rest
- Picture library

Number of Arrows Shot

Keeping account of the number of arrows you have shot is fundamental to ensuring that you are maintaining your training levels, which in turn builds confidence. Although maintaining an arrow count of over 1,000 for one week's training is the easiest way to judge time spent shooting, it is not the arrow count that matters but the quality of those shots. It is the 1,000 shots that you make in a week, each one to the best of your ability, that matter. You have to ensure that you are always shooting well and not just reaching a number at the end of the week. For counting arrows you can use a hand click counter,

A counter enables an archer to keep a tally of the number of arrows shot over a session.

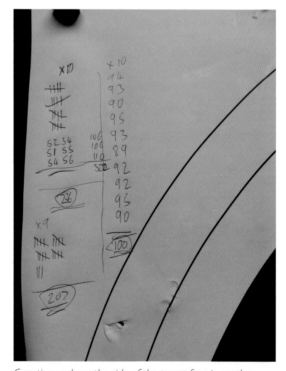

Counting ends on the side of the target face is another way to keep a tally of the quantity of arrows shot and the scores for ends.

which can be bought in most stationery shops or archery shops. You can count the ends you have shot by marking them off on the target face after every end. To start with it is best to account for all your arrows. It is sometimes surprising how few arrows are shot at the longer distances, especially when shooting with others. I put a circle around all total daily arrow counts. Marking down how many arrows I have shot at each distance helps to note not just the total arrow count but the time spent practising at each distance. For thirty-minute full reversals I use a count of 180, circled and underlined to indicate that these were not shot arrows.

Time at Practice

In keeping account of the time spent practising and training, you can cross-reference this with both arrow count and what training you are doing at practice. This enables you to better plan practices and training at future sessions, in conjunction with your weekly planner. There will be times when you have all the time you need for every aspect of your training. At others time will be restricted, perhaps due to travel or work commitments, or you may need to carry out specific training in the limited time

The short range at my club's indoor venue, which is only 6 minutes from home.

between major events. My shooting venue is not far away and is very easy to set up: the indoor range is permanently set up and it takes only twenty minutes to set up two targets on the outdoor range, and the same to take them down. As a result I need to factor in very little time for travel for practice, but depending on the venues used you may need to allow rather more.

Practice Distance and Target Size

Recording the distances shot helps you to keep account of the work put in for competition requirements. Many target archers focus on the shorter distances, as they are easier to set up, and hardly ever practise at their longest distance. Noting down the distance against arrows shot and the time taken ensures that you practise across your full range. You should keep a note of the target size when practising at longer or shorter distances than the face is normally used at, for example when using an 80cm face at 70m.

Focus of Your Practice

You need to make a note of those areas of your shot on which you are working, remembering that adjustments to your technique will take at least 1,000 arrows shot before they become incorporated into your shot sequence. You may, for example, spend a whole week working on your release, building up a picture of the areas that you work on the most by recording the physical actions. You will then be able to ensure that you constantly cover all the areas of your shot and do not neglect any aspect of it.

Competition Scores

The score at a competition is the only one that counts. Archers often complain that they shoot better in practice. When you are doing everything right, they should always be at about the same level. The competition score is a direct reflection of how well you have prepared for that event. As your preparation improves, so the scores at events will also rise. It is not just the total score, however, that needs to be recorded: you should also note the placing at that event and the weather conditions, including the wind direction and how gusty or even the wind was. Wind direction is important and can provide a useful indication of your tuning. A right-handed recurve archer, for example, may find that the score is good when the wind travels from left to right, but it is significantly poorer when going from right to left. This could be an indication that the arrow may be too close to centre-shot. With experience you will be able to judge the score you should have shot for the conditions. Your final placing at the competition is only relevant to the competitors taking part. Gaining a low score but being well placed at an event with good archers is better than a win and a modest score against mediocre archers. In looking at the scores over a period you will start to be able to judge which parts of your training are of most benefit.

Positive Key Statements as a Reminder

When you are working on different areas of your technique, such as keeping your hand relaxed, the draw or the pressure of the shot, the details need to be recorded so you can recap what you have been doing. In writing down the area of focus for the training you will begin to develop a shorthand for keywords that will remind you what to think of when working on certain aspects of your shooting. It does not matter what words you use as they only need to be relevant to you, for example:

Relax hand = plasticine
Draw = deep river flowing
Pressure of the shot = balance

To anyone reading your diary these may seem like nonsense, but the words need to be your own interpretation of what you are feeling or want to feel.

These words offer a simple reminder of what you want to do correctly so that you can focus easily on aspects of your shots when competing. Positive affirmation is an aspect of psychology that is very useful in enabling you to achieve. Choosing words to suit the actions of your training and writing them in your diary creates a series of positive affirmations that are much stronger and more personal than phrases made up to satisfy a list of positive affirmations or given to you by someone else.

Equipment Changes and Adjustments

Any equipment change must be recorded, however small it might seem. This includes clothing, bracer, chest guard, glasses, shoes and anything that might affect your shooting. By recording every change you will be able to reset the bow and equipment to a previous set-up. There may be times when you are not getting the scores that you think you deserve. If you are uncertain whether this is due to equipment or a change in your technique or training regime, you can reset your equipment to an earlier set-up and see whether the scores come back up. In training, three or four small changes to your equipment may seem to make little difference to the groups and scores. The groups may sometimes seem tighter, but at competition you may get 'wild' arrows and lower competition scores. Archers have changed their glasses and seen their scores drop for a couple of months, not realizing that slight variations in the frames put their head, and therefore their arms and shoulders, in a different position. Frustrated and unable to make any progress with their shooting, they have disregarded or forgotten the fact that they have new glasses. Eventually they have gone back to the old glasses and all the shooting issues have been resolved. By tracking every change you can easily see which benefit the scores and which do not.

Strings Made

Although strings come under equipment changes, I keep a separate log of all the strings I have made as there are many variables in string construction. On reflection it would have been better if I had kept a more detailed log before 2003. From then I noted the date, material, end serving and centre serving length, the bow it was for, the colour of material and serving, the length on jig, brace height and the number of twists and performance. Keeping such records enables you to construct strings better, faster and more accurately. Making your own strings ensures that you always have good strings available whenever you need them.

Other Activities that May Affect Your Performance

It is not only the details of exercise duration and activities that need to be included in your diary, such as the distance run and the time spent in the gym. It is just as important to record rest days, whether planned or enforced. Even shopping trips and other 'leisure' activities that keep you on your feet for hours need to be recorded so you can identify any effect they might have on your shooting. Hillwalking for six hours will have an impact, but so too will

#	Date	Riser	Limbs	Colour	Material	Strands	End serving	Loop length	Centre serving	Length on Jig scale	Twists	Brace height	Ren
37	24/03/2008	matrix	G3	yellow	540	10	ANGEL	90	BROWNELL BRAIDED	22 +5			
38	24/03/2008	Nexus	CX900	yellow	540	10	ANGEL	90	BROWNELL BRAIDED	22 +5	40	8 1/4	g
39	07/04/2008	Nexus	CX900	PURPLE	540	10	ANGEL	90	BROWNELL BRAIDED	22 +5			
40	07/04/2008	Nexus	CX900	blue	540	10	ANGEL	90	BROWNELL BRAIDED	22 +7			
41	15/10/2008	Nexus	CX900	yellow	450	9	ANGEL	84	BROWNELL BRAIDED	22+5mm			
42	04/01/2009	Nexus	CX900	yellow	450	9	ANGEL	84	BROWNELL BRAIDED	22			
43	04/01/2009	GMX	CX990	yellow	450	9	ANGEL	84	BROWNELL BRAIDED	21 =21mm			8(BEF FIN ON
44	21/01/2009	CYBERTEC		RED	452X	22	BCY .16	40		53.25"	20		
		CYBERTEC		RED	452X	22	BCY .16	40		40.5	16		
		CYBERTEC		RED	452X	24	BCY .16	40		37.75	10		yoke P
45	14/02/2009	GMX	CX990	PURPLE	450	9	HALO .19	80	HALO .14	21 + 18	60	8 3/4	T LC g
46	04/04/2009	GMX	CX990	BLUE	450	9	ANGEL	82	BROWNELL BRAIDED	21+8	40	8 3/4	g ler
47	04/04/2009	GMX	CX990	BLUE	450	9	ANGEL red	90	BROWNELL BRAIDED	21+8	40	8 3/4	g ler
48	10/05/2009	GMX	CX990	BLUE	450	10	ANGEL blue	90	BROWNELL BRAIDED	21+8	40	8 3/4	g ler
49	15/08/2009	GMX	CX990	BLUE	450	9	ANGEL RED	84	BROWNELL BRAIDED	21+8	45	8 3/4	
50	26/08/2009	bobs		red/black	452x	22	bcy sk75	45		58.5			ser
				red/black	452x	22	bcy sk75	45		40.57			16" 14 s
				red/black	452x	24	bcy sk75	45		39			
51	09/09/2009	GMX	CX990	BLUE	450	9	ANGEL	84	BROWNELL BRAIDED	21+8			
52	16/12/2009	Nexus	CX990	yellow	450	9	ANGEL RED	90	BROWNELL BRAIDED	22 +5	60	8 3/4	bit
53	16/12/2009	Nexus	CX990	yellow	450	9	ANGEL RED BLUE	90	BROWNELL BRAIDED	22 +5	60	8 3/4	bit

Keeping an account of all the strings you make provides a clear record of strings and scores when included in your diaries.

flying a kite or skipping stones. Squash and other explosive muscle sports did not help my shooting and I had to give them up to aid improvement.

Future Events

As with all diaries, put in any future events. As there are many competitions, it helps to track those you want to go to, those you have entered and whether you have booked your accommodation. Without this it is easy to turn up on the wrong weekend or ready to shoot the wrong round. Keeping track of the competitions and rounds entered in your diary ensures that your training plans are relevant to them. Although most of your time will be taken up with shooting, adding details of non-archery events, such as dinner with friends, will enable you to adjust your training routines and still maintain your planned training regime.

Reminders for Future Training

Focusing on one aspect of your training may bring to mind another area needing later attention or it might just be an idea about an adjustment to your equipment. Putting these thoughts and ideas in your diary helps to remind you to carry out the work. It is sometimes the small changes that occur to you while shooting, and that otherwise might be forgotten by the next session, that make the biggest improvements. Just relying on your memory might mean that a month passes before the thought returns and you can implement it – three competitions too late for you to make the team.

Shooting Venue

By including your shooting venue in the log, you will be able to compare scores from venues to see if one of them is conducive to better scores. It is the recording of the small things that can lead to improvements. The lighting conditions at a particular indoor venue, for example, may give better scores. This may be down to the brightness as well as to the type of light. Indoor venues have various types of lighting, such as tube lighting, sodium lights and mercury lamps, and some have windows that let in natural light. In venues with windows the light conditions can vary hugely from bright sunshine to no ambient light at all as the sun sets. Even at venues without windows the type of lighting can affect not only what you see; I find that at venues with sodium lighting, the yellowy orange type seem to affect the nervous system. Wearing a visor when shooting cuts down the direct light into my eyes, so at these types of venues it helped with improving my scores.

Sleep Patterns

Some guesswork is needed here. The idea is to record the amount of time you sleep, not staying awake to see what time you fall asleep. As discussed in Chapter 3, it takes three weeks of testing sleep times to see how it affects your performance. You should continue recording sleep times even when you think you know the sleep pattern that suits you. As your training changes and work patterns alter, you may be able to identify better sleep routines. I rarely sleep or snooze during the day as it leads to poor sleep at night. If you have to sleep during the day it usually indicates that you are not having enough sleep at night. I have also found that the lack of sleep while travelling to competitions around the world means that I take extra naps on the first couple of days at the venue to catch up. Although not directly related to sleep, I make a note of my heart rate when I wake up. I have found that it tends to be raised when changing time zones and returns to normal once I have acclimatized.

Diet Changes or Anomalies

There will be times when you will scrutinize your diet for everything you eat and drink, and it is during these periods that you should be adjusting your diet to improve performance. This is a detailed study; you can note that you are doing it in your log, but it should also be itemized in its own log or table. When your diet is relatively consistent it is only necessary to mention any changes to your daily eating routines, such as going out for meals or dining with friends at home.

You should have a good idea of what you normally eat when going to competitions either at home or abroad. Whenever possible you should try to maintain your eating habits, although in some foreign countries you may end up eating food quite unlike what you are used to.

Keeping a diary of changes to your eating habits also adds to the full picture of what affects your performance. At one shoot I forgot to take my lunch, but fortunately I had a few Mini Snickers in my bag and ate them sparingly during the day. The day's shooting went well, even without my usual rolls for lunch. Curious as to whether it was the change to the eating routine or just luck, I tried it again. Instead of eating everything at lunch, I took less food with me and ate a little at the end of each distance, ensuring that I had the maximum time to start digesting it. This helped in every shoot I went to. Sometimes, when food was provided at lunchtimes, I needed to ensure that I did not eat too much. The after-shoot banquet, if one is provided, is the time to sample the local food to your heart's content.

Check-tune

Check tuning should be carried out every two weeks and the results recorded in your log. Getting into a recording routine ensures that you carry it out. A bare shaft can be used quickly and easily to check your tuning. Plot the position of the bare shaft against the fletched arrows. By checking your tuning with a bare shaft you can ensure that nothing has moved. If the bare shaft is not quite where you expect it to be, first check over your scores and groups. Sometimes changes in the set-up can improve your scores, but checking how your groups and scores are before resetting can suggest what to look for at competitions when groups are not quite what you expect.

Rest

It is just as important to record rest days as those full of running and shooting. Training seven days a week is not a good idea. It is likely that six days of training per week will be better, while some might need to vary their weekly training between five and six days to get the best from their performance. When to take your rest day will also need some experimentation. Many archers prefer to take a day off after a competition. When you think about it, though, while travelling can take up much of the weekend, especially if you live in Scotland, shoots are pretty laid-back affairs: only six arrow ends at the most, twenty minutes between ends, lunch of nearly an hour. In my opinion the rest day is better taken at the end of the week just before the competition, as it lets the muscles relax after a hard week's training.

Picture Library

Now that high-quality cameras are available at a relatively low cost and most phones have cameras built in, it is very easy to record visually every element of your shooting. The pictures can be stored and catalogued using the date that they were taken, as this correlates directly with the written entries in your diary. Both still and video images can be made, encompassing every aspect of your archery. Images taken of your shooting can be compared at a later date to show improvement or to check if anomalies have crept into your shooting. It is also a good way to record bow and equipment set-ups, including button positions. In setting up your bow, a camera is invaluable in checking alignment as pictures can rapidly be uploaded to the computer and scrutinized to confirm the alignment. This is far quicker than standing behind a bow, trying to keep your head still. By noting in your diary that you have taken images you will be able to match them easily to your written log.

Recording Your Log

The way you record all of this is up to you. Some people like to write a small story every day. I tend to use numbers, either underlined or circled, with acronyms to indicate what I have been up to and where I have been doing it. That is fine so long as

you can understand what you have written and are confident it will make sense in a year's time. It has to be pitched at a level that works for you. It may seem that there is a huge amount to record, but you will find that it does not take long once you get used to doing it. I believe it should take as little time as possible, making use of phrases and a shorthand that you understand.

The downside of only using a paper diary to record all you do is that it is not as easy to correlate all your information. There may also be times when you need to produce a record of all your activities for coaching sponsorship or funding. This is where an electronic diary comes into its own.

Electronic Diary

An electronic diary is very easy to set up in a spreadsheet. You only need to enter the key facts as the bulk of information will be in your written diary. Auto Sum takes care of adding up your arrow count and the hours spent training for a weekly and monthly total. Using a limited number of colours to highlight your scores makes it very easy to spot any trends that might lead to improvements in scores and shooting practices. The electronic diary, for example, enabled me to identify a format for peak-

	July							
Days/Dates	24	25	26	27	28	29	30	31
Activity	Sat.	Sun.	Mon.	Tue.	Wed.	Thu.	Fri.	Sat.
Training /Shooting (Arr.Quantity + Time) Plan	250	0	150	200	200	150	100	200
Training /Shooting Actual time at session	4	0	4	5	5	4	2.5	5
Training /Shooting Actual arrows shot	220		170	225	150	180	130	175
Fitness Activity								
Running (Time or Distance)	3 miles			3 miles			3 miles	
Swimming (Time or Distance)								
Cycling (Time or Distance)			10		10			
Multi Gym (Time)								
Hill Walking (Time or Miles)	11.5 miles Mt keen							
Jogging (Time or Distance)								
Power Walking (Time or Distance)								
Special Archery Exercise (Specify)								
Reversals (Sec. Hold/Quantity)		30 min						
Games (Time/Specify)								
Competitions (Programme & Result)								
Squad &Training Days								
Away with work (outside of your home place)								
Travel								
Rest days/Holidays								
Family Commitments								
Other Activities (please, Specify)								

Logs can take many forms. Some may need to be filled out to give credence for funding or for coaches to monitor a squad of archers. A standard log enables the coach to compare archers' progress.

ing that works for me. At one point in my training I would shoot more than 1,000 arrows every week. Then work commitments interrupted my usual three-week run-up to a competition: the first week was at the normal rate of more than 1,000 arrows shot, but then I managed to shoot 850 in the second week and only 650 in the third week. Nonetheless the competition result at the end of this period was very good. I was able to perceive a pattern leading up to a good result and that was the origin of the three-week peak cycle I used to prepare for many competitions. The three-week pattern would not have been so easy to see without the electronic diary.

As you will be keeping a daily diary on paper, there should be no problem entering the information into the spreadsheet on your computer once or twice a week. Although keeping an accurate diary is essential for those wanting to compete at the highest level, it is time that is your most valuable commodity. While you should try to record all the information, you need to keep the time taken by this to the minimum.

Another benefit to keeping an electronic log is that you can insert all the separate activities for the day on a separate line. There is great satisfaction in seeing the catalogue of your training expand and this can spur you on to adding additional tasks, so increasing the lines used each day. This also helps to keep your training varied and extensive.

There will be times when you need to show evidence of what you have been doing in order to make a team or squad, win sponsorship or present to a prospective coach so they can get an idea of what you have been up to.

Some years ago the British squad decided that all the prospective archers would be interviewed as part of the selection. When asked about my training I handed over a printed copy of my electronic log, detailing what I had been doing every day for the past three years. The interview panel was suitably impressed and I was selected.

Diaries for Others

There will be times when you are asked to keep diaries for coaches or as a task when participating in a squad. If funding is involved it is very possible that the funding organization will require evidence of the athlete's training, both in the form of a log from the archer and in reports from their coach that support and, it is to be hoped, confirm the work being carried out. Unfortunately there are some athletes who write a great log, but in reality do not carry out the work. That is why the log evidence has to be supported by the squad coach.

Sometimes you will be able to use the electronic log you are already filling out for this purpose, possibly with a few modifications. At one point the members of the British squad were required to fill out an extensive log listing what we did every hour of every day. It was a complicated log that took a long time to fill out and had to be submitted monthly for review. The results were not reviewed, however, and no feedback was given; it was discontinued after negotiation. When filling out a log for either yourself or for other parties, information should only be submitted if there is a benefit to what you are doing. It should be a means of monitoring your performance and improvements. Coaches and support staff should offer a review of what you have submitted, not just as an acknowledgement that you have sent it in. If you have to submit logs for evidence for funding they should only contain what is required for the funding body. This is not to deprive them of other information, but to ensure that your valuable time is not wasted filling in forms.

Yearly Review

After a year you can analyse and possibly revise the way you are keeping your diary. Whatever changes you make, you still have to come up with a comprehensive method of recording information by which you can retrieve every aspect of training that you have inputted. You also need to be able to review the information easily in order to identify any trends.

Many events are held at the same venues, both at home and abroad. By keeping good records of the conditions at those venues you are able to build a picture of what you may encounter and the prevailing weather conditions. This enables you to ensure that training before an event takes into consideration the likely environmental conditions, so improving your preparations for the event.

CHAPTER 8

FINE TUNING

Fine tuning is about trying to get the best from your equipment, adjusting and changing it to get the best and most consistent groups you can. Initially the bow is set up statically, by measurement and by eye. This puts the equipment into a position from which you can start shooting and then adjust it dynamically.

Archery – The Art of Repetition was written mainly to get the best out of the equipment you have. Fine tuning your equipment to be the best in the world may mean changing everything, but if that's what it takes to get to the top, that's the way it is. Most equipment nowadays, however, is very good and any of the top bows from the main manufacturers will take you to the highest international levels. But there will be one bow and one set-up that could give you the extra ten points needed to be the best.

Although I have taken an interest in compound bows, I have had very little involvement with fine tuning them so will leave that to those with far more experience. The time and care needed to ensure that you are getting the best from your equipment, however, is the same whatever bow or discipline you shoot.

Fine tuning is not something you do at the start of the season and leave it set for the rest of the season. It is progressive improvement of your equipment that goes hand in hand with improvements in your own shooting. Some big changes to the way you shoot may make very little difference during check-tuning to how the bow shoots with its current set-up. At other times seemingly small changes to your shooting may need bigger changes to your set-up and tuning to regain your groups and consistency.

Tuning follows a pattern of initial set-up of the bow, basic tuning that will get the bow shooting reasonable groups and then smaller adjustments to find the best set-up for what you have. You then move on to changing parts of the equipment to see if it will give an improvement. It is making sure that the changes you make to any part of your equipment are based on a logical plan from good information.

Tuning at this level is about constructing a method of proving and testing that can be used on different types of equipment from different manufacturers, testing both the position and adjustment of the equipment. If you have a method of working to find the best groups, you will be able to follow a routine that will ensure that you will get to the best adjustment, and that once you have it you can repeat it quickly and easily time and time again, therefore making the best use of your time. Although tuning is an ongoing process, it has to have its place in training and practice time. Some good archers spend all their time adjusting their equipment trying to get 'super groups'. Groups do not come from good tuning: groups come from consistent shooting. With better shooting come better groups. The better your groups, the finer adjustments to your equipment you can make as the variations in adjustment are more visible to the ever-decreasing group size.

For every level of shooting you will have an optimum group size for your current ability. If yours

Consistent shooting gives good groups.
WERNER & IRIS BEITER CENTER.

is the size of the red at 70m, good tuning of your equipment will ensure that you get the groups you deserve: all the arrows in the red. To get all of your arrows in the eight ring you have to shoot better and more consistently. If your optimum group size for your current level is the size of the gold at 70m, good tuning will ensure that, coupled with a consistent shot, it will go in the gold. Any amount of tuning will not make the group smaller: you have to shoot better. An untuned bow will give you bigger group sizes than you are actually capable of and no amount of shooting practice will make the groups smaller. If your shooting consistency enables you to score 52 points an end at 70m with a well-tuned bow, you will be capable of that score, but optimum points will be lost for every part of the tuning that is out. If your nocking point is a little too high you may lose two points (an end); brace height a little low, lose another two points; button tension a little out, lose another point. For the same consistency of shooting, but with a lack of attention to your tuning, you will go from scoring 312 for 70m down to 282.

Tuning always goes hand in hand with the consistency of your shot.

Before any major tuning takes place, whether this involves new limbs, arrows or riser, you must ensure that the set-up of the bow is correct and that everything is working as it should. Many archers

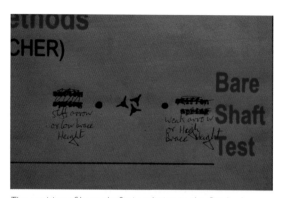

The position of bare shafts in relation to the fletched arrows can be due to the spine of the arrow, the brace height or a combination of both. KAREN HENDERSON

have spent a day working on tuning their bow only to find that the rest/launcher was broken and the whole day was wasted.

Once you have checked to make sure that the bow is set up properly and that nothing has moved, you can carry out basic tuning. For recurve I use bare shaft tuning to get the basic tune. First I get two or three bare shafts level with the group by adjusting the nocking point height. It is best to use at least two arrows for bare shaft tuning. If you use two bare shafts and they go together it is likely that two will do, although you may be more certain if you use three bare shafts and they all go together on the target. Most archers do not have many problems with this stage, but if the nocking point is moved the wrong way it becomes obvious on the next end. The next stage is to consider the horizontal position of the bare shafts in relation to the fletched arrows, seeing whether they are left or right of the fletched arrows. This can be the first stumbling block in basic tuning. If the bare shafts go left of the fletched arrows, the arrows are stiff; the caveat to this is that it could be because the brace height is low. On the other hand, if the bare shafts are to the right of the fletched arrows, the arrow is weak or your brace height is high. When bare shafts go to the right of the fletched arrow group, archers have been known to buy progressively stiffer and stiffer arrows, at £270 a set, in a successful attempt to make the bare shafts move towards the fletched arrows. You can tune a bow using this method but it is expensive and unnecessary. It is not only that the arrow is stiffer but it will be heavier and travel more

---

SET-UP SCHEDULE

Recurve – Right Handed

1. Examine the bow checking for defects.
2. Fit limbs to the riser.
3. Fit the stabilizers to the riser.
4. Find the true centre of the bow.
5. Align limbs to the true centre.
6. Set the tiller (4–6mm positive)
7. Fit and adjust the rest and button.
8. Fit and adjust sight.
9. Set nocking point.
10. Adjust arrow alignment.
11. Set clicker.
12. Adjust stabilizer/bow balance.

For a full explanation, see Archery – The Art of Repetition.

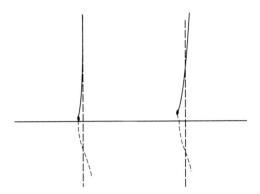

The path of the arrow will be affected if the string hits your arm before the nock is released from the string.

slowly, which is not the best plan for getting good sight marks. If your bare shafts are to the left or right of the groups, change the brace height accordingly. It may well be a cheaper option for getting the bare shafts into the fletched group.

The reason that the brace height influences the arrow's behaviour, making it either stiff or weak, is because it determines at what point of the string's path the nock leaves the nocking point. If the brace height is high, the nock is kicked out to the left and pushes the arrow to the right, making it appear to be weak. With a low brace height the arrow stays on the string longer and the nock is kicked to the right. This pushes the arrow to the left, making it go right and apparently stiff. It also imparts a wider path to the string, which may make it hit your arm. Changing the weight of the arrow either by spine,

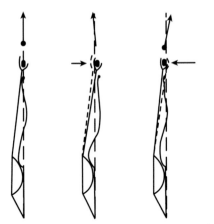

Unless the pressure of your bow hand is directly behind the bow it will affect the size of your groups.

altering stiffness and weight, or by altering the point weight of the arrow will also change the path that the string takes. Changing the brace height changes the path of the string. When the path of the string and the point that the nock comes off the string are correct, the nock will leave the string cleanly. It is then that you will be able to determine if the arrow is in fact stiff or weak. With the nock leaving the string cleanly you will also get better groups. As you are changing the brace height to see if the bare shaft is moving towards the fletched arrows, you are also monitoring the size of the fletched group. There are thus two factors indicating if you are getting to the best brace height and how close you can get the bare shaft to the group.

If the arrow started off appearing to be stiff, you have raised the brace height and yet the arrows have not moved towards the fletched group, then you need to go about making them weaker or buying weaker shafts. The other factor that can give a false reading when comparing the fall of a bare shaft against fletched arrows is the bow hand pressure direction. The pressure should be behind the riser, resisting directly towards the target. If the pressure is across the riser, however, it will torque the riser and offset the direction it moves. On release the string will be carried forward by the limbs towards the target. Because of the torque and pressure direction, the bow will be transmitted to the string via the limbs. It will affect the path of the string and nock, and therefore the arrow will have a tendency to be thrown to the left, indicating a stiff shaft. Minor pressure-torque will make a correctly spined arrow appear to be stiffer than it actually is. Major pressure-torque will make any spine of arrow appear to be stiff.

For initial tuning I want the bare shaft to be in the fletched arrow group at 30m.

Finding *It*

It is quite possible to find that in setting up the bow everything is perfect for you – the elusive *It*.

The chances are that by setting it up visually and carrying out an initial tune you will be able to get the bow shooting reasonably well. To achieve the best set-up for you, however, will require a number of adjustments dynamically to find *It*.

To start with you need to fine tune in favourable weather conditions, ideally in an enclosed venue where you are not troubled by wind. As you are making small adjustments to your equipment, windy days make it extremely hard to judge any changes to group size and consistency. You also need to be shooting in clothing that does not interfere with your form and that you would normally shoot in. If you are shooting in bulky clothing it may interfere with string clearance and restrict the draw arm elbow joint. When I compete I leave my arms bare, not only for clearance on my bow arm but so my draw arm can bend without any restrictions between the upper and lower arm. Therefore when I tune my bow I need to be able to carry out the same movements and bow to body positions. I shoot in sleeved tops if I am practising for strength and it is cold. I am aware that there may be slight interference from the additional clothing, but this is better than getting an injury from cold muscles.

The Plan

The plan is to prove the position and adjustment of every part of the set-up and equipment. When you change parts of your form it can take time before the change becomes apparent. This is the 1,000-arrow marker. When making adjustments to the equipment it will be in three states: better, worse or the same. Be aware that some changes to your equipment may well affect your form. I like a crisp, almost hard-feeling shot and at the moment I use no more than a damper on the long rod. When I was shooting my Yamaha SFF I used a specially made top rod by Jim Buchanan that had a small amount of flex in it. If I added any other dampers to the bow it felt soft, which softened my shot and my groups suffered. Form and equipment have a reciprocal effect. When making adjustments to the equipment or mechanical changes, however, it will generally have the effect of being one of the three states.

This is the effect you can use to tune your bow to its optimum for how you are shooting today.

From the current position of your equipment on every part of the bow, you can change each item by measurable increments to find its best position and place. Any permanent changes need to

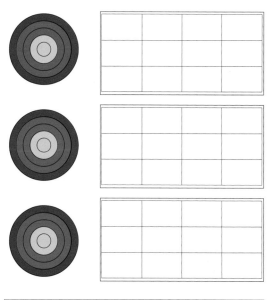

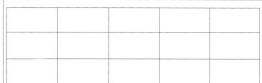

A simple plotting chart can be made using a word processing program. It is not really necessary to put the scores in boxes but it helps to keep them tidy.

be recorded in your diary. Plot and record all your group sizes, either by using prepared paper plotting charts or electronically using Target Plot or a similar app. It is best if you plot the actual position of the arrows relative to the target face as it gives you a far better record of the group sizes and positions than just the score, and it can be easier to review in the future.

All the parts of the bow are interrelated so, although you may be working on the button, for example, you need to see what affect it has on how everything else performs. The shooting of bare shafts will give you a good indication of changes, if any. Bare shaft tuning should be carried out at no more that 30m for this method of tuning. Shooting bare shaft arrows at distances beyond 30m can give erroneous results as the bare shaft may plane or glide, giving false results.

Fine Tuning

To carry out fine tuning you need to be able to shoot consistent, discernible groups at 70m (gents) or 60m (ladies). Your bow needs to be tuned so that the arrows are reasonably matched to your bow for spine (bare shafts in the red/inner blue at 30m) and a good brace height found. (A full tuning guide may be found in *Archery – The Art of Repetition*.)

The method used is to test by shooting for groups and recording the position of every move so that it can be returned to once the best position is proved. Moving one thing at a time, you will go through the proving list once making coarse adjustments, and then through it again on a finer adjustment as the close tuning of all parts of the bow is interrelated. I would suggest that you adopt the following proving sequence:

- Button
- Brace height
- Tiller
- Nocking point
- Strings
- Stabilizers
- Sight rings
- Tab
- Poundage
- Arrows

These are the areas that can be tested through shooting for group size. As they are all interrelated, you will need to go through the list making first-stage adjustments and then again making finer adjustments to get the bow to its optimum performance for how you are currently shooting. As your shooting improves and evolves, you will have to revisit each area of adjustment to keep the bow shooting at its best.

Button

Each make of button has slightly different characteristics. I have found the Beiter button to be robust, hardwearing and reliable. The button has three adjustments that you can make. It is always best to make one adjustment at a time in order to ascertain the change that each adjustment makes. The three adjustments are:

- Position through bow
- Spring tension
- Spring length

Adjusting the button tends to make horizontal changes to the arrows' impact on the target. In adjusting the button position you will also possibly need to make slight changes to the nocking point position and button tension in order to maintain the arrows impacting on the centre of the target. Make an adjustment, shoot for a group and then see if you need to adjust the nocking point or button tension.

Position and Tension

This is the method of finding the best position and tension for your button. Compounds can use the same procedure for finding the best position to the left or right of the launcher.

Pick a direction, either out or in. It does not matter which you choose as you will need to go in the opposite direction afterwards.

At this stage move the button a quarter turn out, shoot fletched and bare shafts at 30m, note the group size and position, and adjust the nocking point and button to bring the bare shafts to the centre of the fletched group again. The reason for moving the button position by a quarter turn is that it is the easiest adjustment to keep track of, since each move can be tracked by the position of the barrel against the locking keyways on the position ring.

Move to 70m or 60m, which is probably your second longest distance or the longest distance at which you feel comfortable shooting consistent groups, and shoot for groups while noting the group

The flat of the button body makes an idea reference when adjusting the button's position collar. KAREN HENDERSON

		Half turn off	Half turn off	Half turn off	Half turn off	Half turn off	Buttons start position Current spring pressure	Half turn on	Half turn on	Half turn on	Half turn on	Half turn on
Set 1	Group size											

		Half turn off	Half turn off	Half turn off	Half turn off	Half turn off	Put button out 1/4 turn From best group size Set 1	Half turn on	Half turn on	Half turn on	Half turn on	Half turn on
Set 2	Group size											

		Half turn off	Half turn off	Half turn off	Half turn off	Half turn off	Put button out 1/4 turn From best group size Set 2	Half turn on	Half turn on	Half turn on	Half turn on	Half turn on
Set 3	Group size											

		Half turn off	Half turn off	Half turn off	Half turn off	Half turn off	Put button out 1/4 turn From best group size Set 3	Half turn on	Half turn on	Half turn on	Half turn on	Half turn on
Set 4	Group size											

		Half turn off	Half turn off	Half turn off	Half turn off	Half turn off	Put button in 1/4 turn from buttons start position From best group size Set 1	Half turn on	Half turn on	Half turn on	Half turn on	Half turn on
Set 5	Group size											

		Half turn off	Half turn off	Half turn off	Half turn off	Half turn off	Put button in 1/4 turn From best group size Set 1	Half turn on	Half turn on	Half turn on	Half turn on	Half turn on
Set 6	Group size											

Recording the group size for every button setting allows you to keep track of adjustments, as these may be carried out over several sessions.

size. You should be looking at shooting at least four ends of around nine arrows to get an idea of group size. The next adjustment is to change the spring pressure for that button position, increasing the button tension by half-turn increments, shoot for groups, recording the group sizes and position on the boss. As you increase the tension on the button the group should move to the left. You will get to a point where an increase in tension either fails to move the group left or the group size increases. When you reach this point, reset the button to the start position and reduce the tension by half a turn at a time, while plotting group position and size. The groups will move towards the right as the button gets weaker.

You may find that as the button tension is increased it reaches a point where not only do the groups get significantly bigger but they also move back towards the centre. When weakening the spring pressure you will tend to find that the groups stay reasonable for longer and just move

towards the left of the boss. Ideally you are looking for a position that keeps the bow pointing at the centre of the boss and gives you the best groups. It will take about 500 arrows shot to complete these two stages. Check your plotting charts and readjust the button tension to the position that gave the best groups.

Next go back to 30m, move the button out a further quarter turn and carry out 30m adjustments. Then return to the 70m boss for group shooting. Plotting the group size, carry on adjusting both button position and tension until the group size noticeable deteriorates. As you reach the point where the group size becomes visibly bigger you can cut down the amount of ends.

Move the button back to its original position at the start of the test and then move the button by a quarter turn, adjusting first at 30m and then moving to 70m. Repeat the position and tension plotting until the groups visibly deteriorate. Looking at the data you have logged from moving the button

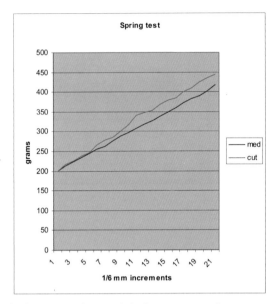

Spring test

As the spring is shortened, the button pressure increases for the same displacement.

Setting up the balance to obtain results for the spring pressure chart. FRANCES KEATS

both out and in, readjust the button to the position and tension that gave the best groups. This process will possibly take a number of training sessions and will also be dependent on the consistency of your shooting. It is for you to judge how many ends are needed to ascertain how good the group is. I like tuning my bow as it requires that you shoot a lot of arrows with good purpose. Not only does it improve your groups, owing to the mechanical changes you are making, but it keeps you shooting consistently. Unless you are just competing at 70m, account should be taken of the groups at both 30m and 70m.

The next stage for readjusting the button is to carry out the same test moving the button only an eighth of a turn, but this should be done only after you have checked and adjusted the other parts of your equipment.

Spring Length

This refinement should be carried out on the second pass of tuning as it should not be attempted before all the other parts of the bow have been adjusted.

The spring length and number of coils of that length determine the rate that the tension increases for the movement of the plunger.

F = Force
X = Length of spring
K = Spring constant
↑ = Increase
↓ = Decrease

$$F = -KX$$

$K = F/-X$ Force per unit (metre) length

If X↓ then K↑

So $F = -KX$ with K↑

Then F↑

Greater Tension

Just stretching a spring will increase the tension. If you cut some of the coils from the spring and then stretch it back to its original length, it will have a greater tension for the same movement than before you cut and stretched it. Just cutting the spring increases the rate that the tension increases, but it limits the adjustment on your button. Stretch-

Cutting the spring to a new length, prior to stretching.
FRANCES KEATS

ing it back to its original length will enable you to make use of the button's full range of adjustment; the Beiter button, for example, still allows you to use the key supplied to tighten it to the bow. The reason for carrying out this test is that, if you have any release issues, it will vary the amplitude at the nock end of the arrow, so varying the pressure against the plunger. This in turn changes the distance travelled by the plunger between shots. Shortening the spring maintains the plunger's initial tension but limits the plunger's movement due to the converse increase in tension, resulting in tighter groups.

Brace Height

You should already have found a good bracing height for your bow, but after altering the button position you will need to check your bracing height again by adjusting and recording the height and plotting the groups. You should not have to move far from the previously measured position to check it. Adjusting by between four and six twists at a time should give you a fine enough change that can be recorded. I always lower the brace height first, as I have found that the groups become significantly bigger when it is too low. Adjust the brace height until it is just above the point where the groups get bigger. Raising the brace height from this point usually increases the size of the group slowly, so a slightly high brace height causes less disruption to group size than a low one.

Tiller

I normally set the static tiller to between 4 and 6mm positive. The static setting assumes that the limbs are perfectly matched and that the stabilizers are set for neutral and dynamic balance, but it does not take into account how the limbs work dynamically in conjunction with the stabilizers and the pressure point of the bow hand. Every new bow I get will carry out 'tiller tuning' using a Beiter rest (for a full description of the method, see *Archery – The Art of Repetition*). Another way to check the tiller is to adjust it

The size of the group changes as the bracing height is increased. To complete the test and find the best brace height for how you are shooting, continue raising the brace height until the groups become larger again.

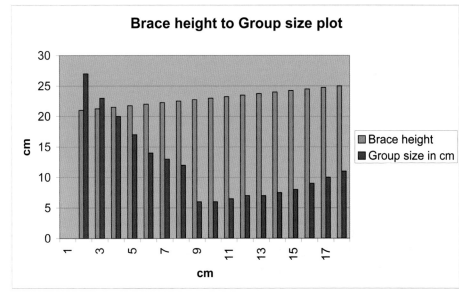

Brace height to Group size plot

cm

■ Brace height
■ Group size in cm

cm

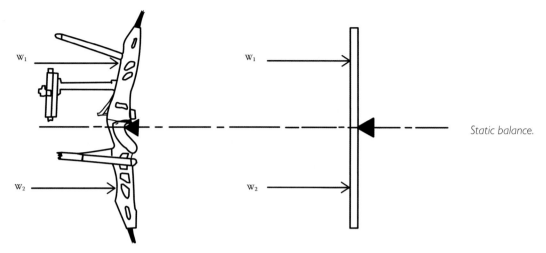

Static balance.

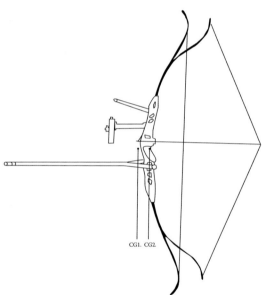

Dynamic balance.

through its full range (from −10 to +10 tiller) and see at what point you feel the bow is shooting the most consistent groups. The problem with this method is that it is a subjective test with no positive evidence that your feeling that it is shooting well is correct. When testing tiller it is important to remember to maintain the poundage on the fingers. This means that both the top and bottom tiller adjusters should be moved by equal amounts in opposite directions. If you adjust the top or bottom on its own you will increase or decrease the weight of the bow, as well as changing the tiller. You would then be testing two

variables at once, which is undesirable; after every adjustment of the tiller you would have to recheck the nocking point position by shooting at 30m, then move to 70m to check the group size and feel of the bow. I prefer the tiller test as it gives an objective result, whereas shooting for feel is subjective. Invariably, a different feeling to that which you are used to is a negative position.

Nocking Point

When testing for the position of the nocking point, you only need to shoot fletched arrows as it is the group size you are interested in. You can move the nocking up and down the string with the flat of a screwdriver blade on a Swiss army knife or a Beiter string mover, but you will need to be prepared to re-serve it after you have finished. Do not be tempted to use an old string as you need to be testing your best equipment to find the best position. The discipline you shoot will determine the distances you will be competing at. Your bow can be tuned for a single distance of 70m, if that is what you are focused on, but if you are shooting a range of distances you should set targets up at least at your shortest and longest distances. You can then move your nocking point up the string by 'walking' it up by 2mm, shoot for groups at both distances and record the group sizes, then move it up again. Once you have checked a range of nocking point positions and found the one from which you shoot your best groups, move to 30m and shoot both fletched and bare shafts. Note the position of the bare shafts in relation to the fletched group. This gives you the position to which you are able to adjust your nocking points on your other strings for you to shoot similar groups. The nocking point position should be set through shooting and not through measuring with a brace height gauge, which gives you a rough idea of where the nocking point should be, but only shooting ensures that it is in the correct place.

Before moving on I will briefly recap the stages of this method of testing: shooting for groups at various distances; making measurable and recordable changes that can be replicated; changing one thing at a time and then plotting your results; and then adjusting the equipment to where it shot the best for that particular test.

Moving the nocking point in this manner enables small adjustments to be made for testing and tuning. The serving may need to be renewed if it becomes damaged or slack.
JAMIE CUTTS

Strings

To find the best string for your bow you really need to be able to make strings yourself. Modern string materials are very resistant to stretch and it is quite easy, with a little practice, to make strings of the same specification. To test your strings, take the one you are currently using as your starting point; using the same material as your current string, these are the changes you can make and test:

1. Make strings with the same number of strands, with the end loops and centre serving the same lengths and construction, but vary the length of the strings on the jig and remember to record the details. When you put the strings on the bow, set it to your current brace height. This will give you strings with a different number of twists for the same brace height, although there will be a slight difference between the weights of the strings as those with more twists will have more string material in their construction. Each string will need to be shot and groups recorded. The range of the tests should go from at least ten twists to about eighty.

2. Make strings with different numbers of strands. If you are currently shooting a ten-strand, you should make eight-, nine-, eleven- and twelve-strand strings, with the construction of the loops and centre servings being the same. The best one of these should again be tested for the number of twists. As you are changing the weight of strands in the string, you will be adjusting the spine of the arrow; more strands should make

the arrow act stiffer or and weaker for fewer strands. At this point you can choose whether to accept that the arrow spine will alter or you can adjust the bow weight to compensate, although this is a separate test.

3. Take the best of the strings you have made so far and change the lengths of the loop size, end serving and centre serving. End loops should be kept the same size and not too small. The transition from loop to end serving should not be at too much of an angle. The length of the end serving must be long enough to protect the string material from hitting the limb and make sure that the end of the serving does not strike the limb. If the loop end serving is too short and touches the limb when the bow is strung but not drawn, it can damage the limb as it will dig into the limb when it is shot. The length of the end servings and centre serving will both change the weight of the string and the stiffness of the arrow. The centre serving only needs to be long enough to cover the area where the tab is around the string and protect the string if it strikes the arm. If it is too short there is a tendency for the centre serving to move on the string when you shoot.

4. You need to try different string materials as the thickness of a strand varies between types and manufacturers. Manufacturers state the thickness of an individual strand so you would think that you could extrapolate the number of

The transition of the end loops to the body of the string should not be too acute. The end serving of the string needs to be long enough so that the string material does not touch the limb. Small gaps in the serving at the transition of the end loop to string are acceptable as long as the serving material is the only contact with the surface of the limb.

strands for the new material from the comparative thickness of your current string. Unfortunately, however, the string thicknesses also vary and you will usually end up with one that is too thick or thin. The best way of checking the thickness of a new string is while it is on the jig. I use No. 2 Beiter nocking points on my current string and I can close them comfortably around a ten-strand string. With the new string material still on the jig, I try to get the nocking point fitment about the same. I can then see how close it is by weight to my previous string by the position of the bare shafts when shot. If necessary, I can then make another string in the new material that is a better match with my last string. When changing string materials you should also observe how

the serving material behaves in conjunction with the new string material. Sometimes servings can be more slippery in conjunction with a different string material, which can lead to servings moving while you shoot.

5. Try using different serving materials. I use Angel serving for the end loops and Brownell braided for the centre servings. I find that Angel is very hard wearing and I do not have any wear issues with it. The Brownell braided keeps the centre serving thin, so I get a positive pressure on my fingers and it does not move very much. When considering serving materials you should look at trying different types of materials and thicknesses. The important factor is how well it stays in place. Servings tend to move over time, but check-tuning should keep this under control. Movement on the centre serving should be minimal. If the material is right for you and is tight enough you may have to adjust its position every 2,000 arrows.

Nocking points can be made using a number of methods. Personally I use the Beiter nocking points and nocks because I know that the nock to nocking point fit will be exactly the same for every string I make, and the fit will be the same for every arrow shot from that string. Nocking points can also be made from dental floss, kept in place with beeswax. The thickness of the string and centre serving should not be determined by the nock fit. Dental floss can be wound over the centre serving to build it up to give the best nock fit. Using beeswax to hold it in place will ensure the nocking point stays in place whatever the temperature. The downside of these types of nocking points is that they are prone to wear and need constant upkeep. Another method of making a nocking point is to use cotton and superglue. Care should be taken when using this method that the superglue does not get on the string material itself as it can make it brittle.

7. Once you have found a string material that you like, you can then try different colours. The colour of the string in combination with the light conditions can make a big difference to the width of the group. As you will not want to be changing strings during competitions, you need

to find colours that give good results for general conditions. The main colours I ended up using outdoors were red, blue and purple. For indoor use straw colour and yellow seemed to come out top after testing. Remember that the string colour needs to be selected for the projected light conditions for the duration of the whole competition.

Stabilizers

In the initial setting up of the bow the stabilizers should have been set for both neutral and dynamic balance. This will ensure that the tuning done up to this point is adjusting the bow to shoot its best without compensating for poor initial set-up.

To fine tune the stabilizers, the two areas you are looking at are the all-up weight of the stabilizers and the adjustment to both the dynamics and static balance points. There should be only slight variations to these balance points but adjustments will help to concentrate the groups. A huge number of stabilizers are available and trying to find the right type and length can be expensive. Where possible it is best if you can borrow rods from fellow archers to get a good idea of what suits you. I like the Easton and Beiter rods. The Easton rods give a crispness to the shot that I like and having one doinker on the long rod seems to work best for me. I find that Beiter rods make the shot a little softer, which means I have to make sure that my shot stays crisp. Adjustments to the stabilizers are more subtle than some of the other tuning adjustments, but with good record-keeping you should be able to track where the improvements are coming from.

1. The weights on the ends of the stabilizers are what do the work. The V-bar adds to the all-up mass of the bow, but it may be of more benefit if the weight can be reduced and redistributed to the ends of the stabilizers. I prefer to use a small, light V-bar rather than a heavy one. The first adjustment should be to keep the same balance but increase or decrease the weight on the stabilizers. The more weight there is in the bow and stabilizers, the slower it will move to get it on target but it will stay still better. Increasing the weight will maintain the balance of both limbs and the extra mass makes the riser a more stable platform for the limbs to work against, increasing the performance of the limbs. Adjusting the weight can include increasing the angle on the V-bars to lower the weight, then adding weight to the top of the riser to maintain the balance. Weight can be added to the top and bottom of the riser either using short rods or directly onto the riser. The downside of adding more mass is the obvious increase in weight in the hand, as you have to be strong enough to hold it up. During some of your training periods it is worth reducing the weights on the stabilizers to a minimum but maintaining the balance points. This will enable you to shoot for groups and see if the size and shape of your group changes. Part of the stabilizers' purpose is to maintain the bow position during the shot; a heavier stabilizer will hide unwanted movement. Reducing the stabilizer mass will give you an opportunity to ensure that the consistency of your shot is how it should be.

Neutral balance is when the weight distribution above and below the pivot point is equal. JAMIE CUTTS

Dynamic balance helps to ensure the centre of gravity stays within the body of the riser at full draw so that vertical torque is kept to a minimum. JAMIE CUTTS

A lightweight V-bar manufactured by Jim Buchanan.
KAREN HENDERSON

2. The other test to carry out with the stabilizers is to make changes to the balance points, moving the pivot point up and down the riser and adjusting the centre of gravity of the dynamic balance. These adjustments involve only slight variations to the initial balance points and can be completed by adding or reducing weights on the rods, or by changing the length and angles of the stabilizers. When changing the balance points you will need to check the bare shaft position at 30m. This is because changing the balance of the mass of the riser will also affect how the limbs work. Moving the pivot point (neutral balance) up the riser will make the top limb work harder and the bottom a little less, and the other way around when moving the pivot point lower on the riser. Changing the centre of gravity alters the pressure on the grip and how the bow reacts on release. Using high-speed photography it is possible to confirm that the riser is balanced, so that it maintains its vertical position on release, and all the work carried out by the limbs is devoted to propelling the string forward. If the riser moves from its vertical axis, some of the energy from the limbs will be lost in moving the riser, which in turn will affect the path of the nocking point. If you could clamp the riser solidly so that it was unable to react, all the work would then have to be done by the limbs. As it is not possible to 'clamp' the riser, it needs to be adjusted so that it is balanced around the pressure exerted by your hand on the grip. Using high-speed photography (see Chapter 9),

looking at the initial movement of the long rod can indicate how much and in what direction the riser is moving. Changing the distribution of weight on the stabilizer tends to make more subtle changes to consistency and group size. Therefore once you have checked that the position of the bare shaft has not moved, it is probably best to shoot a few sessions with that set-up at varying distances to see how it performs.

3. Trying different doinker set-ups and stiffness will also make alterations to your shooting. To my mind the doinker alters the kinaesthetic feedback from a shot. If the shot feels good, the positive feedback helps to reinforce the feeling of shooting well, which in turn encourages you to shoot better. The amount of dampening is very individual and can only be judged by results since dampening can mask kinaesthetic feedback using a heavy set-up, making it harder to notice changes to the bow's feel that may indicate alterations to the set-up.

Sight Rings

To make the best of your sight system, you need to understand both line and point of focus. The eye can take in a great deal of information from an area, but it can only fully focus its attention on a very small area. This is the point of focus. When looking at the 'c' in the middle of the word 'focus' at a normal reading distance, for example, you can focus on either the top of the letter or the bottom. This is your point of focus. The line of focus is a hypothetical line drawn from your eye to that point of focus.

Although it is by testing that you will find the sight ring that suits your needs, it is important to have the utmost confidence in the sight mechanism itself. It should be securely attached to the bow so that the sight ring can be moved accurately up and down, left and right, with a scale that allows you to reproduce any position for changes in distance. Sure-Loc sights are very well made with good fine adjustment. The weak area of all sights is the attachment point to the riser. A close eye has to be maintained on this area owing to the vibrations induced through shooting large quantities of arrows. I use double-sided tape between the sight and the riser to help keep it in position. Care should be taken when tightening the sight screws as you can easily strip the threads if

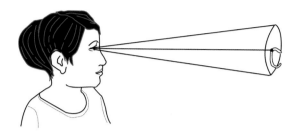

The line of focus is an imaginary line that connects the eye directly to the point you are looking at, the point of focus.

you try to make them too tight. It is confidence in the sight that will enable you to test different sight apertures to get the best from your shooting.

With such a range of sight rings available it would seem that it would take a huge amount of time to find the right one. Fortunately there are really only two types, open or pin (dot comes under the heading of pin). To some extent an archer's choice is influenced by the sight ring they started shooting with. Selecting the right sight ring for you is probably more about a personal mental mechanism than the physical ring itself. An open ring is more relaxing to shoot mentally as your eye is focusing on the target; although you are aware of a slight movement by the ring, it is to hoped that the target remains still. There is a steady imagined line from your eye to the point of focus on the target. The sight ring is then placed centrally over the line. Using a pin-type sight, the dot of the pin is on the line between the eye and the point of focus, so the archer is much more aware of any movement of the dot. It is how your mind deals with the two ring types that determines which type of ring will suit you.

Open Rings

Open rings have three parameters: the diameter of the ring, the wall thickness of the ring and its colour.

Using an open ring is like looking through a window at the target. You look through the centre of the window to the point on the target you have chosen to aim at. The mind is very good at centring the circle of the sight onto the line and point of focus. The ring diameter needs to be the largest size that you are clearly aware of at full draw without having to take your eye from the point of focus to check its position. The smaller the diameter of the

sight ring the more aware of it you are; the more aware of it the more aware you are of its movement, so in use it will become more like a dot sight that you can see through. If the diameter of the sight is too large your attention will be drawn away from the point on the target you are focusing on and your aim will move with it, opening up your groups.

The thickness of the wall needs to be such that it remains visible in all lighting conditions, but not so thick that it blocks your point of focus. If the wall of the ring is too thin it will be indistinct and you will take your focus from the point you have chosen.

Another way of keeping the wall of the sight ring visible and thin is to colour it. This can be done with paint or coloured plastics, some of which are day-glow. The ring needs to be visible, but if it is too bright it may take your attention from the point you are aiming at. The other issue with using day-glow finishes outdoors is that the light conditions can vary and this will in turn change your perception and attention to the target. For more consistent lighting conditions, for example in indoor venues, woods or countries that are eternally sunny, you may find it a benefit to use a day-glow sight ring.

Sight Rings with a Pin or Dot

On this type of sight ring the wall size, colour and thickness have little relevance. The outer ring is mainly for protection of the pin and can act as a hood to maintain a more constant light condition surrounding the pin.

It is the dot size, colour and support that are the main factors. The dot can either sit inside or over the gold, but in both cases it should cover the point of focus on the target. The larger the dot is the further away from the centre of the point of focus you will actually be able to see. The mental aiming mechanism differs from that when using an open sight. You will be covering a portion of the target and it is that matching of the mental image of what you want to cover on the target that you will be reproducing on the shot. For each distance there needs to be a differently constructed image of how the sight will appear. For the target, the images at 70m and 30m are similar, as are those at 50m and 90m. For me, the dot covered the gold at 90m and 50m and I thought 'Dot on dot'; at 70m and 30m I was able to see gold around the dot and thought 'Dot on gold'.

The two rings I favour when shooting either open or dot sight rings.

The square of the Spigarelli ring can help to keep the bow upright.

Holding the hand firmly against the jaw helps to maintain a constant hand position. DEAN ALBERGA

How the dot is held in place is also a factor. A dot stuck to glass can be good for testing different sizes of dot, but it can be difficult to keep clear in rainy or damp conditions. The post that a dot is held on can sometimes be an inconvenience as some are very thick. Personally, I liked the Spigarelli square outer with the dot suspended on a very fine filament, as it appeared that the dot was floating. On some sights you can adjust the position of the dot's post, not only up and down but from side to side. Having it come from the arm holding the pin can make a good image as it appears to be an extension of the arm. If there is a single arm I would tend to keep it either horizontal or vertical as it assists in the vertical positioning of the bow.

The colour of the dot will also have issues similar to that of an open ring. You generally need to be able to maintain your main focus on the target, clear but not distracting.

Trialling Sight Pins

Testing to see which pin suits the conditions in which you shoot in is not quite so black and white once you get down to the final selection. Some of the pins you try will be rejected quite quickly. Dot-type pins would logically seem to make the bow more accurate as you have a positive placement on the target; the downside for some archers will be that it can slow their shooting down as they try to be more accurate and the shot can lose its fluidity. You will need to be aware of any changes to the length of the shot as this will not necessarily be immediate but take a few weeks to creep into the shot. When trialling the open sight, some archers might consider it a less accurate method of aiming the bow as there is no positive positioning of the sight on the target. With practice and good results to back it up, however, it can be a very successful method of aiming. As the open sight enables an archer to shoot with the mind a little more relaxed, it can lead to one being a little blasé with the whole shot. Obviously in selecting the sight you will need to ensure that it performs well at all the distances at which you need to compete. You may also find that the group may move to the left or right as you change the size of the sight ring. This will be due to how you set the string picture. Although it might appear to the eye that the string picture looks the same on different sizes of sight ring, there is likely

to be a variation that could move the groups either left or right. To compensate for this, adjust the windage so that the arrow group impacts on the centre of the target again. Depending on the type of shooting you are doing, you may use the different types of rings for different disciplines. When shooting at varying distances you may find that the open ring suits you better, whereas a dot-type sight may give better results indoors, when you are generally shooting at a fixed distance and there is no wind to interfere. The two sights that suited me the best were the Spigarelli sight and the Arten open ring, with a single insert to make the wall appear thicker.

Tab

When testing tabs you are not only testing types,

The tab should fit the size of the hand.
DEAN ALBERGA

As the backing material stretches it can cover the slot in the tab. This can interfere with the nock leaving the tab faces. Keeping it trimmed will ensure this does not occur.

either aligned with the hand or aligned to the bow string, but the position of the platform and how that impacts on the hand position against your face. If the hand has good contact with your jaw it can assist in maintaining a consistent position.

Tab faces will require to be shot in. They then have a useful shooting life before wearing out, so it is not only about finding what works for you but identifying materials that are easily available and can be reproduced. When testing tabs I would generally test for group size at 30m and 70m: 30m helps to ensure that the arrow is coming off the string cleanly and 70m works on group size and consistency. I want my tab to have enough surface area of the material to protect my fingers and no more: anything extra is just flapping in the wind getting in the way.

Some aspects of testing the tab's faces will give a definite change to the group size; other changes are more subtle and take longer to manifest themselves. Thicker tabs can lead to poorer placement of the fingers on the string. As the feeling of the string is less distinct, this will tend to take a little longer to show. If the tab is too thin and too small, so that it does not protect your fingers properly, it can lead to an unsettled shot due to discomfort. The tab's faces need to be inspected regularly so that any anomalies can be reduced. There is a tendency for the secondary face of the index finger to become distorted with use and partly cover the slot where the nock fits. This can randomly interfere with the path of the arrow, giving off shots. The problem can be solved by clipping off the excess with a sharp pair of scissors as necessary.

Poundage

Although the bare shaft's position was initially set to be in the fletched group, adjustments to the poundage of the bow can be made both up and down, but maintaining the tiller. You will need to check and maintain the height of the bare shaft compared to the fletched arrows, allowing it only to move to the left or right of the group depending on whether you are raising or lowering the poundage. This should be carried out to within one turn higher or lower than your start poundage. At quarter-turn adjustments this will give you eight sequences to test and record. Making a small change to the weight on your fingers will change the amplitude of the string on release and it will also alter the stiffness of the arrow. As usual you are looking for a consistent group size on the small side.

Arrows

The factors you will be testing with your arrows are:

- Nocks
- Fletches
- Point weight
- Shaft types and spine

Starting with the shaft you are currently shooting, it is quite easy to check for arrow consistency by making adjustments to four of your arrows and shooting against four of your current set-up of arrows. If the four adjusted arrows produce better groups, change more of your arrows and shoot six against six. If the results remain good, change all the arrows to the new adjustment. This should be only carried out with shafts of the same spine. Although some changes might give slight variations to height between the groups, it is the size and not the position that you are looking for. Shooting with different spines and types to see what gives the best groups will give very unreliable data as each spine will need to be tuned with or to the bow, owing to the difference in the diameter of the shafts.

Nocks

Tests with the different nocks supplied by Beiter for use with X10s – over, in-out and pin nocks – show that each displays a variation in the way the arrow behaves. Over nocks are longer than the other two types, but fit well to the shaft with little independent flex, and can be made from clear plastic. In-out nocks are shorter but have a slight flex on the shaft (Ace in-out nocks are a lot stiffer on the shaft). Pin nocks are of a similar length, but the presence of the pin means that there is little flex on the shaft. The pin also adds extra weight to the end of the shaft. The colour of the nocks can make a difference to how quickly and easily they can be seen on the boss. Easily identified arrows allow the archer to have certainty of the position of all their arrows, which maintains confidence of their shot. Durability is also a factor to consider as you need a nock that maintains its shape and nock fit. Nocks that are susceptible to a change of nock fit will increase your group size.

It is quite easy to trim a couple of millimetres from the base of the spin wing to produce a lower-profiled fletch, while maintaining its length. FRANCES KEATS

Fletches

You should test the type of fletch, its position in relation to the nock, and the angle on the shaft. The higher the angle of the fletch, the faster it will try to spin the arrow, but it will also slow down more quickly, giving bigger groups at the longer distances. However the fletch will need an angle on the shaft as the spinning of the shaft helps to give it direction and consistency.

Some fletchings, especially spin wings, lend themselves to having their profile changed. I find that the 1¾in wings have too high a profile, so I use a craft knife, a steel rule and a cutting block to cut 2mm off the foot of the fletch. This gives a fletch of 1¾in but with a low profile that gives better groups at longer distances.

Point Weight

Changing the point weight will alter the spine of the arrow. Make sure that you test them in windy conditions as well as calm. As a good guide to the weight of the point, maintain or increase the recommended point weight as suggested by the manufacturer for your shaft size. I do not recommend making the point lighter than the recommended weight because if the point is too light in relation to the shaft it will tend to lose direction and group size will increase.

The length of the insert will also play a part in how the arrow behaves. Although you can use the same weight of point for both the tungsten and steel points available for X10s, not only does the point protrude a different length from the end of the shaft, but the length of the insert is different, altering the flex of the shaft.

Shaft Types and Spine

Not only do you need to decide what type of shaft is going to suit your discipline, but also the spine required. The tables given by Easton provide a good indication of arrows with similar spines to those that you are currently shooting. Having ascertained how your current arrow is tuning to the bow, you will be able to find arrows of a similar spine but different model. By looking in the adjacent boxes on the charts you can find out which is the next spine, either stiffer or weaker, depending on how your current arrows are coming out. The arrow chart only indicates the spine of arrow that will be close to suiting your shooting. Some years ago Jim Buchanan and I were using the same make of bows with the same weight on the fingers, but shot a different spine of arrow. Jim's arrows wereone spine stiffer, possibly due to fingers of differing size and loose. As the chart is only an indication of spine, you may find that you are shooting one spine up from the one indicated. This is quite normal, as fine tuning is about finding the spine of arrow that gives you the best group.

When you step up to a stiffer spine you will also increase the weight of the arrow. After about 42lb the increase of the arrow speed in relation to an increase in bow weight declines, but you do get more mass in the air at the same speed, which will improve downrange velocity. This needs to be taken into account if you are considering moving up a spine weight. If your arrow is a little on the weak side you may be better off lowering the poundage. This may also lower the arrow speed a little and give a slight change to the sight marks, but the next stiffer spine of arrow will give even lower sight marks. To get it tuned you may have to further increase your draw weight, which may put you over your maximum. Maximum draw weight is the weight that you can shoot with and still control the shot. If you exceed it you will not be able to fully control your shot, however much you train.

Another solution to increasing stiffness to the shaft on tapered type arrows is to shorten the arrow from the back of the shaft. In cutting from the back you are shortening the taper, which stiffens the arrow significantly more quickly than cutting from the front of the shaft. With ACE arrows (620s) I found that if I cut 5cm (2in) from the back of the arrow it more or less stiffened the arrow to that of a 570 shaft, although it did not perform well. I therefore would not usually cut more than 2.5cm (1in) from the back. If you are going to cut from the back of your shafts, shorten them by small amounts at a time and test. The benefit of this is that you can shoot to your maximum bow weight with an arrow to suit.

Another consideration for cutting from the back of the arrow is the arrow's final overall length once it has been cut. I shoot a 28in arrow from point to nock slot with 45lb on the fingers. If I cut my arrow to length only from the front, it makes the back tapered part of the arrow proportionally longer than the front parallel section, putting the logo towards the front half of the shaft. Although I can get the arrow to tune, I feel I end up with an arrow that has a whippy back end. Cutting from the back of the arrow maintains the ratio of parallel to tapered shaft.

I shoot X10 550s with 2.5cm (1in) cut from the back of the arrow. This stiffens it and gives a good proportion of front to back. If I shoot X10 500s, even if the are just cut from the front, which I am not keen on for my arrow length, in order to get them tuned I need to increase the bow weight to 57lb, which puts me over my maximum draw weight. Arrows are expensive, but finding those best suited to you may well mean having to test at least the two adjacent spine weights in the range to which you are currently shooting.

First Pass of Tuning

This concludes the first pass of fine tuning. In each area you are proving, by adjustment and noting the group size, the best position and adjustment for all the areas. This involves, in effect, detuning the bow so that the group size gets bigger on either side of the adjustment you are making, then using the detailed notes of your results and setting it to the middle best point. Because all the factors given above have a bearing on each other to a greater or lesser extent, every area needs to be visited before further finer adjustments should be made. All the areas of the list can now be revisited. The first pass of fine tuning will put your equipment in a state of mutual cooperation, but all the changes are inter-related. Changes to the tab will affect the amplitude of the string, which in turn changes the best point for the nock to leave the string, which changes the pressure and angle of the arrow against the plunger. Each area will therefore have to be revisited to recheck and test for its best setting. The adjustments made on the second, third and subsequent passes of tuning will, on the whole, be smaller and more refined as each tuning pass gets the bow closer to best adjustment.

Check-tune

At the end of a tuning session, even with all the changes to settings recorded, you should shoot both bare shafts and fletched arrows at 30m and record the position of the bare shafts in relation to the fletched arrows. You will probably find that they are no longer in the fletched group. This new position should be recorded as it gives an account of how your bow needs to be set to keep the bow shooting at its best. With no other adjustment made, you should carry out this test weekly to ensure that nothing has altered on the bow. A change of position in the bare shafts indicates that something has changed on the bow or with your shooting. If you are going to be setting up a new bow, you would initially set it up so that the bare shaft to fletched group position bears a similar relationship, enabling you to set the bow up close to your current set-up.

Finding the Right Bow

Any of the top bows will give you a top score, but there may be one that gives you a better score. The only way to find out is to try them out. As you get to the top of your sport you may be lucky enough to be sponsored. This is great, but it will make you reluctant to try other manufacturers. Fortunately some manufacturers have a good selection of great bows. As you will need a second bow, this is when you can acquire and try a different model. You will have a primary bow that you want to shoot competitions with. It would be foolish to put in all that practice, travel across the world and have an issue with your only bow. A second bow ensures that you have one that is well set up for you and should shoot just as well as your primary bow. I refine the tuning on my second bow until it is better than my primary. This will then become my primary bow and the other becomes the secondary and will be the one to be adjusted. Even two bows of the same model can shoot differently, with one always giving better results. When you are looking for a second bow, think about getting a different model. The new one will either be better, worse or the same, but at this level worse is 1310 not 1320. Both will shoot well, but if it is better you might go to 1330. There may be no difference in groups or score. If it is the same and you still get 1320, it means you are shooting the best bow for you, so you just have to learn to shoot even better.

To summarize: tuning is an ongoing process that needs to be carried out to get the best from your equipment with your current shooting style. As your style and technique change and improve, readjustments to your equipment will be necessary if you are to continue to get the best from your equipment. Tuning only gets the best from your current shooting style. You cannot tune to better scores above the level of your technique, so a balance needs to be maintained between these two areas. If you are lucky enough to be able to tune in indoor conditions, further tuning must be carried out in all weather conditions.

I feel that to get the best consistency of score, the bow needs to be adjusted so that it forces the arrow to bend the same way every time it leaves the bow. This is for both recurve and compound, so when you shoot a good shot the arrow bend = X. Even with a poorer shot the arrow bend is still very close to X. Many recurve archers have their bows set either slightly stiff or weak. With compounds this is achieved by setting the nocking point slightly high. This helps to ensure that a specific bend and direction of bend is induced into the arrow, which in turn gives consistency to the group.

The initial run through the list will take some time as you will be testing for more major changes to your set-up. The subsequent adjustments can be carried out within normal training. You will be shooting, perhaps working on your release, and every three dozen arrows you can make minor adjustments to your button tension. At your next session it might involve changes to your brace height that you can carry out. Although the major part of the result will come from your technique and mental game, if the brace height is just 5mm too low you will not achieve your potential score, however well you execute a shot.

CHAPTER 9

TRAINING AIDS

Practice makes perfect, but it is what you do at your practice that makes the difference to how long it takes until you become perfect.

The books by W. Timothy Gallwey, including *The Inner Game of Tennis* (1974), *Inner Tennis: Playing the Game* (1976) and *The Inner Game of Golf* (1981), are of particular interest to archers. Much of their content is about the mental aspect of the sport and this can easily be translated to archery. What is particularly relevant here is his observation that it is far easier to adjust your body's position by thinking about the position of the bone and the position and direction you are trying to achieve, than by trying to describe and think about which muscles to tension or release to achieve the same movement or position. It is about making your body more aware of its position by amplifying and exaggerating, using the body's built-in natural balance. From general observation and the experience of practising yoga, it is apparent that limbs and other parts of the body do not always do what you think they are when they are out of sight. Very little of your body is in view when shooting. Trying to adjust your stance or posture by observations and comment can be slow and laborious. By introducing external stimuli to balance and vision, changes to stance and posture can be made to an individual far quicker, and in some areas without the need to have an extra body on hand to monitor the areas being worked on. By using the body's natural balance and visual input, some aspects of an archer's stance can easily be adjusted.

The areas covered in this chapter are:

- Feet together practice
- Balance board
- Tripod on stick
- Arm weights
- Spirit level – recurve
- Speed meter
- Mirror
- Cameras: photographs, video and high-speed video

Feet Together Practice

This practice is one of the simplest to help you ensure that the weight distribution is the same for both legs and that you remain upright during your shot. All you have to do is stand on the line with both feet as close together as possible. Having your

Shooting with your feet together will make you more aware of your vertical alignment and the weight distribution for each leg.

feet together will make you less stable, highlighting any imbalance in your weight. Adopting this posture when standing will help you get the feel of a more even distribution when standing, and how that feeling is on your hips. While shooting with your feet together you will become more aware of changes in balance, as to stand still you will have to maintain your centre of gravity within the small area that your feet are in contact with the floor.

Balance Board

Balance boards are very simple to make. The accompanying photograph shows examples with discs 8cm and 12cm in diameter: I feel the 8cm is a little small and the 12cm works better. It is important that a circle is used so that all-round balance is tested. The discs are made from 18mm (¾in) thick MDF and the boards used here were salvaged from old kitchen doors. The balance board needs to be placed on a hard surface to get the best results. The position of the feet on the board is also very important: the centre line of the disc should coincide with the centre of the foot's arch. Moving the heel away from the centre line makes the archer balance with more weight on the toes, so changing the body's vertical position. The board can be angled on the shooting line to take into account the stance of the archer. Once the correct foot position is ascertained, the board is marked and the archer can get on with

practising. Most archers will be able to find their balance quite quickly throughout the whole shot sequence.

As with all the previous practices, you need to allow for shooting about 1,000 arrows or a month of shooting, whichever is shorter, to find the new 'feel' of the shot.

Stick on a Tripod

In many activities that that you may well already participate in – walking, running, riding a bike, motorbike, driving, skiing – where you look determines where you go. Look at the gap, and you will go through it. In archery it is the same.

Many archers seen in both recurve and compound competitions would benefit from standing upright and still during the draw, especially as they execute the shot. For others a slight modification to their vertical stance would make it much easier for them to execute good shots. Simply saying 'Stand still and lean forward a bit', however, would not be a satisfactory or consistent way of achieving this. It takes a lot of training time to get it right. As it is all about consistency, ensuring that you are in the same vertical position for every shot might involve someone standing behind you and directing you to the correct position at full draw. This would not only be an onerous task for the helper, however, but would invariably lead to a protracted time at

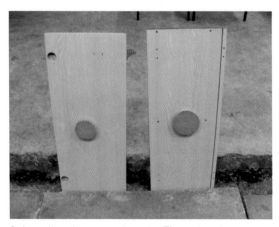

Balance boards are easy to make. The various sizes enable archers of different abilities to start with a more stable base.

The position of your feet on the board will enable you to work on maintaining the correct balance throughout your shot.

A broken arrow can be attached to an old tripod so that the height can be easily adjusted.

The height should be adjusted so that the end of the arrow appears to be on the gold.

full draw while you are guided to the correct position. Fortunately there is an easier way of ensuring that your vertical consistency, position and point of focus are maintained for every arrow. This can be achieved easily using a do-it-yourself performance-enhancing tool, which can be very useful for archers and coaches of all disciplines.

With a simple tripod and an old arrow, or simply sticking a bamboo cane in the ground when outdoors, the 'line of focus' can be utilized to enable you to maintain your vertical body position during the shot. Place the tripod about 12 to 15m in front of your position on the shooting line with the tip of the pointer in line with the gold. You may need to move your feet on the line to get the arrow-pointer and body in the correct position. Once found, your foot position can be marked so that the same position can be maintained throughout the practice. I usually use this device at distances of 50m and above, as the arrow needs to pass over the tip of the pointer. For indoor shooting and shorter distances a plumb line can be used.

All you have to do is shoot at the target maintaining the pointer's relative position on the target face. It does not necessarily need to be absolutely central on the face, but within the nine ring at 70m. If the end of the stick appears to stay still in relation to the target face it means that you must be keeping your head still. You will need to shoot at least 1,000 arrows to ensure that you have this feeling instilled in your shot sequence. Although the distance between the archer and the pointer is not critical, your movement is more apparent the closer the pointer is to you, since the stick's position and movement against the target face become more apparent. I usually start by placing the pointer slightly further away at about 20m. As you get used to working with it, it can be moved closer so you can iron out the smaller movements. Remembering that the shot finishes only when the arrow hits the target, the stick should stay in position on the target until the arrow impacts.

Compounds can also use the pointer to help keep the bubble centralized by making it appear that the

Compounds can carry out this exercise with the same ease. Movement will be more or less apparent according to how far the stick is placed from the archer.

LEFT: The archer's vertical position can be maintained throughout the shot with minimum supervision.
KAREN HENDERSON

RIGHT: By maintaining the end of the pointer on the gold but moving their feet along the line, an archer can easily realign their vertical body position.

bubble is balancing on the tip pointer. It is important that the pointer stays on or very close to the line of focus. It should also stay motionless against the target face throughout the whole shot. The same principles can be used for short-range work indoors by using a string or plumb line suspended through the centre of the target. It is better to use a thin string, since an arrow will hit a solid pointer. As the arrow's flight is below the line of sight, it is much

safer to use a string as it will move out of the way if the arrow touches it.

This simple pointing aid can also be used with the help of a coach to adjust your vertical body position. Stand on the line so that the pointer is aligned with the gold. If you move your feet backward (heels back) slightly along the line, but maintain the visual position of the pointer on the target, you will have to lean forward, transferring more of your body weight onto your toes. If you move your feet forward on the line, again maintaining the visual picture of the end of the stick in the gold, it will transfer your body weight onto your heels, making you more upright. Once you are in the vertical body position that you want, the position of your toes can be marked on the floor. You can then start your practice knowing that, with your toes in the same position and the position of the stick maintained, you are in the same vertical alignment for every shot. As a coaching aid this allows the coach to set the body position that they want the archer to achieve and leave them to it as they work with other archers.

Once you are used to working with both the stick and the balance board they can be used in conjunction with each other. This makes it very easy to adjust your vertical position while ensuring that your centre of gravity remains stable, so reinforcing your shooting platform.

Arm Weights

Originally I bought sets of weights that could be attached to the ankles and a lighter set for wrists so that when carrying out exercises I could get additional benefit fro the exercises I was doing. I thought I would try shooting with them on to help strengthen my shoulder muscles as dual training for shooting and strength. It did help but I also found that it kept the bow arm far steadier as the additional weight dampened down the movement of my arm. It had a similar effect to putting more weight on the stabilizers to steady the bow. Putting the weight on my arm, however, did not affect the dynamics of the bow. It meant that I could easily vary the weight placed on my arm, so working on strengthening the shoulder and getting a better feeling for how a steady arm should feel. I tried putting the weight on my draw arm but found that it only got in the way and was of no real benefit. In Chapter 8 above I mentioned that most weights can be removed from the stabilizers, while maintaining the bow's balance points, to demonstrate how much of a dampening effect your normal stabilizer weight arrangement has on your group size. If, when you shoot with the wrist weight on with your normal stabilizer set-up, the group gets smaller, it is an indication that work needs to be carried out on steadying the front arm.

Spirit Level

If you have a tendency to tilt the bow while shooting, one method of getting a correct feel for maintaining the bow's position is to secure a small spirit level bubble to the sight. You may be able to borrow a bubble from a compound shooter that will suffice.

Placing additional weights on your bow arm.
KAREN HENDERSON

A bubble can only be used in training, but it enables an archer to experience what an upright bow feels like.

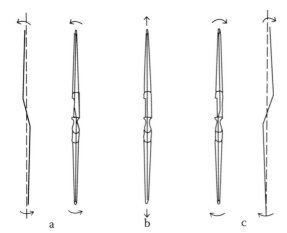

Keeping the finger pressure on the string vertically aligned with help to bow vertical, torquing the string will make the archer tilt the bow away from vertical.

It is important to ensure that with the bubble attached it is in fact keeping the bow upright. Probably the best way of checking this is to use a Beiter square large insert sight ring, which has a fitting to take a level bubble. While this can only be used for training, practising with it for a few weeks will give you the feel of how to maintain the bow's vertical position. As it is the vertical position you will be working on, it is probably best to shoot at a target set at 5m. This will enable you to focus on keeping the bubble central without concerning yourself with where the arrows are going. Your bow may not be upright because the string is resting on your chest, which should have been rectified for clearance, or it could be due to the angle of the draw hand. You should find it very easy to maintain the bow in the vertical position if you set it up with the reversal sling. It is also easy to tilt the bow left and right because it is only the bow hand that is altering the bow's vertical position. If the draw hand is not maintaining the string in a vertical plane, not only will it impart a tilt to the bow but, with the bow hand trying to maintain the vertical position of the bow, it will impart a twist to the string.

Speed Meter

The 'shoot through' speed meter is a useful addition to any range, I have never quite understood why some archers get so worked up about how fast their arrows go because it makes little difference to the group size. In addition, variations in lighting conditions, the length of the arrow and its position when it passes through the frame of the speed meter will

When using a speed meter indoors a permanent light will help to give more consistent readings. The long rod points at the meter body ensure that the arrow passes above the meter.

all give different readings. It is of benefit, though, for working on the consistency of shot and tuning one bow to another.

To get reasonably consistent readings, the light above the meter needs to be constant. That is not too much of a problem in sunny countries, but if you have varying weather conditions it is best to set it up inside with a good light source above it.

The other issue in using this type of speed meter is that is has a tendency to get shot. A good rule of thumb is either to get someone to look from the side to ensure that your arrow will go through it or, if you are shooting on your own, set it so that your long rod is pointing at the readout on the front. This should ensure that the arrow goes through the frame and not the machine. Once you have found a good position and height, use foot markers to help you keep the same place for all your shooting.

Although the speed readings may not be strictly accurate, they are reasonably accurate between shots on the same day. Readings should therefore be used only on that day and not compared with those from other sessions.

A speed meter can be used for trying to make the arrow speed consistent between consecutive shots. When shooting through it you will notice that any movement of the head or body while at full draw, or made during the shot, will make the frame seem to move across the face of the target in a similar way to when carrying out the tripod and stick exercise. When you remain in position, the frame will stay at the same position against the target.

This equipment can also be used for comparing the speed of different bows and set-ups. The same length of arrows must be used for all the tests. When comparing bow speed you will need to ensure that, as far as possible, the arrow goes through the frame at the same height and position. In matching arrow speed between bows you will be able to set each bow to a closer match, if that is what you are looking for. Once you have matched them for speed, you can use one as a 'control'. By making equipment changes or tuning adjustments to one of the bows, you will be able to see what changes, if any, it makes to the speed of the arrow. A couple of points for film buffs: in *Blade: Trinity* (2004) the arrow speed should remain constant when shooting a compound arrow through a speed meter; and in *Avatar* (2009) the arrow is on the wrong side of the bow.

Mirror

A full-length mirror placed on the shooting line can be useful in monitoring your position during the shot. After making a simple adjustment you can get a feel of how the position looks. It does have its limitations, however, as at full draw you need to be focusing on the target.

Cameras

Getting instant feedback nowadays is very easy. Nearly everyone has a camera with them all the time. Most mobile phones have them built in and these can usually take both stills and video. Traditional cameras generally take higher-quality pictures and video, while cameras are available that have the ability to take reasonably high-speed sequences at about 1,000 frames per second, allowing you to see what happens as the arrow leaves the bow.

Both phones and cameras give the opportunity of instant feedback. In conjunction with your shooting log this can be used as a record of progress and changes. Video is especially useful as coaches can monitor shooting form from afar. Postings on YouTube and other online sites make it possible to watch top archers around the world in action.

A full photo from the front enables you to keep a record of weight distribution and alignment of arrow and elbow.
KAREN HENDERSON

A full view from behind, with the string running centrally down the centre of the limb, gives you a photograph that can be easily reproduced so that body and bow alignment can be recorded and reproduced for comparison. KAREN HENDERSON

This shot gives a clear record of the hand and finger position against the face. KAREN HENDERSON

Photographs

Photographs are very good for recording your progress, particularly if you can take three or four key shots from different angles: full facing the archer; full from behind the archer, showing the elbow and the line of the string down the centre of the limb, including feet and all the bow; a close-up shot of anchor and elbow; and, if possible, a high shot from behind showing the line of the arrow with the string down the centre of the limb.

Other angles can be taken, but sets of photographs taken from the same angles but at different times will let you monitor any changes. You need to ensure that these key monitoring shots are taken once you have settled at full draw. It is also useful to see photographs of yourself shooting at competition, although care needs to be taken when comparing these photographs as they may have been taken just prior to your full draw position. These will help you gauge whether your shooting at competition is the same as when you

If you can get a shot from an elevated position directly behind the archer, you can observe the alignment. JAMIE CUTTS

Recording good groups helps to reinforce good shooting at practice or competition.

are practising. You also need to ensure that they are taken as part of your normal shooting sequence, as specially posed shots may be out of your normal alignment. Taking stills from video sequences will help ensure that you get the right part of the sequence. Photographs can also be linked into your spreadsheet diary with pictures of equipment and good groups, which can help with reinforcing good practice sessions.

Video

Video shot from similar angles can be used in a similar way to photographs. It is best if you can use a tripod as this will ensure that you have no movement on the camera. You will then be able to judge an archer's position and movement by comparing it with the background. If the camera is only handheld it can be difficult to see if the movement is from the camera or from the archer being videoed. One area that is worth focusing on is a close-up shot of your eye and face. When playing back the sequence you will be able to observe any movement of your eye, which should remain focused on the target

Gauging an archer's focus by monitoring their eye during a shot. DEAN ALBERGA

throughout the shot and behave the same at all the distances that you shoot. An ideal sequence would be hearing the clicker, the string releasing, the arrow hitting the target and then the eyes blinking. Close observation of your eye will verify if you are maintaining focus throughout the shot and whether or not you are anticipating the shot.

With video you should be able to produce still shots from any part of the sequence. Using a simple video editing program you will be able to scrutinize an exact moment taken from the whole sequence of the shot. When watching the video you should also follow the action in slow motion and speeded up. Watching in slow motion will give a better idea of what is happening in local areas of the shot. Not many people watch video sequences speeded up, but when watching an archer shoot nine or ten consecutive arrows on fast forward it is much easier to see if the archer's body moves or sways during the shot sequence. The movements that are usually picked up are from the upper body, movement forward and backwards, side to side or a combination of both, together with tilting of the bow. The other area to observe is the hips, during and just after the shot. If the hips are not well supported they twist or rotate as the release takes place. If they are not held well in place, the back will also

be poorly supported, which will affect your shot. When viewing this area at normal or slow speed the movement is not obvious, but running the same sequence at between five and ten times the normal speed shows it well.

As with all aspects of your shooting, look at the good bits, analyse how you do it and see if you can improve. When watching clips of yourself shooting you need to think about how the shot feels to reinforce the feeling of that shot. Watching video of top archers can also be of great benefit, but in the same manner you should be emulating the movement and timing of their shot, working on how that feels. This is best done by mimicking the shot in front of the screen in real time. If you only run through how the shot feels in your mind you will tend to speed up the shot. Pick sequences from actual events, watching and copying one of the archers in a match. Try to emulate not only the body movements and how they feel, but also consider what that person might be thinking. By looking at the archer's eyes you will get a feel for their area of focus while between shots and that will help you build a picture of their mental state.

The best use of video is to make sure that your mental picture of how you want to look is how it is in reality.

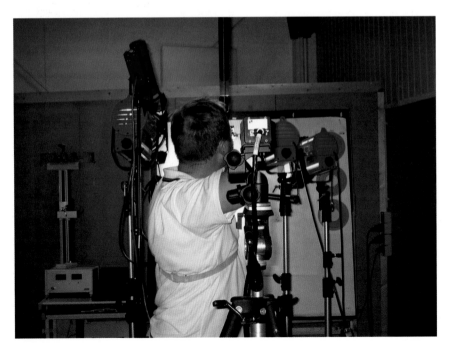

Werner Beiter has the best archery facility in the world. I have had the privilege of visiting on a number of occasions.

High-speed Video

Until recently it was not possible to shoot high-speed video at home. Only places such as the Werner & Iris Beiter Center in Germany had the facilities to make detailed high-speed video sequences for analysis and then were able to utilize the resulting images to improve your set-up.

Following the introduction of cameras such as the Casio High Speed EXILIM EX-FH25, which can take video at 1000 frames per second, it is now possible to take high-speed video sequences at the club that can benefit your shooting. It is not enough to have such a camera. You also need a planned shooting sequence, and the ability to interpret the sequences that you take, or the technology is just a waste of time. A high-speed video booth set up at a coaching workshop often attracts flocks of archers simply seeking a video to take home that shows their arrow coming out of the bow 'Sloooowleeey'.

High-speed video can be very useful if it is set up well. For a start you need to be shooting consistently with a reasonably well-tuned bow. You can make more of the data you collect from the sequences that you shoot. The more consistently you shoot, the fewer retakes of each area you will require, which will enable you to make more accurate adjustments. You will also require good light, an appropriate backdrop, so that you can see what is happening, a laptop and a planned sequence of shooting so that you make the most of your time. With this in place you can upload the images immediately and waste no time while checking the results, making adjustments and reshooting.

A good source of light, such as two 500W floodlights, is needed when setting up for high-speed shooting indoors.

Lighting

A reasonably good source of light can be made from two 500W floodlights. They need to be easily adjustable for height and to swivel so that the maximum light can be directed onto the subject. They should not be too close together, however, as you will want to be able to work the camera between them.

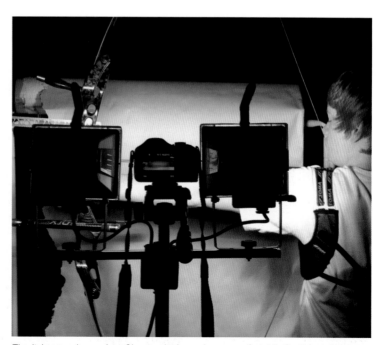

The lights produce a lot of heat, which can be uncomfortable for the archer.

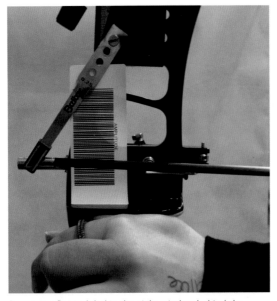

By using a Dymo label in the sight window behind the arrow you should be able to see the arrow clearly, especially against a dark riser. The lines give a good reference when checking the rise and fall of the arrow as it leaves the bow.

Backdrop

A light-coloured backdrop not only helps to reflect the light back onto the subject area but enables you to see the movement of the equipment and body more easily. A backdrop with grid lines on it can also aid in picking out movement and alignment. Another, with a graticule design, should be attached in the bow window behind the arrow. This highlights the contrast between the arrow and the riser so that any movement can be observed accurately. Printable Avery labels or Dymo labels may be used for this.

Video Shooting Sequence

Shooting plans or sequences for recurves and compounds are more or less the same. Using a camera does have some limitations. Overhead shots, for example, would be ideal, but you will tend to be too far away from the subject to be of benefit. A typical sequence is shown below.

1. The first shot enables you to study the hand and nocking point behaviour before and during the release.

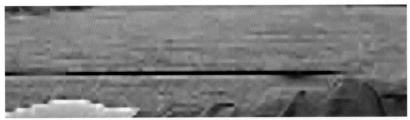

2. On the second shot you are able to track the first part of the travel of the nock.

3. The third shot is taken from the arrow side and should include as much of the arrow as possible, including the arrow's detachment from the string point.

At 60 frames a second the arrow stays in the bow for one or two frames. At 1,000 frames per second the arrow is in the shot for about 22 frames.

The shot sequence is as follows:

1. Nock end of arrow on release
2. Nock and as much of shaft as possible
3. Arrow and detachment point from string
4. Bow window
5. Front of bow window to sight block

The reasoning behind this sequence is that you want to observe what is happening to the string, D loop and nock on release, then the path of the nock while it is attached to the string, what is happening at the bow window and finally what path the arrow takes as it leaves the bow. Using this sequence you will be able to check the results and make any necessary

4. The fourth shot enables you to study the behaviour of the arrow against the riser, rest or launcher.

5. The fifth shot follows the path of the arrow in front of the riser. Some sights are positioned so you can follow the arrow's path using the sight track as a reference.

adjustments as you go through it. Unless you have observed what is happening to the nock on release, by videoing the launcher or rest first to see what it is doing, you will not be able to correlate any movement you observe and will be wasting your time.

Nock End of Arrow on Release

Initially the camera and lights need to be set up so that you can get a good close-up shot that shows the nock at and just after the release, and the fingers just prior to the release. The first observation of this shot is to note the finger movements that are made to activate the release.

Compound

With compounds it depends on what type of release aid is being used. When using a thumb release you are making sure that the only movement in the hand comes from the digit activating the release. The body of the release aid should remain in place without movement, as should the fingers supporting the body. For back tension release, the angle of the release aid to the D loop changes to allow the release to take place. The observation for this type of release is that the fingers should remain in place on the body of the release aid: when operating this type of release there is a tendency to activate it by changing the finger pressure to tilt it.

Recurve

Recurve shooters should examine the finger position on the string and that the fingers remain in place on the string prior to the release. There should be no discernible movement in the hand. You should then check that all the fingers release at the same time and that the string appears to pull through the fingers, pushing them out of the way. Once the string has passed they should go back to their original position and start to move back along the line of the face.

Study the movement of the fingers before and during the release.

Recurve archer's fingers pushed out of the way by the string.

Then relax back as though still holding the string.

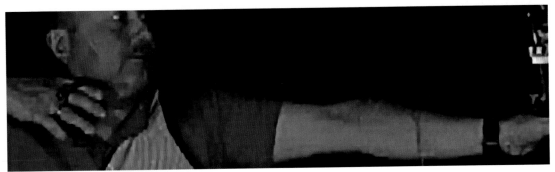

The track of the release hand past the neck can indicate the tension in the hand prior to the release.

Nock

Close observation of the movement of the nock on release will enable you to judge the nocking point position and tiller of the bow. If the nock moves directly forward, this indicates that the tiller and nocking point are set at the right positions. If the tiller is set correctly and the nocking point is incorrect, however, the straight line travelled by the nock will instead travel up, if the nocking point is set too low, or down, if the nocking point is too high. If the nock initially moves in a curve, either up or down, it indicates that the limbs are out of balance, as one is working harder than the other. Up indicates the top limb is working harder. This can be more noticeable on compounds shooting with a D loop. Not only should the nock move directly away from the release aid but the D loop's vertical position should also remain constant. If the string between the D loop is observed tilting, it also indicates that an unequal balance is being exerted above and below the D loop. This could be due to issues with the cams as well as the tiller.

Before seeing these details you need to upload them to your laptop. By holding the edge of a piece of paper against the line of the arrow, you will be able to see any vertical change in the height of the nock. You can then make adjustments to the bow to maintain the nock's horizontal trajectory on release. Sometimes you will come across limbs of

Holding a sheet of paper against the screen enables you to see the path of the arrow. JAMIE CUTTS

unequal strength and you will need to significantly offset the tiller to make them work better. If the top limb is significantly stronger than the bottom limb, normally you have to make the tiller a much larger positive or you can change the limbs around, putting the top limb in the bottom. This may well give a more balanced tiller position, but you will have to fend off helpful archers pointing out that your limbs are the wrong way round.

Nock and as much of the Shaft as Possible

Once you have corrected the initial movement, change the camera angle to one from where you can observe as much of the arrow as possible, while keeping the nock at full draw in the shot. You are then able to observe the arrow and the nock's path while it is connected to the string.

For compound bows you will expect to see the arrow flex downwards. The nock path should be fairly level throughout as the arrow should only be flexing in the vertical plane. For recurves the arrow and nock ought to have a flat trajectory as the shaft should only be flexing in the horizontal plane. This means that it is easier to set up a recurve bow correctly in this key part of an arrow's trajectory.

To observe the vertical placement of a compound arrow, you need to have the camera above looking down or below looking up; the latter is harder to set up and you will not be able to get as close to the arrow. Any major deviations in the arrow's trajectory can be made by adjusting the launcher or rest. By observing a longer movement of the nock while it is still connected to the string, you should be able to observe the nock's path more closely, giving you the opportunity to appraise the position of the nocking point. The other anomaly that you may come across from time to time is an imbalance of the limbs' power release performance. This occurs when one limb differs in performance on release during the power stroke. This will be indicated by an anomaly in the path of the nock two or three inches from the point of release. With compounds it may be an issue with the cams, but for recurves it indicates imbalanced limbs or excessive vertical torque by the bow hand.

Bow Window

Close-up shots of the bow window give the best views of the rest and launcher position. With recurves you are looking for the arrow to main-

The vertical displacement of the arrow is relatively small compared with a recurve's horizontal displacement bend.

This view shows the flex of the arrow clearly. The only contact is where the nock is attached to the nocking point.

tain its vertical height as it passes the rest's position, remembering that the nock is still attached to the string for 45cm (18in) of the arrow's forward movement. It now becomes more apparent why it is important to deal with the nock end of the sequence first. With compounds you will initially observe the front of the arrow lowering on the launcher, then raising off it so that the remainder of the arrow clears the launcher. In order to observe any horizontal displacement of the arrow, rig up a mirror above the arrow set at an angle of 45 degrees. This will enable you to look down on the arrow above the rest or launcher. The mirror should be plastic and firmly attached to the bow. For recurves you will expect to see the arrow press into the button for about 5 to 7cm (2–3in) of the arrow's forward movement. This is the equivalent of a compound archer's arrow dropping onto the launcher and then moving away from the button. There should be no further contact: if the fletches contact the button you need to change the angle at which they are set. With compound arrows the arrow should remain directly above the launcher, as any bend should be in the vertical plane.

Front of Bow Window to Sight Block

The final video frame of this sequence is to observe the arrow passing the sight carrier on T-type sights. In this shot you will be able to check any movement of the sight against the background. This provides feedback on how steady the bow is on the shot and you will be able to observe the trajectory of the arrow with reference to the bow. A recurve arrow should pass the sight in a flat trajectory, with both the front and back of the arrow passing the same point. A compound arrow will be seen to flex vertically, but the front and the back of the arrow's trajectory should follow the same path.

As with other forms of tuning, once you achieve good, consistent results you can record these set sequences with high-speed video equipment. This record of the dynamic set-up can be used as a guide to setting up a second bow or for checking for changes in your current set-up.

Coaching Programs and Apps

Software programs made by Dartfish have been available for some time on Windows platforms.

They are regularly updated and allow you to view and compare shots using video overlay. You can also draw lines and shapes over the video sequence to make it easier to analyse the archer's position and movement during their shot sequences. It is a good means by which coaches can demonstrate an archer's body movements and alignment. By super-imposing sequences you can easily confirm the consistence of an individual's shot or illustrate the differences between new and old shot sequences. It can be used in conjunction with high-speed video sequences, but a piece of paper against the screen usually suffices when working down at the club. Just observing an archer shooting will in most cases be enough for a coach to see all that is necessary, especially if there is a fixed background to judge movement against. Dartfish programs are very useful for checking on an archer's position when there is no fixed background against which to judge their move-ment and alignment. Provided a tripod has been used, you can mark the image position and note any movement.

The increasing availability of communications equipment such as smart phones, iPads and other tablets has introduced coaching applications that give instant replay similar to Dartfish, but at a much lower cost. A current example is Coach's Eye, which is available for iOS (iPad, iPhone and iPod Touch) and Android devices. Using this you can overlay video clips taken with your device and make simple comparisons of shots and movements for consist-ency. In a single package this provides instant video feedback, illustrating what you want the archer to see and feel. You can also pause it, change the playback speed and draw lines and circles over the image to illustrate positioning or movement. It can be used, for example, simply to check if the head is stationary during and after the shot. A line can be

Using Coach's Eye on an iPad.

Lines can be overlaid so that the archer's movements can easily be seen.

drawn against the arrow or bow to check where the movement comes from when initiating the clicker or positioning a release aid. Due to the size of some tablets, pictures or video footage of less experienced archers can be taken with less obtrusive mobile phones and then transferred to your tablet or iPad by Bluetooth. (You will have to use this method with the original iPad as it does not have a camera.)

With all the advances in technology to keep ahead of the rest of the game is to find and use anything out there that will enhance your training. It is not just following the instructions of what others have used the technology for, but inventing other ways to use it to check, adjust and record what you do.

If you cannot find what you need for your training you can devise your own apps to do what you need. Glen Croft has come up with two apps so far: a 'reversal timer' with which you can use an iOS device to help you time and count your reversal training, and an AIArcher that generates scores for head-to-head simulation so you can train using your device as your opponent.

I am waiting for the app that will map your movements in three dimensions. You would be able to overlay all the movements you make during a shot in 3D using video taken from any angle. This would show whether what appears to be corrected from one angle is producing an imbalance on the other side at the same time. It is not enough for the shot to look great from whatever side the camera is situated. The same shot has to look great from every angle. This can be achieved using three cameras, followed by endless editing to get them all into sync and proportion, by which time the archer has moved on. 3D single-shot imaging is what is required. In summary, it is the use of training aids, used on their own or in conjunction with each other and shooting practices, that improves your progress faster, making you more consistent.

CHAPTER 10

ARCHERY FIRST: MENTAL FORM

The concept of 'Archery First' applies to everything you do or think. Archery should be your first consideration and this concept should determine your goal setting.

On many occasions I have been taken as someone who spends most of his time on equipment, setting it up and tuning it to get the most out of it. As Jay Barrs pointed out in his video *The Mental Game*, however, equipment makes up only 10 per cent of the picture, with shooting technique taking 20 per cent. That leaves the remaining 70 per cent to the mental game. At the practice field I give serious attention to the 30 per cent – equipment and technique – that is visible. What you do not see is the time spent utilizing the mental techniques I have learnt, not only at the practice field but throughout the day, from waking up to going back to sleep.

It is a bit like being a Formula 1 driver. Even if the car has been set up for peak performance, the driver will not win if his skill and mental game are not as good as his rivals'. If the car is not set up at its best, it takes more than good technique and mental tenacity to win the race. When the equipment is set up well, consistent skill and a strong mental attitude will enable him to win. The skill in archery is the ability to be able to reproduce your shot, time after time, whatever the conditions. Setting up your equipment to make it the most forgiving will give you the best opportunity. Relying on equipment and a consistent technique alone, however, is not enough. It will take you to reasonable scores and a long way towards success, but without combining it with a strong mental game you will not be able to reach the top. Each of these three areas needs to be in balance with one another. The area that takes the most effort to improve is your mental attitude, yet for many archers it is the area they spend the least amount of time on. It is easy to allot time to working on your equipment, physical training and shooting, and recording it in your diary, but how do you allot time to your mental game? If you spend five hours a day on the physical side of your shooting, it would take twelve-and-a-half hours of mental training a day to reach the equivalent 70 per cent. Put the two together and you have seventeen-and-a-half hours spent on archery and six-and-a-half hours left for everything else, including sleep. But it's not like that. Martin Eubank, a sports psychologist on the British squad, asked me to record how many hours I spent in mental training and what I did during them. After a bit of thought I decided it was easier to say when I wasn't thinking about some aspect of archery, generally only when I was watching a good film or an episode of *Star Trek*.

From waking in the morning, taking my pulse and deciding what archery I wanted to do for the day, until going to bed, reviewing the day's activities and considering my plans for the coming days and weeks, the first priority in my mind was 'Archery'.

'Archery First' is the first priority in all that you

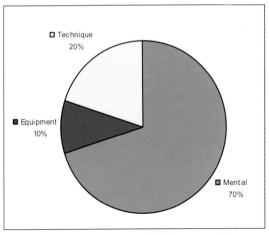

The proportion of time spent on the three areas of attainment.

do. It does not mean that you are unable to do anything else, but you need to factor in how that would affect your archery. If it is for archery and you believe it will help, then do it. If it is outside archery and does not have a negative impact on your shooting, do it. If it has a negative impact, don't do it. It is this single-mindedness that keeps you on the path to success.

Belief

Mental training or management, as it is termed by Lanny Bassham, works, but you have to embrace it and believe in it entirely. The first stage is finding the key that opens the door to trusting that mental management works. The two keys that opened the door for me were Jay Barrs's *The Mental Game* and my first encounter with neuro-linguistic programming (see Chapter 1). As they say, 'Saw the film, read the book'. I was hooked. Perhaps I found it easy to get hooked on the belief that mental management works as I have always been a positive, 'can do' sort of person, willing to have a bash at most things. This helped me see the mental mechanisms behind what I already did most of the time. I was then able to reinforce the generally positive practices that I unknowingly employed. I can see that those who might not be positive by nature will need more convincing. If you are looking for a good introduction to the power of mental management, Lanny Bassham's book and CD *Freedom Flight: The Origins of Mental Power* (2008) will set you on the road to believing and understanding the underlying principles. Lanny Bassham is a USA Olympic gold medallist in rifle shooting. At his first Olympic games in 1972 he took the silver medal. That was not good enough, however, so he put together a mental management system that took him to the gold medal in 1976 and made him a dominating figure in world-class rifle competitions. He wrote *With Winning in Mind: The Mental Management System* from his personal experiences. The books, CDs and DVDs that followed show the way to success in many areas of endeavour. What I like about Lanny is that he devised his management system to help him get an Olympic gold. His published works are a by-product of his original intent and I believe that makes his system far more realistic.

Mental management is about goal setting – getting what you want by working out what you want. Once you know what that is, you can then work out what you are going to do to achieve that goal. The visible effort will be the physical things that everyone can see – the shooting, exercise, equipment and logs, the physical evidence of a goal-setting programme of short-, medium- and long-term goals – but to do all of that you need to nurture a 'can do' attitude. It is the mental mechanisms that you put in place and work on that will enable you to do the physical things designed to move you forward that you have been told about, while thinking up new training schemes to help you improve. Everyone starts at a different level of the 'can do' attitude. When I was introduced to mental management my attitude was already fairly strong and I tended to work out what I wanted to do. Many people are very good at making lists and telling everyone what they don't want to do, although it is easy enough to change that around to making lists of what you do want. Some will need to make more changes to their current mental mechanisms to get the best from their thought processes. You might see this as some kind of brainwashing and falsely believe that, if you change how you think, you will no longer be who you are. Mental management does not change who you are, but it helps you be the best you can be. You may have noticed that successful people appear to be successful in all that they do. This is because they employ the positive mental mechanisms of 'Just do it' in everything that they do.

In embracing the benefits of mental improvement you can get the best from yourself in everything you do. It is about altering your thought processes to give you the best chance of achieving what you are after. Although this book is about archery, the mental mechanisms that you utilize have to be applied to every aspect of your life. It is not just for the archery, it is about turning yourself around and reinforcing current good mental practices to encourage success. By using this in every aspect of your life you will be able to achieve more. In conversation I have found that some archers, while claiming to be positive in their archery, display negative thought processes when talking about the rest of their lives that will always impact on what they perceive to be their positive outlook on shooting.

Once you believe, the rest is easy.

A selection of reference books on psychology.

Aim

The aim of this chapter is to introduce some of the aspects of how your thought processes work and how they differ from individual to individual. This is only the tip of the iceberg. It is up to you to look deeper into the subject and expand on this introduction. The mind is a fascinating subject. The more I read about it, the more I wonder at its mind-boggling complexity and how it accomplishes so much. There is a huge quantity of books on the many aspects of the subject, not all of which seemingly have a direct relation to sport. During the winter months I put time aside to read books on various areas of the mind. Some are a little offbeat and do not seem to have much relevance to improving my better understanding, but they may contain one paragraph that fits into and improves my understanding of how I can think better. It is worth reading that book for just the one paragraph.

Primary Sense

What is not generally apparent or realized is that everyone has different levels of sensitivity in each of the senses – sight, sound, touch, smell and taste – and one of them will be your primary sense. This primary sense may be way ahead, with the other senses widely spread in sensitivity, or they may all be of a similar sensitivity with just one out in front. It is

like having a volume control for all your senses that is predetermined and set. The senses all have their own volume and can be arranged in an order of sensitivity to each other. If your primary sense is negated, then the next in line will take over. My primary sense is sight (visual), then touch (kinaesthetic), sound (aural), taste (gustatory) and smell (olfaction), although I feel that the last two are at about the same level. For me visual input is way ahead of all the others.

To decide on your primary input and which ones follow, think about objects such as a bed, car, tree, curry, settee, bike or bow, and make a note of the first impression you get from each. I find that a picture comes to mind for all these words. Continue thinking about each word and see which senses then come to you. For me it is generally how it feels, then how it sounds. For curry, however, I still get a picture first but then the smell is the next impression. What you are determining is the order in which your senses come into play as you think. If the senses' input is closer together you will find it harder to identify the primary, secondary and subsequent senses. This is a direct method of ascertaining senses. An indirect method is to listen to or read the words that an individual uses in conversation or in written text. People tend to use words and phrases that indicate their primary sense ('If you see what I mean').

It seems that about 70 per cent of the population have visuals as their primary input, with kinaesthetic as their secondary. The next biggest group has kinaesthetic as their primary input, with visual as their secondary. The other three senses are less common as primary inputs, but you will come across exceptions. Understanding between individuals is linked quite strongly by primary sense inputs. Individuals with similar types and levels of input are more likely to share a better understanding. Where the primary inputs are dissimilar there is

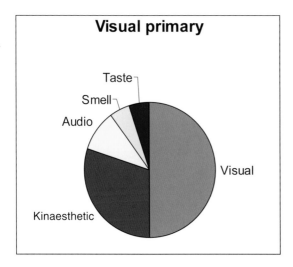

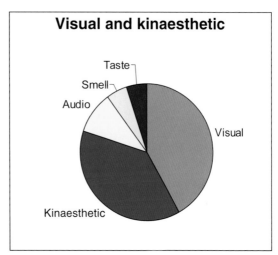

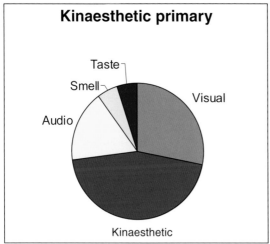

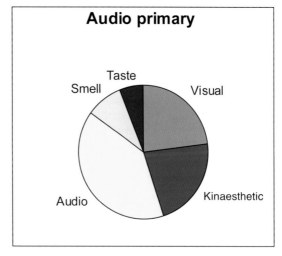

The five senses, showing variations in primary senses.

more likelihood of misunderstanding: while a visual person is thinking in pictures, an aural person is thinking of the sound.

In your quest to improve your understanding of what you are trying to achieve, it is important to gather as much information as possible from many different people. If you are only able to comprehend information from those of a similar input type, you will curtail the amount of information available to you. An insight into other mindsets will enable you to translate more of the available information. Since I am strong visually, and the bulk of shooting well is how the shot feels, my shooting practices are engineered to reducing the visual inputs and amplifying the kinaesthetic aspects of the shot. A kinaesthetic person will naturally be able to 'feel' those aspects of the shot but may have to amplify the visual aspects of archery. Training practices will need to reflect that. With a little effort I can practise the feeling of thinking and be better understood by a kinaesthetic person. Most of the time, once you have deduced what type of person you are, you will have to translate information given by those with a different primary input. Coaches and teachers who understand this concept are able to alter their coaching phrases to suit the individual they are instructing, making their advice far more effective.

Five Senses

Speech and Hearing

Be aware of the power of words. It is the words that you speak, write, hear, think and read that will shape your attainment.

What you say is directly linked to how you think and how you are thinking; when you hear someone speaking freely, what they say and how they say it will enable you to have a good idea of their thought processes. When initially wanting to gain insight into an individual, either listen to them talking about their archery or ask innocuous questions that allow them to talk freely about themselves. With archers it is easy because you just ask about their archery, equipment, shooting, events, scores and so on. Many will quickly give away the areas that are holding them back, even if they are not referring directly to what they see as the perceived problems. These are the areas that they need to work on. If you pay attention to what you are saying when you talk about your own archery the same will be true. It is best if you are not listening to an internal dialogue. Talking to other archers to help them improve at coaching weekends and workshops, and giving them the opportunity to ask questions about any aspect of shooting, allows me to verbalize what I currently do and think. I can later review what I said to see if there is an area of improvement. It is similar to talking about your shooting to someone you trust within or outside the sport.

The England hockey goalkeeper once visited the British squad for a session on how he approached his mental game. He said that sometimes after making a mistake he would then tend to make two or three more. He was working with his coach on reducing the number of mistakes after the initial one. We suggested that he worked on not making the mistake in the first instance. It is this interaction with others that can let you view the area you are trying to improve from a different angle. What you are listening for in your own words and thoughts, and those of others you are helping, is an indication of areas to work on, not only the physical form but altering and improving how they talk about it. In changing how you talk about something you will change how you think about it.

The common plea to 'Please can you have a look at me and tell me what I am doing wrong?' infers that you or they think that they are doing something wrong. What should be asked is, 'Please can you look at me and let me know if there are any areas I can work on to improve?' Unfortunately many do not believe there is a difference between the two statements or that it makes a difference. They are wrong. If you are saying it, you are thinking it. Other people's words can be just as invasive to the way you think. If you hear, read or see it, you will think about it. If you hear 'Don't drop your arm', all you will think about is dropping your arm. 'Keep your arm up' is what should be said and thought about. Your first line of defence is to make sure that those around you are saying it in a way you want to hear, as this can only be controlled in a local environment such as your club and training venue. I help the archers in the club to shoot better not only for their benefit but also for mine. If I can get them to shoot with a good style then the archers all around me at the club are shooting in a way that reinforces what I want to be doing.

Your second line of defence is to translate mentally what others are saying into the positive: 'Don't move your head' becomes 'Keep you head still'. By thinking about keeping your head still it will work towards that end. This should be used all the time: at archery, work, watching TV, overhearing conversations and at home. Listen to what people say and translate the negative statements into ones that they should be saying and you want to hear. In doing this it becomes a habit. While it might be annoying for others, you end up telling them how to do things while they focus on what they cannot do. Once a habit, others telling you what you are doing wrong enables you to pick the best out of it, to ensure you do more things correctly.

Your third line of defence is to walk away and turn your attention to something positive. When shooting I am more than happy to hear how someone shot a ten, or two tens or six tens. At competitions, however, if archers are talking about how it all went wrong, as they usually do, I walk away and talk to someone more positive or more likely to be telling jokes. If someone is shooting with poor style, I prefer to look along the line and focus on another shooting well or something else entirely.

To start with, listen to what you say and make sure you are saying what you want. One of the easiest ways to start working on this aspect of your

Most bows are now fitted with a type of damper. DEAN ALBERGA

thought processes is to work with someone who also wants to improve themselves. This does not have to be someone wanting to improve in archery, but it needs to be someone with whom you have quite a lot of contact. Simply listen to what your 'friend' is saying and then 'mention' it when a statement is in the negative, changing it around to the positive. It is about working out what to 'do', and not what 'not to do'. When your statements are not positive, they will obviously be 'mentioning' it to you. This can also be used effectively during team weekends or even at the club if most people are willing. You can just annoy any archers who won't join in. By working with others to find ways of saying things the right way, and therefore helping them to think the right way, you start to become more aware of what you are actually saying, ensuring that what you say is what you mean.

Kinaesthetic and Visual

Why do doinkers work? The first stabilizer damper that I came across was being used by French archers when they came to Scotland in the early 1990s. They had a short piece of rubber tubing on the end of their long rod between the rod and the weights. A friend described it as a passing fad. After all, they did not change the tuning of the bow. But they do make the shot feel smoother and consistently the same. The feedback to the archer is that every shot feels the same; therefore the shot is the same. Without the dampers the difference between shots would be more noticeable, leading to a feeling of inconsistency.

There is more to the effects of dampers than just this, but what is pertinent to this chapter is the feeling it gives to the archer. The feeling of the shot is its main constituent. It is the feeling of the shot that makes the shot. Those archers who do not experience feeling as their primary input, however, will find that dampers make a good tool for aiding with the feel of the bow. Even when you close your eyes to shoot, to help enhance your kinaesthetic awareness, you will still find yourself trying to imagine visually what is going on around you. This needs to be suppressed and the feel of the shot brought to the fore. That is why closed eyes release is an excellent part of a training programme for strongly visual people. At times you will want to close your eyes and feel the shot while imagining how the sight

looks on the target. Other parts of the training will want to focus on just the feel of the shot, trying to minimize any visual awareness. When focusing on how the shot feels, this should be how all of the shot process feels, not just the final part of the draw and release.

To do this, start by standing next to your bow on the equipment line. Think about the feeling you experience with every stage of the shot:

- Be aware of how your clothing feels and how the belt of the quiver feels around your waist
- Reach for the bow and sense how it feels to pick it up
- Putting on your sling
- Walking to the line
- Putting on your tab or holding your release aid
- The feeling of the proper position of your feet on the line.
- Placing your bow on your foot (recurve)
- Touching your arrow
- Feeling the decals on the shaft
- Withdrawing it from the quiver
- And so on

Making yourself more aware of what comprises the 'feeling' of the shot is by far the most important aspect of producing a strong, consistent technique. If you think about when you shoot, how much can you see? By bringing to the fore the sense of how things feel for each action, you will improve your understanding of what happens to your body when you shoot.

I have been lucky enough to be hooked up to an EEG that monitors brain activity while shooting. When I was shooting my best, I felt that I had tunnelled, focused vision and really only saw the target and sight, greying out all the other visual inputs. The monitor confirmed that there was less activity in my visual cortex when I was getting it right, enhancing the feel of the shot and closing down the visual input of thoughts that occurred naturally. This allowed my body to feel the shot.

To get the body into the right position there is nothing better than being able to see it for yourself. A mirror can be used in the initial part of the draw to see in real time what you are doing and become accustomed to its feeling. Using photographs and video connected to a screen, you can view straightaway what you have just done. Connecting the camera directly to a projector so you can see what is happening in real time, however, is limited in its benefits as you need to be focusing on the point of aim, and not at the screen. Even delaying for a few seconds to see each shot directly after it was made has the drawback that it is a visual input and needs to be translated to a kinaesthetic one. Much the same as when you are translating negative statements into positive ones, you need to work on translating visual images into how that image feels, so that you feel what you see. A practice adopted in Korea has children who are starting archery standing behind established top archers for the first months, mimicking the movements that they make. This ensures that when they eventually pick up a bow, their body knows what movements need to be made. This can be demonstrated by the way you find that your body moves with what you are seeing when you are engrossed in a film or when watching sport or dance. 'Mirror Neuron' is the term to describe this happening. It is the firing of neurons in response to seeing an action take place by another. This effect can be used to improve your own movements when carrying out a task. When watching a video of yourself shooting you should be looking at the position of your body and how that feels, using the information you can see to improve your body position. By watching yourself over and over again, you will just be repeating what you do and therefore the score that you get. You can easily find video images of archers shooting the best scores in the world. Watching these clips over and over again will help you feel the shot sequence and timing that they are using, since the neurons in your brain will be firing more closely to the way theirs are. This is part of the principles of neuro-linguistic programming. Following what the best in any branch of human endeavour does gives you the opportunity to do the same – be the best. At the end of this book some of the best archers in the world give their advice on what they do or have done to get to the top. This offers an insight into what it takes to be the best. If you currently shoot 1150, you could emulate a 1200 shooter and then become one. Then emulate a 1300 shooter and become one, and so on. As an 1150 shooter, looking towards a 1400 shooter from the start will help you to reach your potential far more quickly as you will be learning from the best.

It is not only the feeling of touch that incorporates the kinaesthetic. There is also your spatial awareness in your immediate surroundings, knowing what position your body is in without having to 'see' what it is up to. This can be practised and actively improved in an individual. In the Marines we had to shave every day, even when we were on exercise. To start with this seemed impossible without a mirror, but very quickly we found that it is quite simple. You know where your face is and you just get on with it using the sense of touch alone. Practise putting a pencil on the table beside you, turn away and then pick it up without looking at it. Try the same with drinks, but start with cold ones. We also had to be able to strip and reassemble weapons in the dark. All these exercises improved our sense of touch. Try walking around your house in the dark, feeling your way around. It becomes even more interesting when there is random stuff all over the floor. I am quite good at that kind of navigation. It is being able to take a drink from a glass on the bedside cabinet during the night without switching on the light or spilling it. Remember where you put it, remember what else was near it when you put it down, then carefully reach out, locating by touch the surrounding area, and move gently towards the location of the drink. Spending time with tactile games enables you to move your body how you want more precisely. As a mechanic there are times when you need to reassemble parts of a vehicle without being able to see them. Even simple jobs can seem impossible to those who have not tried to improve this aspect of their awareness. Some may find that putting a flat washer, spring washer and then a nut onto a bolt that is out of view is impossible.

Taste and Smell

I do not find these two senses have a direct connection with the physical aspect of making good shots, but they have a place in helping to trigger mental rehearsal sequences. The taste of shooting well is orange: at competitions I usually keep to fizzy orange drinks and so, as I only remember shooting well, for me orange is the taste of success. As for smell, it is beeswax and cut grass.

Of all the triggers to which the brain responds for recalling memories, smell is the best. This is possibly because smell is the only sense that is directly connected to the hippocampus, which plays an important role in the consolidation of information from the short-term memory to long-term memory and spatial navigation. Humans and other mammals have two hippocampi, one in each side of the brain. Smell can be associated with past events and memories by accident or it can be reinforced deliberately by introducing a smell. The smell of lavender is supposed to aid with sleep due to its properties, but I find that using it at home, where I sleep well, helps when I am away owing to the associations that come with the smell. This can be used for triggering mental rehearsals associated with shooting at your practice field. If you shoot well in practice there, associate a smell with the shooting field and the other feelings you experience when shooting there. At competitions you can use the smell as a key to all the feelings of executing a good shot. This might be a manufactured smell, such as a scent, which you can put onto a handkerchief, so that it appears you are wiping your nose when you are actually activating the feeling of shooting well. We shoot at a maltings, where barley is malted for making whisky, and there is always the smell of the drying grain mixed with the smell of burning peat, which is used in smoking the grain for a peaty taste. This makes it easy to recall the smell of the field, which in turn helps with bringing to the fore the feeling of shooting well. My scores for practice and competition have always been very similar, but that is only part of it.

It is the combination of these five senses that needs to be worked on to ensure the right balance for achievement. The fact that every individual has these senses in different measures and levels, coupled with a varying degree of positivity in their personality, means that each of these areas requires different amounts of attention to bring about the better use of your body and mind. I sometimes wonder what it would be like to be someone who has touch as their primary perception, as it would mean having to work on bringing the visual sense to the fore and my training would need to reflect that.

Mental Rehearsals

Some people use the term 'visualization' when they are describing mental rehearsals. Visualization, though, only takes into account what you can see and what you think you can see. Mental rehearsals are the combining of all of your senses to practise shooting without shooting. It often happens that we think about telling someone something, but later are uncertain whether we actually spoke to them or just thought about telling them. Still worse is when we say the same thing twice without realizing it.

Whether you actually do something or just think about doing it, the same neurons fire in the brain. The good thing about only thinking something is that you will have practised always getting it right. Mental rehearsal for archery enables you to shoot shot after shot in your mind, always shooting the perfect ten. Each of the senses can be broken down into its individual track. It is like listening to five instruments playing the same song individually; once you know what each instrument is playing you can then recombine it to get the full sound. The difference is that each of the tracks is one of your senses and it is about adjusting the volume of each so that on playback you have the full shot. When carrying out mental rehearsals you must perform the full sequence of your shot and not just the release. This can be combined with the actual physical movement of the shot, although you may get weird looks if you start doing it in a checkout queue. Some people are able to spend half an hour every day shooting arrows in their mind. My mind seems to wander after three or four shots, so I prefer to rehearse my shooting throughout the day. Mental rehearsals can be used for practising anything you intend doing. We use them in everyday life as a matter of course, for example when running through everything you need to create a meal. Using them for your sport, you need to ensure that what you are rehearsing is exactly what you want to do and feel yourself doing. It should also be used for running through match sequences, collecting medals, shooting at venues and so on. Before going to an event at a venue that is new to you, talk to other archers about what the venue is like, find pictures of the venue and the area you are going to, even what your accommodation looks like. Incorporating all these mental reviews enables you to be far more at ease when you get to the venue. Mental Rehearsals (MR) are not limited to something you do at home; they can be used before every shot that you make.

- MR your shot
- Shoot the shot
- If the MR shot and the real shot were the same, congratulate yourself and MR the shot
- If the shot was not how you rehearsed it, forget it. MR how you want the shot to be
- Shoot the shot

When you come to the end of the shooting, judge the percentage of the shots that were shot the same as the MR and record it in your diary. Work towards getting it to 100 per cent of your shots.

The mental rehearsal for shooting should include rehearsing how the sight looks on the target as well as the feel of the shot, since it presents a different view at every distance, and how the string looks in that picture. When shooting in windy conditions, I 'aim off'. Before every shot I decide how far I am going to 'aim off' and visualize how the sight will look, even during the draw. As the wind is changing I will be adjusting how I want the sight to look against the target on the release.

Raising Comfort Zones

In everything that you do there will be an area of expectation in which you feel comfortable, that is 'like you'. When asked what score you get for shooting a round, your answer will reflect the sort of score you usually get. The mind is very good at ensuring that you get what you think you should. If you start poorly, and below average, at a competition you will tend to dig in to shoot above average and end up with your usual score. On the other hand, if you start very well you may think you are heading for a personal best, but it tails off and you end up with your average again. Using the same method as when mentally rehearsing the shots, you can up the levels of expectation. This can be done in two ways. The mental approach requires believing that you are getting scores just above what you normally shoot and that your groups are one ring smaller than you actually shoot. This raises the expectation of your result so that you always expect the best of how you think you shoot. It can also be adjusted physically by moving the targets closer, so you actually shoot 70m at 65m but still think of it as 70m. When you go back to shooting the correct distance

there is still the expectation that the groups are at the slightly shorter distance. Some archers make a good start to the outdoor season because they have spent the winter shooting arrows into the gold. The expectation is to hit gold, so when they shoot they still have a high expectation of hitting gold. As the season goes on, however, the expectation of gold decreases and the scores can fall back.

Flash Cards

Flash cards are a good way of helping to improve your expectations. The more you talk, write or think about something the more likely it is that it will happen. Talking about how you shot a ten improves your chances of doing just that, and also those of the person listening to you. If you hear someone talking about how they shot a great ten, it improves your chances of shooting a ten. Even talking about how someone else shot tens improves your chances. The more areas of the brain you can activate when learning and teaching increases the likelihood that you will remember it. Talking about something activates two areas of the brain: the speech area, to say it, and the auditory area, as you hear what you are saying. Writing adds another area of the brain, and this further requires adding another area to read it. Talking to yourself is considered a sign of madness, but this activates more areas of the brain, which can help you solve problems more quickly.

You can use this to your advantage in producing flash cards that can be carried around in your pocket. They should consist of between ten and twelve small cards with positive statements that help raise comfort zones. They can also have statements encouraging you to do training that you are not so keen on. Running is one of the best short-time exercises that can give good returns on cardiovascular fitness, but it may not always be a task that you relish. The encouragement should say something like 'I enjoy the feeling of finishing my morning run' or 'I enjoy running to the coast in the morning to see what the sea is doing'. The statements must be realistic and set at the next level up from your present status. If they are too ambitious and well above your present level, they will be unbelievable and not have the desired effect.

Carry your flash cards with you and read them out to yourself whenever you have a spare moment. They should be handwritten and renewed and revised at least once a week.

Your cards should be written by hand, as this makes the statements more personal. They should be rewritten every week, when you can make adjustments or substitute new cards for those that have served their purpose and raised your expectations. Carry them around with you so you can use them throughout the day, ideally reading out loud what is written on each card. Where circumstances make this awkward, for example on a train, you may read them to yourself. Read each statement word for word and mentally rehearse what is on the card.

FLASH CARD IDEAS

- 90m is my most relaxing distance
- At 70m most of my arrows hit the ten
- 50m is my strongest distance
- At 30m I get my highest score
- I enjoy shooting in the wind
- My morning run starts me off for the day
- I usually shoot 335 for 50m
- My loose is so smooth
- All my arrows are in the 8 ring at 90m
- I enjoy and am good at my work
- At 70m all my arrows are in the gold

In Sight, in Mind

Leaving things in plain sight reminds you what needs to be done. Put them away and it is easy to forget about jobs that need doing. Around your environment you need to leave reminders of what you are trying to achieve. If it is the Olympics you are going for, put Olympics posters and images around the house and shooting venue. Display some positive affirmations and statements (the back of the toilet door is always a good place for one of these). A positive affirmation is like a big flash card displaying a short statement that reminds and reinforces what you are trying to achieve: 'I am always good at shooting in the wind', 'I use the time available wisely', 'I see the wind blow and bend with it to shoot my arrows into the middle'. I keep my reversals bow in sight in the living room. This not only encourages me to carry out reversals but reminds me of the scores and shooting I did with it when it was my competition bow. I wear an Olympic ring. I am not one for jewellery but it always reminds me of what I do and why I do it. Preparation time for any Olympics is four years: having visual reminders around you keeps you focused on what you are trying to achieve. The kitchen is another good area for posting motivating statements as you can read them while your tea is brewing. The screen saver and wallpaper on your PC is somewhere you can have a little fun with and send yourself positive messages, perhaps choosing photos of all your arrows in the ten. (My screensaver read 'I only shoot tens'.) I keep all my accreditation cards hanging by my bed so that one of the first things I see in the morning is a visual reminder of all the great shoots I have been to.

Put used target faces from high scoring competitions around the house; 40cm faces are good since the target shows your group size, as you are the only one shooting on them. Put up photographs of your arrows crowded in the ten ring. Some archers even put them up on Facebook. Yes, it is for show but it is also about being proud of what you can do.

Predicting the Shot

Here is a good game that can be played at home or at the practice field: 'Predicting the Shot'. The best way of playing it in the field is to have someone to spot for you. Set up the target at 70m and shoot. After every shot tell the spotter where the arrow is going to land on the target. This is not about how well the arrow is shot but where it will land because of the way it is shot. In knowing where the arrow will land you will start to understand what it takes for the arrow to hit the middle. This is an extension of 'learn how to shoot a ten', and then keep on doing that. At international competitions I have seen archers who do not appear to be shooting consistently, but their arrows are all in the middle of the target. It is about learning how to shoot a ten and there is more than one way. The more consistent you can keep the shooting the easier it is to maintain a simple method of shooting tens and be less prone to errors. By practising this, initially at 70m, you will get more of a feeling of what it takes to put the arrow in the middle of the target. Once you have started to get the feeling of prediction you can use it at all distances. The reason behind starting at 70m is that it gives you arrow flight time to make the prediction; by the time you get to 30m you should be able to predict for yourself. This is part of the reason of why if you use a scope on the line in competitions, you should use it during most practices (you can put

By hanging your accreditations near your bed, you will be reminded of what you do as soon as you wake.

the scope aside when volume or speed shooting). The scope allows you to spot every arrow, giving instant feedback from every shot and confirming your predicted fall of shot.

This game can also be played by watching others shoot, either during an event or at home on the TV or computer. Predicting the fall of shot and the result of matches by watching the archers closely can alert you to the nuances of how to shoot tens. It is not just the body language you are looking at but the focus on committing to the shot.

Body Language and Facial Expressions

Actions speak louder than words, not only to others but to you. While watching athletes compete at any sport, you will notice how they hold themselves and their facial expressions. From their behaviour you will start to be able to predict the outcome of a shot or a match. It is not only how they are reacting but how their opponent responds to what is 'on show'. Body language and facial expressions are a double-edged sword if you are projecting confidence through how you hold yourself and positive facial expression. Your opponent will see what appears to be confidence even after you make an error, and you will maintain your level of threat to them. At the same time your body will respond to the positive posture and you will remain confident. The interesting fact about posture and expression is that your mental state can affect your posture, but your posture will also affect your mental state. This means that positive emotions will lead to positive posture and behaviour: positive posture and behaviour will lead to positive emotions.

This works in reverse for negative emotions. If your opponent seems to be struggling with their shooting and manifesting negative postures through their body language and facial expressions, not only are they reinforcing their own negative emotions, but empowering you as your response to their negative attitude will be positive. To work on this, think about how you act and hold yourself when you are shooting well. Are you aware of any facial expressions? You can, for example, introduce a small nod after each good arrow shot as a physical manifestation of a strong mental attitude. The mind picks up on your strongest emotion. You need to make sure that when things go well there is a strong emotional acknowledgement of your success. Negative results should have no emotional accent and should be forgotten. You are working towards shooting every arrow perfectly, and observers should never be able to tell by watching you if you have made a good shot or not. Malcolm Gladwell, the author of *The Tipping Point: How Little Things Make a Big Difference* (2000), illustrates this in *Blink: The Power of Thinking without Thinking* (2005). Two scientists are cataloguing the muscle groups used to produce different facial expressions. Both start to become depressed when they start cataloguing the negative expressions and realize that, in producing negative expressions, they are also producing negative emotions.

Concentration

The levels of concentration and focus required when shooting vary throughout the day. Total focus on the shot is required during the shot sequence. One of the best ways to approach this is to give yourself a start signal to switch to total focus for the shot; this should be a motion that is part of your shooting sequence or a deliberate physical action that indicates the start of total focus for the shot. It can be a deliberate movement that is not part of the shot sequence, such as tapping your leg or tapping the finger and thumb of your draw hand against each other, or you can use part of the shot sequence or an equipment adjustment as the signal to yourself to start paying attention to what you are about to do. It should be broken down into two parts. A 'get ready' part first draws your attention to getting ready to shoot; at this point you should be aware of what is happening around you, looking for indications of what the wind and weather are doing, and then carry out a mental rehearsal of the shot. The second indicates the start of total focus on the shot. My initial signal is putting my hand on the shaft of the arrow ready to draw it from the quiver; my second comes after putting my fingers on the string, with a slight pre-draw ready to shoot. From this point I am totally focused on the shot. After I have put the arrow on the string, if I find that I am not focused enough to start the second signal I adjust my chest guard and quiver position to bring me back to the 'ready to shoot' focus. Most times when I come down from full draw it is because I am not focused enough. I then do the chest guard and quiver sequence again to get me back on track. This anchors the shot sequence to a specific start point. For me the shot sequence finishes when I have spotted the arrow on the target. I feel the shot after the release, the shot itself finishes when the arrow hits the target. I mentally review the shot, giving it marks out of ten to how the shot compares with the 'Mental Rehearsal'. From the feeling of the shot I predict where I feel the shot has gone, then look to see where it has actually hit so I can see how well I

A competitor's frame of mind can be gauged by their body language. DEAN ALBERGA

have judged the weather. That completes the shot. If at this point I feel that the shot was not how it was rehearsed, I 'feel' the 'Mental Rehearsal' and then prepare for the next shot. You will see that many archers 'do' something before the start of their shot.

Improving Technique

Part of winning is being able to improve your technique faster than your opposition. In incorporating a different physical movement to your shot more quickly, you can bring forward the time that your scores improve. This may bring the improvement forward to before a shoot-off rather than after it. The mind is very good at following a sequence as instructed. If you need to change part of your draw sequence, it takes longer to incorporate a new movement into your current sequence than into a totally new one, as your mind will keep trying to revert to the original sequence. By incorporating it into a totally new sequence you will not be restrained by the old way. This means that you will have to start the draw sequence in a different way to move away from your established sequence. The focus of the new sequence is not the whole sequence but the area of the draw that you really want to change. Once you have established the new movement after 1,000 arrows, you can go back to your original draw but incorporating the 'new' part of the sequence. There may still be some residual tendency to revert to what you did before, but overall the new step will be incorporated more quickly. This will also be reinforced by the 'Mental Rehearsal' of the part of the sequence you want to change.

Confidence

Confidence is going to an event 'knowing' that you have carried out everything you planned to do and that there is nothing else you could have done beforehand. No matter what the outcome of the event, if you can say, hand on heart, that there was nothing more you could have done then what more could be asked of you? After the event, however, you can evaluate if you are going to make any changes to your training prior to the next. In trying to ensure that they have done more than anyone else, some

individuals do too much and are too fatigued to use what they have done. That is why you should have a good training plan. Do the training you have planned, with minor changes incorporated to enhance what you are doing, and record it in your diary so that you can judge how that plan worked.

Confidence is making the case for why you should do well: because you train well; because you shoot the arrows; because you do the cardio-vascular training; because of your experience; because your equipment is in the best condition. It is belief in yourself. If you let doubt creep into any of these areas, it will try to drag you down. You may perhaps be going to an event after a slight illness and have not done all you wanted. This is when you look to why you will still shoot well. It takes three weeks to start losing muscle tone, but you were only off for three days, you are fit and the rest will have helped. It is always finding a reason that you can do it. I have made shoot-offs when I had the flu.

It is about reasoning why you 'can', but the underlying self-belief comes from all the training you have put in. The confidence in your shot is knowing that you can shoot it well. Hoping that it will be a good shot or that it will go into the middle is not enough. It is the 'switch' that you know where to aim the arrow and there is no doubt it will go into the ten. Perhaps the wind will blow it off course after you have shot it, but there is absolute certainty that the arrow will go where you want it to.

What can be most upsetting is when an archer feels that the shooting is good but the arrows do not go as they feel they should. If they feel that their shooting is poor on that day, however, the poorer score is acceptable and can be worked on. Poor scores when the archer feels they are shooting well tend to be down to a technical failure and this must be remedied quickly as it can affect confidence. First look at the bow to see if anything has come loose and then check your diary to see if any changes have been made to the equipment. The bow can be reset to an earlier known good setting to help determine if it is the archer or the equipment.

Arousal Levels

At opposite ends of the scale are fully relaxed, when you are still just about awake, and hyper-excited.

You first need to be aware of where you should be on the scale to be shooting at your best and then be able to employ mental and physical aids to keep you there. When I first started competing for Great Britain, everyone kept telling me to 'Relax'. I was very good at it and would be very laid-back on the line, doing as I was told. I soon realized that being so relaxed was not helping my scores. I had to find the level of arousal at which I shot my best. On a scale from one (relaxed) to ten I would be about a three, which is generally right for most archers. Alan Wills, however, shoots at around eight or nine and it was no help when he kept being told to relax and be calm on the line. He explains his approach:

> I like to compete with a high arousal level. I think being happy or pumped up gives me a different approach. It makes me more focused for a short space of time. I know that if I have to do something or shoot a ten when needed 99 per cent of the time I will.
>
> Alf Davies and I worked a lot on controlled aggression as you can sustain it for short spaces of time, such as head-to-heads.

The best time to think about the level you are at is when you are shooting well in training. Stop shooting and think carefully about your thoughts and arousal level. Finding the one at which you shoot your best is quite easy; the trick is to be able to keep it at that level. Most tend to get too excited when they compete, so they need to relax to lower their arousal levels. There will be times, however, when they need to bring it up slightly.

There are a number of techniques to help you learn to relax. Most include lying down and calming the mind towards a 'golden place' where you feel you are happy and relaxed. They may also include tensing up individual muscles and then letting them relax, the idea being that the muscle will go into a more relaxed state after it has been tensed. It takes thirty minutes or more to bring yourself to a relaxed state, which you might have during a lunch break, but not between arrows. The aim of these exercises is to bring you to a relaxed state while awake. Once you have experienced the feeling of being deliberately relaxed, you can work on shortening the time it takes to relax to a single breath. At first it might take the time between ends to get your arousal levels down

to where you want them, but with experience you will get there. Fill your lungs to the bottom, then let all the excitement drain out as you breathe out. So that you do not give anything away to your opponent, this can be disguised as a yawn. If you have relaxed a little too much, a couple of coughs can help clear the airways and raise the arousal levels slightly, keeping your opponent none the wiser as to your arousal levels and how you are feeling.

Situation Planning

Have a plan to cover everything that might affect your shooting; this is the 'what if' game. Draw on your own experiences and what you have done in the past to get around issues. Listen to others talking about the issues they have faced and what they did to remedy them. If other people only tell you about their problems, think about how you would remedy them. Lastly think about all the issues that you might come across and come up with a plan of how to deal with them.

An early experience that threw me was at the British Championships, held in the National Indoor Arena, Birmingham. After the first dozen arrows I was aware that I was on the leader board, which I had not experienced before. My plan for the day was not to look at it but to get on and shoot. As we came to the last dozen one of the archers said, 'You're still in the top ten'. Needless to say I wasn't by the end of the final dozen. At the next opportunity, I took a photograph of the leader board and have never been bothered with leader boards since.

Some of the things you have to plan for are outside the course of the competition, but others may be issues within the competition that a good knowledge of the rules will help you overcome. Any of the following might arise:

- What do you do if your serving comes loose? Where is the spare?
- If you have a flat tyre on the way to a shoot, do you have tools and a spare?
- Your bow is not on the plane. Whose can you borrow?
- Have you forgotten your lunch?
- What do you do if the person on your target is using the same coloured nocks?

Leader board at the British Indoor Championships at the National Indoor Arena, Birmingham.

- A stabilizer snaps?
- You lose your tab?
- Your finger sling goes missing?
- The sight comes loose?
- Your grip snaps?
- What if the archer next to you keeps bumping you?

Not every judge has a comprehensive grasp of the rules. Judges have been known, for example, to be about to allow a score from an archer who shot before the whistle in a head-to-head, but fortunately the senior judge set them right.

Luck

The more I practise, the luckier I get. You will have heard it before but I do believe there is an element of luck in competitions, especially when shooting alternately. It is luck that you go to a competition and find yourself on the part of the line that is sheltered from the wind. Someone has to be on it and today it is you. When shooting alternately it can happen that it has been calm every time I have shot, but windy when my opponent has had to shoot – or the luck might go the other way. You can win because an opponent's arrow passed through a boss or was deflected out of the gold when it hit another nock, or you might be standing next to someone whose bow explodes as you are about to release.

Your Companions

Mental management is not only about making sure you are managing your own mind. You will also need to ensure that those around you are not going to detract from what you are trying to achieve. This means that your coach or shooting partner also needs to be working on the same aspects of mental management to ensure that what they say is attuned to what you want to hear for your development. The archers who are around you when training or travelling to and from training, or more importantly competitions, need to be sympathetic to your training. It is no good having done all the right things if your travelling companion then goes on about how badly they have been doing and how they don't think you are doing it right. Although I have suggested ways of translating negatives into positives, sustained exposure to the opposite of what you need to hear can only be damaging. Even the smallest comments from well-meaning coaches and trainers can do the most damage. A bit of idle curiosity said at the wrong moment, such as 'Do you hear the clicker of the person next to you?', may leave you wondering if you do instead of what you should be thinking about. Companions may not be a help to what you are doing, but do not let them be a hindrance. At least you can turn up the music in a car, but it may be better to get the other person to work on their mental game or tell them straight that you only want to hear positive things or nothing at all. Otherwise travel to the competition on your own. Why spend

months training for an event to have it undone by someone sharing the car and petrol just to save a few pounds. You should also look out for those who deliberately use their knowledge of psychology to try to unsettle you. Fortunately this does not happen often, but you will come across it: forewarned is forearmed. If you are aware that this kind of mental intimidation may be used against you, it is far easier to detect it, and once detected it is easier to ignore.

To summarize, the content and direction of this chapter is of the greatest importance as it can enable you to succeed at whatever you do. It is, however, just an introduction to some of the concepts and practices found in books specifically on the subject of mental management and training. Most of the references are not directly about archery so you will need to alter the information to enhance your shooting. Suggested material can be found in the reference section of this book.

CHAPTER 11

INDIVIDUAL AND
TEAM ROUND PREPARATION

Archery has had to change how a champion is determined in order for it to remain on the world stage. The changes have been driven by the media seeking an exciting show that can be televised and easily understood by the watching public. No doubt it will continue to evolve. That is the way it is and you need to adapt to changes as they are introduced if you want the gold medal.

To my mind, a competition to determine the best archer would involve shooting a full round across all the distances. The archer with the highest score would also be the best all round, as they can hit the target more consistently at every distance. If archery had stuck to that format, however, it is unlikely that it would still be in the Olympics and would now be a marginal sport across the world. So if you want to be World or Olympic champion you need to forget about this purist approach and shoot to the current rules, whatever they are and whatever changes they introduce, with an attitude of 'I can do that, and win'. You need to be able to encompass any rule changes and embrace them, incorporating them into your training. In accepting rule changes with good grace and planning, it is how

Teams will be on adjacent targets when shooting qualifying rounds. DEAN ALBERGA

you use them to your advantage that will keep you on top of your game.

There is a big difference between the individual and team rounds and the practices that need to be carried out for both. In the individual round you will be very aware that you are shooting against an opponent, especially when you are shooting alternately. When shooting in the team round, I think it is far easier to maintain the focus within the team, but to reach either part of the event you will first need to qualify.

Qualifying

Every event seems to have its own way of interpreting the rules as to how many will make the cut for the individual rounds, since byes now seem to be quite acceptable. This tends to turn quite a lot of the qualifying rounds into seeding rounds. At the Olympics, the seeding rounds are shot before the event starts as there is no real competition and no one is knocked out. Before you get to the event, find out whether you need to qualify or whether your score will just rank you. If there is a seeding round, while you will want to seed on the table as high as you can, you can afford to work on shooting to the conditions of the field as a competitive practice, so that when you get to the knockout rounds you have a better shooting feel for the field. Whether it is a seeding or a qualifying round, if you finish higher up the table there is more chance of getting a bye in the first round or an opponent who is lower down the table. This gives you a psychological advantage, as long as you do not become overconfident.

When shooting with teams your teammates will be on the adjacent targets during the qualifying round. Make use of this to compare shooting conditions with one another concerning how far the conditions are moving your arrows from the centre. During squad sessions and team practices you should have worked on how different weather conditions affect each of your arrows' deflection from the gold. The same wind conditions will produce different amounts for drift for each archer. In knowing how much drift each of you has compared to each other, you are able to compare group size and shooting performance. This results in increasing confidence in your performance or draws attention to an anom-

aly in your shooting or equipment, giving you an opportunity to rectify it before the main part of the competition. Working with your teammates during this part of the event can also help settle an individual's excitement, as it brings a level of normality to the routine of shooting.

Individual Round

The first thoughts that go through every archer's mind when the lists are published are, 'Who am I shooting against? Where am I seeded and where was my opponent seeded?' These questions are the start of the match. How you deal with them will have a bearing on how the match progresses. The name of the archer will have 'points' attached to them and the seeding will either add to or subtract from those 'points'. You need to make sure that you do not fall into this trap, as top archers tend to be given 'points' by their opponent even before the match starts because they are in awe of them. When looking at the seeding, archers often give away more 'points' when they are lower in the rankings. Take every match for itself. Shoot every arrow the best you can and finish the current match before you move on to the next match and opponent. Plenty of matches have been lost by good archers who were complacent about shooting against a much lower-ranked archer and did not put in a good performance, while the lower-seeded archer relaxed and shot smoothly without any expectations of winning. Building a reputation for being consistent in shooting good groups in all conditions and rounds is worth points to you when you are competing in the head-to-heads, especially in individual events. In the team round an individual's reputation can be diluted if their teammates are perceived as less of a threat.

There may be an opportunity to enhance your shooting kudos when practising at any event or even during the warm-up before matches. If you have shot great groups, let the other archers remove their arrows first, leaving your group in the centre of the target. If the group is not quite so good, remove the arrows earlier so the poorer group is not apparent. Even when you are shooting on a boss on your own, if you shoot three stunning Xs, stop there and collect. Let other archers notice your performance

Archer and support staff. DEAN ALBERGA

as you may come up against one of them in the head-to-head. There is nothing better for your confidence than an archer telling their teammates how well you are shooting at the moment. Remember that the same tactics can be used by your opponents or the 'helpful' teammate who points out that you will be shooting against a former world champion tomorrow morning (I won that match). It is down to you to shoot consistently and push everything else aside in order to win your match.

The support you are given will vary depending on the event's format. In some events all the early rounds will be shot at the same time with your opponent on the same target. In most cases the limited number of support staff available on the field may leave you without any contact with your team or the person present may not be your first choice of immediate support. At the training camps you should work with all the support staff and archers who may be going away with you to make sure that they have a clear knowledge of what you want to hear from them and see them do. I need someone who appears calm and asks 'How was that?', as it allows me to focus on how it was and how I want the next shot to go. If you are on your own due to the seeding of the archers, plan a routine you can follow to keep you on track. I usually have a drinks bottle next to my bow stand, which allows me to use the stand as a location point and, if time allows, something to do in taking a drink.

In some events you may be shooting grouped individual matches from the start. As not all of the team will be shooting at once, you should have one of the support team with you or one of the archers who is not competing on that day, possibly from another discipline. This will give you a point to return to away from the shooting line, which can help to maintain your focus. At events where the matches are not concurrent, you should share with the archers still to shoot any relevant information about the conditions. This is especially so where the head-to-head is taking place in a venue set aside just for the matches, such as an arena, stadium or a staged shooting lane. Although you may have had a chance to practise in the competition area, the conditions may have been different when you practised. Any information that can be passed on to your teammates about how the shooting conditions may have changed and are moving the groups can help archers of all disciplines to make a better start to their own matches.

Every arrow must be shot the best you can, down to the very last arrow of the match, whether you are ahead or behind. The oddest things happen in head-to-heads. Many matches have been lost because the trailing archer gives up and shows it by putting in poorer scores, but then the leader shoots an unexpectedly poor arrow and anything can happen. You should take notice of Suvaporn Anutaraporn's advice, 'Fight until the last arrow'.

Head-to-head alternate. DEAN ALBERGA

Head-to-head alternate in the final team rounds. DEAN ALBERGA

Your opponent will be as much aware of you as you are of them. You can make use of this on a number of levels. Sometimes you will be quite wrapped up in shooting your shots in the time allotted and won't be thinking about what your opponent is doing, or possibly may not really want to. At other times you may want to play your opponent. In matches when you are shooting simultaneously, for example, you may realize that your opponent does not like to shoot when you are at full draw. Delaying your shot would mean they have less time to make their shots, putting them under pressure to make mistakes. When shooting alternately some like to shoot fast and others slow; with fast opponents you can take your full time and with slow opponents you can up the pace to give them less of a breather between shots. All of this is dependent on how you feel and your confidence levels. You must do whatever it takes on the day to execute the best shots you can.

Body language plays a big part in the outcome of matches in individual events. The way that you move, hold yourself and talk when you are shooting your very best is how and who you should be whenever you are on the shooting line in competition or practice. When an opponent appears to be struggling and gives off negative 'vibes', it will tend to boost your confidence and settle your shooting. If you are the one giving off negative signals, it will affect you in a negative way but your opponent will gain from it. With matches being decided by so few points, you must make sure that everything counts in your favour.

Team Rounds

Team rounds are the oddity in all your shooting. Until you shoot such an event everything is about what you do as an individual to get a result. It is the only time you have to work together and rely directly on each other to get a result. Good results come from having a good plan for training and practice. Teams who have done very little work

Positions for a team round. DEAN ALBERGA

in this area tend to finish up with three individuals shooting the event and relying solely on their individual skills. Before you make national teams there is little opportunity for you to practise team rounds. Ideally national squads should publish the formats and routines they are using to compete as a team. This would give aspiring archers advance warning of what is expected of them.

Good practice drills for a team round enable the archers to focus fully on their shooting.

Timing

The main consideration for this round is the time you have to shoot your arrows. At the time of writing the three archers in the team have two minutes to shoot their six arrows: twenty seconds per arrow, not counting getting on and off the line. It is important that each archer uses their forty seconds allocated over the two shots and no more. An individual should not try to shoot faster to make time for a teammate they perceive to be slow. The shooting should involve a fair and equal division of the allocated time. All the team members should know by heart the time left and how many arrows have been shot: one minute means three arrows shot, three arrows to go; forty seconds left means two arrows to shoot, and so on. When calling time, it should be given after the fall of shot has been called by the observer. Depending on the remaining time it can be confirmed by:

60 seconds – on time
53 seconds – plenty of time
65 seconds – behind time, speed up

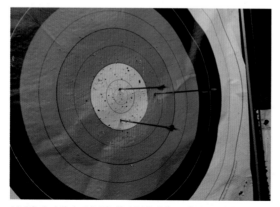

Mid 9, 6 o'clock. Mid 8, 3 o'clock. X, good shot.

By monitoring the time all the way through and adjusting for the remaining time left, you should always have enough time to shoot your arrows well without being squeezed for time. Some key matches have been lost purely through running out of time and shooting after time, even when that team has been comfortably ahead on points.

Calling the Score

All the archers will be required to call the fall of shot on the target so that the shooter knows where the arrow has landed and whether they need to adjust. The calling must be clear and concise, but most of all it must follow the same format of calling. This ensures that there is no misunderstanding of where the arrow has hit and that every time the shooter can assimilate the information in an expected order.

First call = Inner – Mid – Outer
Second call = Score
Third call = Position on boss using a clock face
Mid 9 @ 6 o'clock
Mid 8 @ 3 o'clock
X – good shot

In my opinion you need to call every shot to where it hits. Some archers call 'tens' to try to upset the other team. Most of the time the other team is so involved with what they are doing that they do not hear the call, while the archer who has just shot gets poor feedback from their last arrow. This practice may cause more disruption to your own shooter than the other team.

Rotation to the Line

No 1 = first archer to shoot
No 2 = second archer to shoot
No 3 = third and last archer to shoot

The rotation to the line should always be clockwise, whoever is shooting, even if there are left- and right-handed archers shooting together. This is to ensure that if an archer comes off before they have shot they know which turn before going back on. Archers should practise moving on and off the line. To get on the line a right-handed archer steps off with their right foot one pace, pivots on the right toe and brings the left foot over the line into their shooting position. It should be possible to get off the line in one pace by pivoting on the right toe again and then

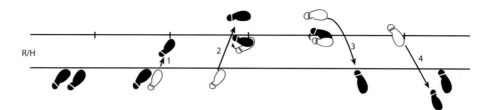

Position of archers as the team round progresses.

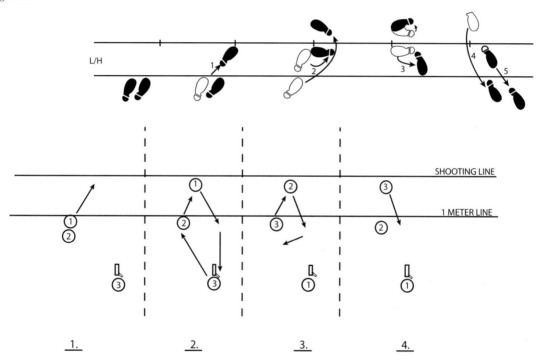

stepping over the waiting line with the left foot in one step. Left-handed archers need to step off on the left foot and then pivot anticlockwise onto the line. To get off the line they must back off, leading with the right foot. The minimum time is used when moving on and off the line efficiently. Any archer preparing for the event can practise keeping the same clockwise rotation on and off the line. The routine is the same whatever order you shoot and whether you are left- or right-handed. During an event it might happen that an archer comes off the line before completing their shot. In such a case it is always clear for the next archer to go straight on to shoot. The archer coming off can then move into position to go onto the line without interfering with the shooting archer's exit from the line. If there

are still two archers to shoot at this point, they can quickly discuss where the archer slots back into the rotation while the shooter on the line gets on with the shot.

Best Guesser

As part of your training practices you should all be able to shoot in any position in the team round. Although you may have come up with a good combination for good weather, changes may need to be made for adverse conditions. This is where your best guesser for shooting in the wind comes in. As part of the preparation for shooting team rounds, you need to know how much each of you has to aim off compared to one another to get the arrow in the ten. Some team members will aim off by the same amount, but others may need to aim off more or less. The archer who should go first in the team round in adverse conditions is the one who is best able to guess the wind for that day or week. If the first archer to shoot can determine where to aim to get the arrow in the ten, as they come off the line they can say how much they were aiming off. From this the next archer can determine where to aim to get their own arrows in the ten. The third archer then ends up with any informa-tion the other two team members can offer. The best guesser can be determined on the first arrow shot during practice or during the qualifying round. On the day, the choice can be finalized during prac-tice prior to the event, since every point counts at these events.

Encouragement
Within the team you need to be aware of what encouragement you want to hear and what you

First archer shooting, second waiting, third spotting.

Second archer shooting, third waiting, first spotting.

Third archer shooting, second timing, first still spotting.

need to say to your teammates to keep them shooting at their best. Above all it needs to be sincere and real. The same words can mean different things to each archer (see Chapter 10). An understanding of the words your teammates need will help to ensure that they are performing well, provided they are said at the right time. When shooting with Roy Nash on the occasion we won the European silver team medal, I was the No. 2 in the rotation and you could see that his draw elbow sometimes relaxed slightly. When this happened the key phrase he needed to hear while he was at full draw to make the shot good was 'keep it strong', but it could only be used when the elbow relaxed. At any other time it would have upset the shot and Roy. I was happy with congratulations on a ten or an X, but not for anything else. Trust in knowing that your teammates will say the right things at the right time needs to be worked on at training camps. It can be hard to be candid and confide in those you are usually shooting against for a place on the team, as there is always a concern that if you let them know what you want to hear they will use it against you later.

The Round

When the round involves shooting two arrows at a visit to the line, No. 1 should be behind the waiting line before shooting with No. 2 directly behind,

making sure they do not step forward prematurely. No. 3 should be on the scope ready to call the first shot only, as No. 1 will be coming off and spotting for No. 2, and will also be able to see their own second arrow.

When the whistle goes for the commencement of shooting, No. 1 archer should step onto the line to shoot. No. 2 should be ready to go on and meanwhile has to monitor No. 1 archer's shooting and check the time taken in order to keep them on track. After the first shot No. 3 gives the arrow's position, then No. 2 calls the time, always in that order.

After No. 1 has shot, No. 2 should make sure that the line is clear before taking their place on it to shoot. No. 3 immediately takes their place on the waiting line, ready to step on. No. 1 takes over on the scope and continues there for the remaining arrows for that end. No. 3 then monitors No. 2's shooting and calls time after No. 1 has called the shot. When No. 2 comes off, they monitor No 3's shooting and call the time. The final time should be called at ten seconds, with a countdown for the final five seconds in a clear, steady voice.

Following this routine ensures that it can be well practised by any archer at any time, so that when you come to shoot the event for real you will be able to get on with your shots with confidence in what to do. All the positions can be shot by any archer, knowing what is expected from them at every position.

Making the routine slick will maximize the amount of useful time on the line and ensure that there is a slight delay between one archer coming off the line and the next crossing it. This should be timed so that the judge does not catch the movement and decide that two archers were over the line at the same time, which might lead to penalties being awarded. Leaving a slight pause between archers crossing the line helps to ensure that there is no doubt in the judge's mind.

Mixed Team Round

The mixed team round has been introduced at competitions since I finished competing. It brings an interesting element to a competition and I would have liked to compete in this format. It follows the same routine as the team round, but with two competitors from the same discipline shooting two arrows each in eighty seconds. The ranking of the mixed teams comes from the combined highest scorers from each gender of a discipline during the ranking round. The country can then choose to select which archer they want to shoot from each gender, or by default they will be those with the highest scores. This gives a total of nine possible mixed team pairings. If the Ladies and Gents recurve and compound teams have the same practice routines, it ensures that any combination of archers selected will be able to work together smoothly.

To summarize, whatever the competitions evolve into, planning is essential to ensure that there are no errors in competition. Maintaining a set routine means that a reserve can step into the team at any time knowing what is expected of them. The rules and routines will no doubt change in the future, but devising a good but simple plan to make the best of what you have to work with will give you the best chance of success in any competition format.

Larry Godfrey and Naomi Folkard shooting the mixed team round against Spain. DEAN ALBERGA

CHAPTER 12

COMPETITIONS, FITNESS AND TOP TIPS

Planning Competitions

It does not matter how well you shoot in practice or what scores you can achieve, the only scores that count are the ones shot at competitions. At first every competition you go to will be a test of how well you have been practising. As you aspire to rankings and have ambitions to make country squads and teams, you must pay attention to the shoots you have to attend and the scores and placing you will need to qualify for those teams. You also need to be aware of any requirements for attracting funding. These are not usually the same as the ones for qualifying. However obvious this may seem, many archers do not make the team because they do not know the full requirements that they must meet.

When planning the season's competitions you will need to set your priorities, starting with entering competitions that will qualify you for the team. Then enter competitions that offer practice in formats similar to those in your qualifying competitions. You can then add in any other competitions that might be appropriate, either because you enjoy the format or the location.

Given a choice of venues for a particular day, pick the one that has the better ground. Some venues are better sheltered and lend themselves to better results.

The number of competitions you need to get to during the season will depend on the weekends you have free and the recovery time you have between them, especially if you are working full-time. Trying to compete every weekend will give you little time for recovery; you also need to give yourself enough time to have a good day off and a full quality day of practice and improvement. The benefit of working part-time or not at all is that you can fully recover on the Monday and make better use of the rest of the week. Once you have picked your events and decided which are the most important for making teams, these are the ones you have to plan to peak for. All the others are for training and preparation for the main events. When you make the national team, the main events become the international ones where you are representing your country. It is important to prioritize the competitions and change the priority as the level you compete at changes. Non-priority competitions can be used as practice for testing equipment and making technique adjustments; this might mean getting a lower score than you would wish at that event, but in the end you will be able to raise your score levels.

The best way to plan and record your competitions is to put a year planner on the wall in a prominent position in the house. Many archery magazines give away year planners around Christmas, so you do not have to buy one or make one. Putting all your events on the planner makes it easy to work out which you want to go to. You can then use it to record whether you have booked accommodation and entered the shoot, to insert details of the event and track what you are doing. It also enables you to plan rest days and meetings with family and friends. Erika Anear knows what it is like trying to juggle archery and a social life: 'I actually book them into my diary … I did have to book lunch with my mother and sister three months in advance once. Otherwise they're all just used to me being socially useless.'

Fitness and Training

I have deliberately left this until later in the book. It is not that fitness is unimportant, but invariably fitness is substituted for shooting instead of being additional to it. As always it is 'Archery First': you must ensure that you have carried out all the shooting training you need before adding fitness to your schedule. If you do not have enough time to do everything, however, fitness training should be one of the first things to go. Ambitious archers with full-time jobs cannot afford to cut 300 arrows from their weekly total to spend two evenings a week at the gym. Much of this comes from outside pressure to carry out fitness training with an alarming emphasis on squats, much as Blackadder was recommended a course of leeches. The amount of effort needed to shoot arrows and then to pull them out of the target, together with the distances walked to collect them and setting up the field, can itself be fairly rigorous. Try to allow some time in your routines for working on fitness. I enjoy hillwalking, but that takes most of a day and eats into the time you can set aside for exercise. Running is the best and quickest means of exercising; about 40 minutes per session is all that is needed. I also like cycling as there is little or no impact during this type of exercise.

Too little is often explained about the basics of doing exercises. 'Go running' sounds easy. It's a bit like walking, but faster and your body should leave the ground, whereas in walking it should always be in contact with the ground. The rhythm of breathing that you use while running is very important. Panting does not help as it increases your heart rate and you will soon be out of breath. It restricts you to taking partial breaths that fill only the top of your lungs, lessening the amount of oxygen entering the bloodstream and hindering your running. You can choose to do aerobic or anaerobic exercises, or a combination of both. Your body is like an engine and the food you eat is the fuel but, as with a car engine, you also need oxygen for it to work properly. Walking is an aerobic exercise as the amount of oxygen drawn in is more than enough to sustain the slow movement of walking. As you move up to a jog you will need more oxygen, so you will need to breath more deeply. As you get faster there will be a point, depending on how well your lungs work, when you are unable to take in enough oxygen to keep you moving. You will now have moved into anaerobic exercise, which can only be maintained until oxygen deprivation slows you to a pace that puts you back into aerobic exercise mode once there is sufficient oxygen entering your body to maintain your move-ment. If you exhaust the oxygen too quickly, as in a sprint, you will have to stop and breathe very hard to replenish your oxygen levels.

Breathing should be in a rhythm that ensures the breath entering your body does so efficiently in a manner linked to your pace, breathing in for two steps and breathing out for two steps. This method is used to regulate your speed and stride according to how efficiently you bring oxygen into your body. Start running at a slow pace. The plan is to change the length of stride, while maintaining the breath rhythm to the pace. Slowly increase the pace and stride while staying within your aerobic level. If you go too fast you will not be able to get enough breath. Cut the pace slightly so that you stay in the aerobic area and maintain your running. Through practice your body will become more efficient at bringing in oxygen and you will be able to increase and maintain your pace for longer. On downhill stretches you can increase the stride as gravity will assist you, but on uphill sections you should reduce the stride but maintain the pace. This way you will find that running becomes much easier. An additional aid to maintaining oxygen levels is to slightly restrict the out-breath in your throat. This increases the pressure in the lungs and helps to get more oxygen into your body. Parachutists use a similar method during high-altitude jumps to maintain oxygen levels. This breathing pattern can be utilized for any aerobic fitness training. A fiendishly simple exercise that will tax your breathing system fully when time is short should take only three-and-a-half minutes to complete. It comprises four sprints of thirty seconds duration, with thirty seconds of recovery time in between. It sounds quite simple but is very effective. Sprint as fast as you can in a straight line for thirty seconds, stop, catch your breath for thirty seconds, sprint back for another thirty seconds and then repeat. The session is over in just four sprints. This is an anaerobic session and you would not believe how long the final thirty seconds can feel.

Cycling is another good way of maintaining fitness, although more time is required to get the same benefit. The benefit with cycling, however, is that it is low-impact and helps to reduce the chance of sustained jarring to the joints to which some people are prone. When cycling you should generally look-ing at riding 15km (10 miles) or more per session. The longer distances usually mean that you can vary

A draw board makes it easy to check the timing of your bow.

your routes more than the limited opportunities offered during a run.

Even hillwalking has tricks that make the experience more enjoyable and easier. Walking on the flat, downhill or on slight inclines does not usually tax those taking up this form of exercise, but the steeper inclines can feel exponentially more tiring than they should be. This is usually down to two issues. Not taking in enough oxygen, through not breathing hard enough, puts you in an anaerobic exercise and you have to keep stopping to catch your breath. In addition, many people starting out continue to take the same length stride as when walking on the flat. Shorten your stride when walking or running up inclines, by ensuring that the heel of the foot going forward only just passes the toe of the foot currently on the ground. This ensures the leg does not have to bend so much and straightening it becomes easier. Perhaps squats might help with hillwalking after all.

Setting Up a Compound

Compound bows are quite fascinating mechanically and I have talked to a number of top compound archers as a means of bringing back information to help those in my club. It was also decided that the club would buy a bow press, an Apple, for the compound archers.

Bob Provan was getting on well with his Hoyt compound bow. He had been shooting it for about three years, changing the strings and making odd adjustments. At a training session I asked him about the bow and the set-up. Bob knew more or less what needed to be done, but seemed less clear on the best way to do it. As there was little guidance on the internet, I asked an expert at Quicks Archery to explain some of the mysteries about a Hoyt compound bow and the order in which to set it up.

The bow in question was fitted with a Hoyt Cam & ½ Plus system: 'Set the axle length with the bus cable. This sets the brace height. Adjust the cam timing with the control cable. Then using the modules and/or the string length, adjust the draw length.'

First we had to find out the composition of the bow, the 'deflex' of the limbs and the cams fitted to it. The 'deflex' of the limbs was necessary in order to set the cable's distances. It is marked on the end of the limb, but that meant stripping down the bow and putting it back together before setting it up with the information we had been given. We found that it was relatively difficult to hold the bow steady at full draw to check and measure the cam timing accurately. Fortunately I was able to put together a substantial draw board in my garage, which made it far easier to set up the cam timing.

Ian Simpson, a top compound coach from Oxford, had always maintained that a bow that was well set up would not need doinkers on the limbs. Bob's experience, however, was that the bow did not shoot well without them. Once we had set up the bow timing on the draw board, he shot the bow not realizing that we had forgotten to refit the doinkers. The bow felt fine without them. Now we

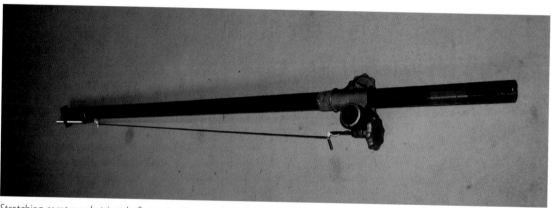

Stretching compound strings before using them can help to ensure that fewer adjustments are required as the string settles to length. KAREN HENDERSON

were on to something and tried all sorts of experiments with the bow. It seemed a good idea to start with the string material. The suggestion was to use 452×24 strands for the Bus cable and 22 for the other strings.

Bob's shooting was getting better and he was reluctant to make any changes to his bow before competitions. We made a set of strings for the bow, with 24 and 22 strands respectively, and these seemed to make the bow work better. I also made a string stretcher to help with stretching the strings.

The loan of a Hoyt Seven 37 from Les McPherson of Quicks Archery made it possible to carry on experimenting without disturbing Bob's shooting, while Bob himself supplied a spare sight and wrist release. The choice of using a wrist release came from seeing recurve archers who were starting out on compound bows letting go of the release aid.

When tuning recurve bows it is important, once the bow has been set up statically, to set it up dynamically. This gets the bare shaft level with the fletched arrows, meaning that the arrow leaves the bow in a flat trajectory when seen from the side. With a compound, the arrow needs be set to the dynamic centre shot, so when seen from above it comes straight out of the bow.

Setting Up a Hoyt Seven 37
With all the cables and string on the bow, it was suggested that the cams should be set to position 'E' on the cam adjusters. It was also suggested that after the cables have been fitted, adjustments to cable or string length should only be full twists (360 degrees) in order that the cables maintain the same 'set'. I then set the tiller at 2mm plus.

Bus Cable Adjustment
The bus cable splits into two parts and attaches to either side of the top cam, with the bottom end attached to a peg on the bottom cam. Putting more twists in the bus cable shortens it and therefore shortens the axle length. The axle is the round pin in the centre of the cam that attaches it to the limbs. The measurement is taken between the centres of the top and bottom pins. Adjusting the bus cable sets the brace height. If the axle length is increased, both the brace height and peak weight drop. To a certain extent the power of the bow can also be controlled with the bus cable.

Control Cable Adjustment
This is the single cable that is connected to and sets the timing of the cams. It is much easier to set this using a draw board. If the timing is out, the cable will need to be twisted. The easiest way of finding out which way to twist the string is to put in three twists: if the timing gets further out, you know you are twisting the string the wrong way.

Ensuring that the release aid is directly behind the nock can help to reduce many shooting anomalies.

String Adjustment

To get the draw length close to where you want, you will have to fit a D loop to the nocking point. I initially set the nocking point to 3mm above flat. Once the D loop has been tied on, an extended bottom nocking point is usually required so that when the release aid pulls on the D loop the release aid catch is directly behind the nock, in line with the length of the arrow.

Major changes to the string length can be made by changing the module position; smaller changes can be made by adjusting the twists in the string.

Peep Sight

It can be fiddly to get the peep sight to a reasonable height, and then to get it to a position where you can see through it. The easiest way is to draw the bow back and get another archer to mark where the string is in front of your eye.

Finding Centre Shot

It seems that the commonest error in setting up a compound is setting the centre shot. Although it can be set close statically, to get it right it must be set dynamically. One such method used by experienced archers is known as French tuning and involves shooting at both 5m and 50m and getting the arrow to stay central at both distances. This is fine if you have a range up to 50m and calm conditions, but I considered if it were possible to set up a compound dynamically for centre shot in an 18m range.

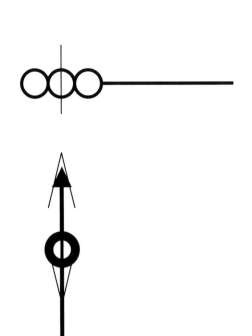

Looking from behind the bow. the sight needs to be set directly over the arrow.

The first sight rings were made from steel washers welded onto an old sight bar.

Compound Centre Shot Setter (Three Seashells)

Initially I welded three 8mm (ID) washers together on a small piece of threaded bar as a triple sight ring.

To check the centre shot, set the compound so that the limbs are clear of the ground and supported. Put an arrow in the bow and align the arrow with the string using the peep sight. Then adjust the central ring to lie directly above the arrow and in line with the string.

At 18m, draw a thick vertical line on the back of a target face and position it in the centre of a boss, in order to ensure the arrows stay on the boss. Shoot three arrows at the line on the target face using the centre sight; next shoot three arrows at the line on the target using the left sight ring, then three more using the right sight ring.

If the three groups are equidistant from each other, this indicates that the bow is set to centre shot. If the groups are not equidistant, reset the centre shot using the following guide:

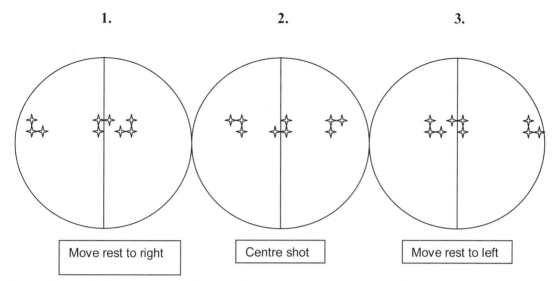

1.

1.   **2.**   **3.**

| Move rest to right | Centre shot | Move rest to left |

Pattern of arrows in relation to the vertical line, with the rest adjustments needed to get the correct alignment.

Pattern 1. The arrow is too far to the left: move the rest/launcher to the right.

Pattern 2. The arrow is on centre shot: the rest is in the correct place.

Pattern 3. The arrow is too far to the right: move the rest/launcher to the left.

I then fitted the scope and set it so that the arrow hit the centre of the target.

After you have set the pattern so that the bow is shooting centre shot, you may find that when you come to shoot at a target face the sight position needs to be moved a little for the arrows to impact

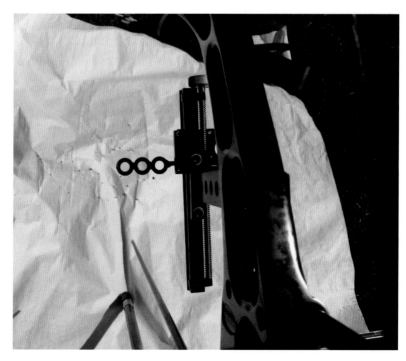

When using the first version it was necessary to remove the scope.

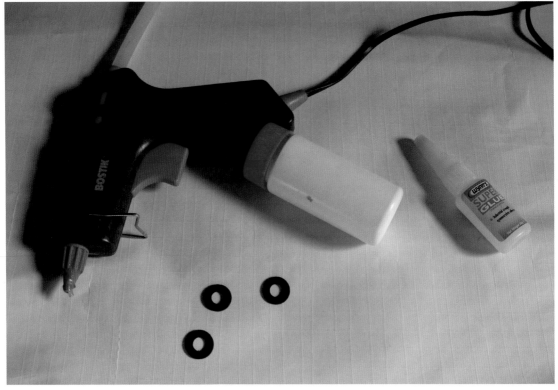

Parts needed to assemble a clip-on version.

in the centre of the gold. This will depend on the type of bow and the set-up of the cams or the position of the cable guard and the amount of side pressure that it exerts.

Making a Better Version

The device with three washers welded together seems to work very well, but the downside is that the scope needs to be removed in order to use it on the threaded bar.

There seemed to be a need for a home-made version that would fit on a scope so that archers and coaches can check the dynamic centre shot of compound bows. This can be made using three rubber washers with an inside diameter of 8mm (do not use metal washers as they tend to fly off), a plastic medicine container of about the same circumference as a scope, a hot melt gun, superglue and scissors.

• Glue the three rubber washers together with super glue, making sure that the overlap is

exactly the same for all the washers. A ruler helps in lining them up.
• Cut the container so that you end up with a curved half section that fits over or under your scope.

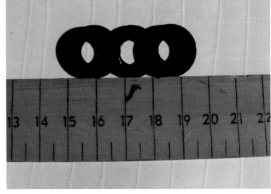

Rubber washers, shown lined up ready to glue, were substituted in order to reduce the chances of any damage during testing.

Cutting the tablet container to make the cover that fits onto the scope.

Gluing the assembled sight rings to the container.

The assembled centre-shot sight.

- Using the hot melt gun, firmly glue the centre washer to the centre middle of the container piece.

The completed centre-shot checker can easily be attached to a scope with a couple of elastic bands, remembering to move the sight position as necessary to compensate for the position of the rings. It is now possible to check the dynamic centre shot of the bow.

I have found that this device is particularly useful for coaches when setting up compounds as they can easily check the centre shot without disturbing the other archers.

The centre-shot sight can be easily attached with elastic bands.

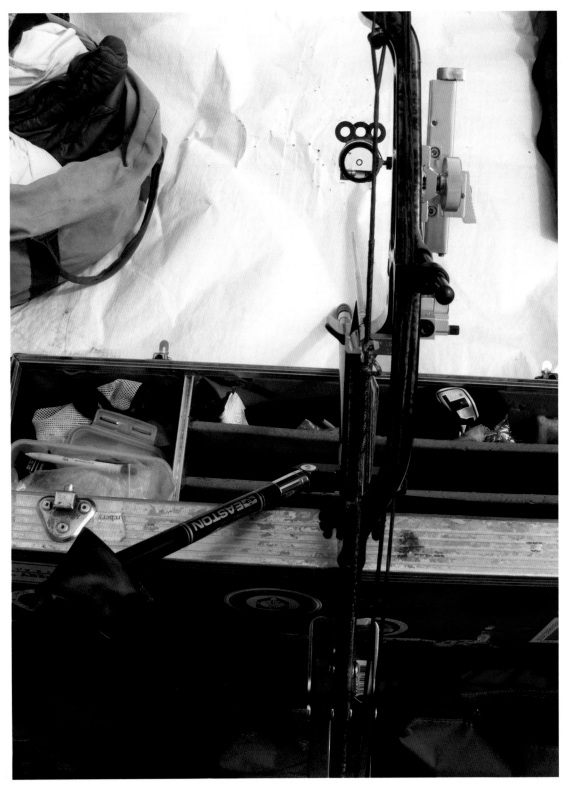

Line-up for using the right sight ring.

Line-up for using the centre sight ring.

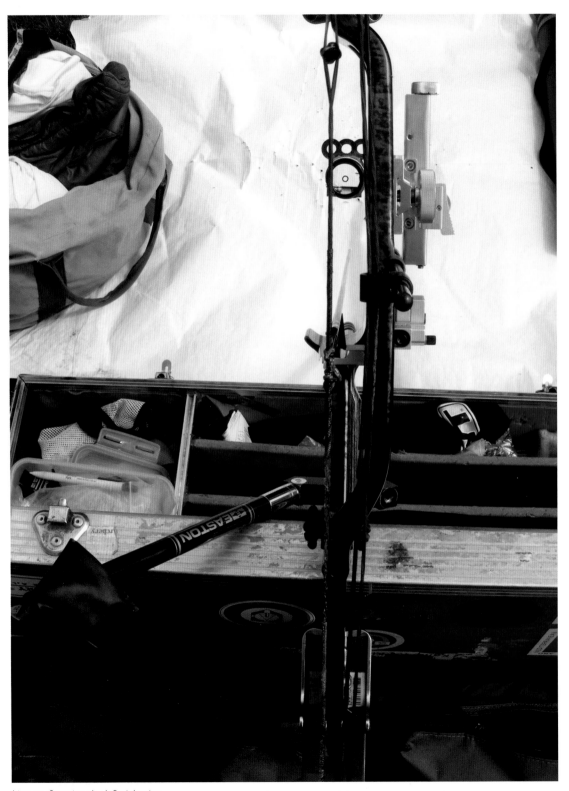

Line-up for using the left sight ring.

Stabilization

The initial balance points for a compound are similar to those of a recurve, with the dynamic balance a little lower than the pivot point and the static balance point about an inch forward of the riser. Due to the additional weight of the compound sight, launcher/rest and sight window, adding additional weight to a V bar on the opposite side seems to help.

Equipment to Get the Best from a Compound

Various items of equipment will help a compound archer make the most of their shooting. These include a bow press to make changes and adjustments, a draw board on which the cam set-up can be set accurately and consistently, and a source of strings and cables. The cheapest option is to make your own strings. There are a number of ways to stretch them once made, such as hanging a dead weight on them or making up a piece of scaffold with an eye bolt. The selection of different string materials and varying numbers of strands and twists can make as much difference when shooting with a compound as it does with a recurve.

Full set of limb gauges to check alignment. JAMIE CUTTS

Further Adjustments to Recurve Bows

Werner Beiter has made further refinements and additions to the limb alignment gauges available, including one that can be placed along the limbs to aid with their further alignment. The new set also incorporates a draw bar so that your bow can be set to your draw length at full draw. Archers can now check the alignment with the bow strung

at the correct brace height and when set at their full draw.

Although this can be used to check the alignment, it does not take into account any lateral misalignment of the limbs. This can be checked using parallel shafted arrows secured to each limb with an elastic band. Depending on the type and make of riser, adjustments can be made to realign the limbs. In my opinion a misalignment will result in the same

With the bow set at full draw, the alignment can be rechecked to ensure that there are no anomalies.
JAMIE CUTTS

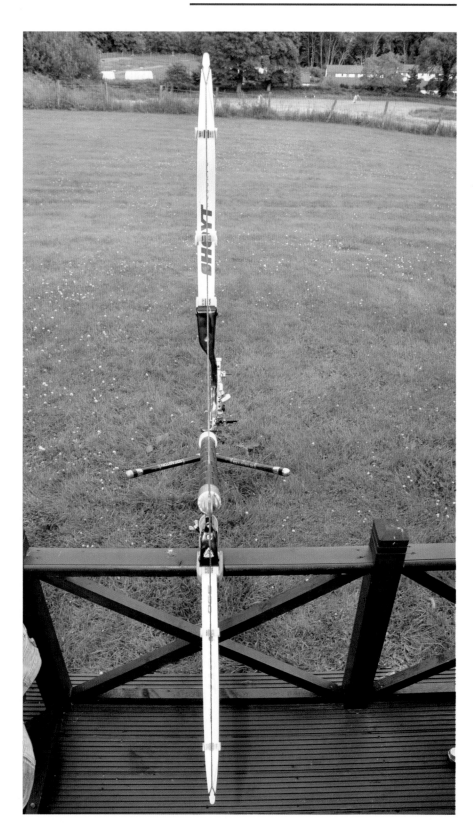

Gauges fitted to
the front of the limb
can help to check
the alignment of the
limb tips.
JAMIE CUTTS

constant error for every shot. I would not make any permanent modifications to the riser itself in order to avoid having to file the riser again to straighten it up when fitting subsequent limbs. I would advise either using shims or only filing parts that can be replaced, such as the alignment pins on a Hoyt, to attain the correct adjustment. To shim the limbs you need to ensure that the material used is both resistant to wear and does not wear the limbs or riser. If the material used for shims compresses as

If the arrows are parallel, the limbs are aligned with each other. If they are not parallel, you will need to determine where the twist occurs by examining the string alignment to the limb tip or with a spirit level. JAMIE CUTTS

Rubber bands will hold the arrows firmly against the limbs while you check the alignment. JAMIE CUTTS

you shoot, the alignment will change and give you problems with the bow going out of tune as the shim compresses. Feeler gauges used for adjusting cars are a good source of shim material. They are cheap, come with a full range of thicknesses and can be held in place with double-sided tape or a contact adhesive.

Another method is to adjust the alignment by modifying the alignment pins. These can be easily replaced and any permanent modification is of no consequence as the riser itself is left untouched. Whichever method you use to align the limbs, you must decide which limb you are going to adjust. If the limbs are out of alignment with each other, you need to find a method that aligns the limbs to the vertical axis of the riser. Initially you can use limb gauges to see which of the limb tips are out of alignment with the string. Using the same method of

Checking limb tip alignment to string. JAMIE CUTTS

Feeler gauges make good permanent shims to adjust the alignment of the limbs. FRANCES KEATS

ascertaining the true centre of the riser and aligning the long rod to that centre, you can then use a spirit level to put the long rod into a vertical position and then another on the arrow attached to the limbs to indicate which limb requires adjusting. This will ensure that you will be moving the wayward limb to centre, rather than moving the aligned limb away from centre.

Using spirit levels to determine where the misalignment of the limbs occurs. JAMIE CUTTS

EPILOGUE – AFTERWORD

To be the best at whatever you want to do takes hard work. There is no short cut or magic wand that will get you to the top without it. However it is not just a case of working hard. You also need to plan how you are going to apply yourself to the task in hand. Hard work is rewarding and satisfying. No matter how much money you have it cannot be bought.

This book has been intended to outline methods and ideas about how to go about succeeding and having your plan of what you are going to do to reach the top. At every practice you should know what you are going to do when you get there and have alternatives ready if required by the circumstances and training outcomes. You can use the plans laid out in this book, but in the end it is the creation of a plan that suits your physical and mental personality that will help you succeed.

You must do something because you want to. Being made to do it does not breed success. You need to find out what makes you go out and shoot. I like shooting arrows, so I find it easy to just go and shoot. Even now when I am not shooting so much, I still have the urge to shoot at every opportunity. Think about other ways of getting the results you want, using the autonomic functions of your body and mind to enable you to maintain consistency in all conditions. Listen to how others reach their goals. If someone has a better idea, use it or at least try it.

In many sports it is youth that has the advantage, but this is not the case with archery. Participation in the sport as a junior will give you a good grounding, but there is no real upper age limit to competing. Your limiting factor may be that your body starts to fail. I am no longer competing, not because I love the sport any less, but because I want to try other things after giving everything to it for twenty years. In that time the longest I spent without training was two weeks. On average I was training six days a week and that level of commitment would be necessary to compete at that level again.

I now enjoy motorcycling and would like to qualify as a Mountain Leader to help on the Duke of Edinburgh's Award scheme. I can do things without having to make up for the missed training time. Even when walking in the hills, however, I find myself factoring in training times: the goal setting and planning described in Chapter 2 can be applied to any activity to help achieve what I set my mind to.

I hope that *The Competitive Archer* will enable archers around the world to raise their game to compete for their country. I have made so many friends through this sport, many of whom appear here. Maybe it will be you who wins a gold medal in the future, but you will find that making friends in the worldwide archery family is even better.

Some of the equipment I have used for competing over the last twenty years.

ADVICE FROM ARCHERS

At one point I considered asking archers to answer a short questionnaire to include in *Archery – The Art of Repetition*. That didn't happen, but it was something I really wanted to if the opportunity arose again.

The views and methods described earlier come from my approach to success. I have also found that the effort required to succeed is often diluted by suggestions that the route can be made easier and accomplished with less effort. To help give readers a balanced idea of how world-class archers think, train and approach their sport, I contacted many of the finest archers from around the world.

I would like to take this opportunity to thank all those who have passed on their advice to help others follow in their footsteps.

Alan Wills

Club: Sellafield
Country: England
Bow type: Recurve
How did you start in archery?
    I just fancied trying it when I was twelve.

Alan Wills: represented Great Britain for 13 years. 2 times Olympian (Beijing and London), World Field Champion 2010, European team gold 2011.

How many times/years have you represented your country?
    I think about 100 times. I have been on the junior and senior teams since 1997.
What motivates you to practise?
    For me it's the enjoyment and the addiction of bettering myself.
How many arrows do you shoot a week?
    At the moment I shoot about 1,000 a week.
How many hours/times do you spend shooting a day/week?
    From one hour to eight hours a day.
Do you work? If so, how many hours?
    I work part-time two or three days a week.
How do you deal with the limited time you can spend with family and friends?
    I try to make the best of the time I have with everybody and I have a very understanding family and girlfriend.
Do you see a physiotherapist regularly?
    I try to go for regular treatment to keep my body working right.
Who tunes/looks after your equipment?
    It's all me, I take advice from others such as Larry Godfrey, Werner Beiter and Simon Needham.
Who coaches you and helps you shoot better? Why do you trust them?
    Alf Davies is my main coach. Lloyd Brown helps me too. Peter Suk had a big impact on how I shoot today. But I mainly watched a lot of the top archers to see why they did what they did.

What was your most memorable event and why?

There have been a lot, but the best was winning the world field champs in 2010.

What is your advice to archers wanting to get to the top?

You have to be in it for the long haul and enjoy it. Just keep plodding on and the hard work will pay off. Have an open mind and a lot a dedication. I like to compete with a high arousal level. I think being happy or pumped up gives me a different approach. It makes me more focused for a short space of time. I know that if I have to do something or shoot a ten when needed, 99 per cent of the time I will. Alf Davies and I worked a lot on controlled aggression as you can sustain it for short spaces of time, such as head-to-heads.

Ana Umer

Archery club: Ankaran
Country: Slovenia
Bow type: Recurve

How did you start in archery?

At school I played handball, the violin and did gymnastics. I decided to try to shoot with a real bow, starting with a barebow, and after a few years I changed to an Olympic bow. I could not carry on doing all of these and decided to continue only with archery

How many times/years have you represented your country?

I have been representing my country for five years. My first competition with the Slovenian national team was the 2006 Junior European Cup in Germany.

What motivates you to practise?

My goals are my motivation. Normally I don't have a problem with motivation. I practise at least once a day and it's the way I live. If 'hard times' come, my motivation is seeing my archery friends at practise.

How many arrows do you shoot a week?

In the summer I shoot 1,300 to 1,500 arrows a week. That's not many in comparison with other world archers. The number of arrows is lower during the indoor season. It's a big problem that my club doesn't have full-time use of the hall.

How many hours/times do you spend shooting a day/week?

I shoot six days a week. Five of these are for practice and normally at weekends there is a competition. One day is free for recovery.

Do you work? If so, how many hours?

I am a student, but help at the club for four hours, coaching beginners and competitors.

Ana Umer: represented Slovenia for 4 years. Gold and Bronze Junior World Field Champion.

How do you deal with the limited time you can spend with family and friends?

I still live with my parents but see less of my sister, who lives in another city. I see my friends when I can. My closest friends are archers and we spend time together anyway.

Do you see a physiotherapist regularly?

Once a week.

Who tunes/looks after your equipment?

My coach and sometimes me – if he lets me.

Who coaches you and helps you shoot better? Why do you trust them?

My coach, Matija Žlender, represents Slovenia in international competitions. He was largely self-taught, but he has studied at the faculty of sport and is very knowledgeable. Since I started to shoot seriously with the Olympic bow we have practised together like teammates and he has always been ready to help me as a friend. In 2009 he became the club coach and selected six of us to work with: three others are in the Slovenian junior team and we hope the other two will make it soon.

What was your most memorable event and why?

One of my favourite moments was the 2008 Field Archery World Championship in Wales when I won in the junior category. But the best event was the 2011 Universiade in China 2011. The feeling that comes from living in the Village with more than 10,000 sportsmen is incredible. The Chinese are very good organizers as well.

What is your advice to archers wanting to get to the top?

Zig Ziglar said, 'You can't hit a target you can't see, and you can't see a target you don't have.' Find your target and do your best to get it. On the way to the top everybody feels ups and downs. If your reaction is positive you are on the right way up. Just keep on going.

What sayings do you use to help with your archery?

My coach sometimes reminds me about going 'Step by step'. This always motivates me to march towards my goal. And I like Zig Ziglar's one.

Andreas Lorenz

Club: Arcieri Bolzano – Bozner Bogenschützen
Country: Italy
Bow type: Recurve Olympic

How did you start in archery?

Through my parents. They started shooting when I was six and I used to go with them on the fields at weekends. I began shooting arrows at seven and when I was thirteen I knew I wanted to shoot at a high level.

How many times/years have you represented your country?

I've lost count, but it was over six years.

What motivates you to practise?

At different ages, there have been different motivations: first being with my family, then meeting people (still a main motivation), travel and last, but not least, training to become better and to go to the Olympics.

How many arrows do you shoot a week?

About 100 arrows a week, two weeks before an event. I didn't shoot regularly for almost ten years, but started again this year. During my 'active' period I would shoot four to five times a week, 100 to 250 arrows a day, depending on the programme.

How many hours/times do you spend shooting a day/week?

At present maybe one hour a week.

Do you work? If so, how many hours?

I work nine to twelve hours a day.

How do you deal with the limited time you can spend with family and friends?

I share as much time as possible with my family and try to involve my friends in archery. Many of my friends are archers.

Do you see a physiotherapist regularly?

Yes.

Who tunes/looks after your equipment?

My dad did until I was sixteen or seventeen, when I started doing everything by myself … except strings … my dad still does them better.

Who coaches you and helps you shoot better? Why do you trust them?

My mother was my coach (she was head coach of the Italian team in the 1980s). Then came Andrea Polloni, the Italian national coach. After 1992 I coached myself.

What was your most memorable event and why?

The 1988 World and European Field Championships, where I became World and European Champion.

What is your advice to archers wanting to get to the top?

Train, enjoy and pay attention to your material.

What sayings do you use to help with your archery?

Every arrow that leaves my fingers cannot be shot again. The next arrow will be the best arrow!

Andreas Lorenz: World and European Junior Champion, Italian Champion.

Anna Artemova: represented Russia for 4 years. Russian and European Youth Champion, World Cup team gold.

Anna Artemova

Country: Russia
Bow type: Compound

How did you start in archery?

When I was twelve my school started an archery club.

How many times/years have you represented your country?

I have represented Russia twenty times.

What motivates you to go and practise?

My hopes for the future in the sport, the big competitions, to see the world, the medals … The hopes of my mama and my coach.

How many arrows do you shoot a week?

About 600 in the winter and about 1,000 in the summer. It's not that many, but I'm sure my results would be better if I shot more. I do as much as I can without getting tired and keeping good technique.

How many hours/times do you spend shooting a day/week?

Every time it's different. Some days it's two to three hours, others it's three to four.

Do you work? If so, how many hours?

I work twenty-seven hours a week, but they vary.

How do you deal with the limited time you can spend with family and friends?

It's not limited. I do what I like with my sister. I always see my mama at home in the evenings. I have to study and work, but that's with friends so I never feel it's limited.

Do you see a physiotherapist regularly?

We have a full check-up every six months.

Who coaches you and helps you shoot better? Why do you trust them?

My coach is Aleksandr Yalishev, who coaches the Saint Petersburg team. I trust him because he knows all about the sport and he's been very successful. He

helps me whenever I need it and we are friends. Every win of mine is also his.

What was your most memorable event and why?

The European Youth Championship in Turin in 2008. It was my first individual medal (or any medal) at an international competition. Before that I won the Russian championship and broke a record, but when I arrived in Turin I was shooting very badly, only 280 or 282. Nobody believed in me after the qualifying round, but somehow I was lucky and won a gold medal despite a poor result.

What is your advice to archers wanting to get to the top?

Believe in yourself. With belief, luck will be on your side.

Chris Bell

Club: Saints and Sinners
Country: England
Bow type: Compound

How did you start in archery?

I loved the archery scenes in *Robin Hood: Prince of Thieves* and started making bows with pieces of wood from the garden hedge. My mum didn't like all the holes appearing in the hedge and took me to a beginners' course at the local club.

How many times/years have you represented your country?

None so far. I hope to in the near future.

What motivates you to practise?

I spend a lot of time thinking about archery and working on ideas relating to form and equipment set-up that could help me be more accurate. Practising means I can test these ideas and see how well they work. Usually the ideas work better in my head than they do on the range, but every once in a while something works really well. For me there is no better feeling than improving my scores because of an idea.

How many arrows do you shoot a week?

This varies dramatically depending on what else I have on, how well I am shooting and what tournaments are approaching. It could be as few as 150, or as many as 2,000. The average is usually about 800.

How many hours/times do you spend shooting a day/week?

I usually shoot five or six days a week for three or four hours.

Do you work? If so, how many hours?

I work but in a self-employed capacity with flexible hours. This September I am starting a full-time job, so my practice time will have to change.

Chris Bell. GB series winner. PB 1398. KAREN HENDERSON

How do you deal with the limited time you can spend with family and friends?

It's not too much of a problem because of the nature of my work. I can adjust my schedule to find enough time for everyone. I think it's important to follow your passion, regardless of what those around you think. Compromises have to be made from time to time but if someone loves and respects you, they will understand how important your passion is to you.

Do you see a physiotherapist regularly?

Never.

Who tunes/looks after your equipment?

I do. I don't see how anyone can better understand what you are looking for and how it is shooting than you can yourself. If someone else is tuning your equipment for you, you need to learn more about it.

Who coaches you and helps you shoot better? Why do you trust them?

Many people have helped me improve, but the two most influential have been Braden Gellenthien and Liam Grimwood. I trust them because they are both world-class archers. Liam has taught me almost everything I know about how to get a bow to shoot well. Braden has taught me about form and execution. Without their help I would not be anywhere near my current level.

What is your most memorable event and why?

Making the 2012 National Series final. I had been working extremely hard all year, but you don't really know how well you are doing until you shoot against the top guys in the sport. On this occasion my hard work paid off and I came out on top.

What is your advice to archers wanting to get to the top?

Use as many information sources as possible to improve: books, DVDs, personal coaches, YouTube videos. Keep a diary of what works and what doesn't. Spend time on your mental approach. Go to big tournaments and ask the guys who are winning as many questions as possible.

What sayings do you use to help with your archery?

'I can do this.'

Chris Marsh

Club: Audco Archers and Bogenschützen Pilatus Luzern
Country: Great Britain and Switzerland
Bow type: Recurve (Olympic bow)
How did you start in archery?

I'm not sure where it came from. It was something I always wanted to do and we do not have a history of shooting sports in my family. My local sports centre suggested contacting the closest club, Audco Archery Club. I was taken to an introduction session and fell in love with the sport immediately. I have now been a member of the club for twenty-four years, but sadly I no longer shoot with them as I moved away in 2005.

How many times/years have you represented your country?

England/Great Britain between 1998 and 2004, Switzerland from 2006 to 2009.

What motivates you to practise?

Motivation was never a problem as it always seemed to come naturally. I just loved to shoot my bow. The feeling of a good shot, seeing the arrow go into the 10

Chris Marsh: Swiss No. 1 2006–09. Competition Manager for the 2012 Olympics and Paralympics.

and, of course, the satisfaction of shooting well and winning was addictive. My competitors also motivated me. I am very competitive and if I wanted to beat them I could not miss training sessions and my practice session had to be quality. Losing fuelled the motivation to perform the many reversals I did when I was unable to shoot when travelling or living abroad.

How many arrows did you shoot a week?

My parents taught me that, in order to achieve any of my goals, I would have to work hard. I have also always needed to practise a lot to build up my confidence. I was never sure how many arrows I should be shooting, so I would read magazines, articles and books to find out. I also asked those shooting the scores I wanted to reach, how many arrows they were shooting.

Their answers ranged from 90 arrows per day to 1,000. All I knew was that I would need to shoot between 150 and 200 arrows at a competition. I had to make sure I could exceed this total if I were to be fit enough to shoot the last arrow as strong as my first.

I used to shoot between 1,300 and 1,600 arrows per week, depending on whether I was competing in tournaments at the weekend. This could be at various distances, 5m to 90m, with or without a target, eyes open or closed, and focusing on specific aspects of the technique.

The major factors that determined the quantity of arrows and type of shooting were the training time I could fit around my job, the facilities and the weather, as there were few indoor facilities. The main aim was to enjoy my shooting, not injure myself and make it focused and purposeful. Arrows shot without purpose wasn't training, but sometimes I would just shoot arrows with my club members to relax and enjoy the social aspects of shooting. I would encourage everyone to do this from time to time.

How many hours/times do you spend shooting a day/week?

This was always a tricky balance with a demanding job that involved international travel. It all depended on workload, where in the world I was working and the shooting facilities available. When I wasn't travelling I used to get up at 5:30am, cycle thirty minutes to the range, set up the targets and shoot for ninety minutes, cycle back, shower and start work at 8:30am. After work I'd go back to the range and then go to bed. It was very challenging. When I was away on business I would take my archery equipment and try to find a local club. If there wasn't a club, I would do either

one hour of reversals or shoot with a rigid Formaster (shooting with a cord) in the hotel room.

Do you work? If so, how many hours?

Between fifty-five and seventy hours per week.

How do you deal with the limited time you can spend with family and friends?

This was down to my career as well as to archery. I used the telephone, SMS, email. I would arrange to shoot at the same competition or club to catch up with archery friends.

Do you see a physiotherapist regularly?

No, as I have been fortunate not to get injured. However I would have liked the opportunity to work with a biomechanist to verify that I am using my body correctly and check I have my joints in the correct place, to ensure that I am using minimum effort for maximum output.

Who tunes/looks after your equipment?

At first my coaches did but then I learned how to set up, maintain and tune my own bows myself. If I am unsure I will ask a few select people.

Who coaches you and helps you shoot better? Why do you trust them?

Currently no one, due to my work commitments. I refer to what my former coaches have given me and learning experiences, and take videos of myself shooting. I trusted former coaches because they made it enjoyable, worked with what I have and gave their time and patience to get me to shoot better and achieve my goals. I am fortunate that I have always had someone willing to listen and help.

What was your most memorable event and why?

That's a very difficult question. What is memorable to me is probably not considered so by others. All the baby steps I took as an archer come to mind, such as winning the club, regional, nation championships for the first time or making the regional and national teams. Achieving my 1000, 1100, 1200 and 1300 FITA stars. There were also times when everything clicked, such as timing or a positive feeling in the execution of my shots. This could be in a match, distance or event, or in times of bad weather.

What is your advice to archers wanting to get to the top?

Enjoy shooting your bow. To succeed at anything, you must enjoy it. It is not easy to be the world's best in any sport. It takes dedication, determination, hard work and lots of quality practice and training. The more you do from the start of your sporting career, the easier it is later on.

What sayings do you use to help with your archery?

It depends on the situation, how the training or competition is going, what I am working on or my state of mind, so I have many. The most memorable are 'elbow', 'expand', 'strong', 'have no regrets', 'it doesn't matter, just enjoy' and 'learn from your loss and savour your win, then move on'.

Chris White

Club: Rugby Bowmen
Country: Great Britain
Bow type: Compound

How did you start in archery?

My parents used to shoot when I was six and I used to run around and get in the way. They bought me a little take-down recurve bow and I went from there.

How many times/years have you represented your country?

I'm not sure. I was on the junior team for a year and also made the senior team as a junior in 1996–97. Since then I've made it onto one or more of the GB indoor, field or target teams every year. As a rough guess I would estimate maybe fifty or sixty times.

What motivates you to practise?

Wanting to be better, always believing that I can improve, making my equipment that little bit better, perfecting my form a little more and knowing that more success will come from it. I still get excited trying something new in the hope of finding that extra point or two. I think the day that stops is when I will take a back seat, but I hope that isn't for a while yet!

How many arrows do you shoot a week?

I don't keep track of arrows shot. At the club I will offload my quiver each end, anything from ten to twenty arrows at long range during the outdoor season. This helps to ingrain my shooting form into my head and teach my body what it should be doing over and over. Taking that repetitive form into competition, when shooting only three to six arrows at a time there should be no issues with fatigue, as can easily arise from the kind of weights I am pulling and holding all day. This allows me to concentrate on my shot process.

I don't have a set practice routine, mainly because of my everyday life away from the sport, but I try to get to the club two or three times a week before a major event and do any work needed in the back garden to keep my form repetitive and check that the bow and the other equipment are working as they should.

Chris White (centre), with Duncan Busby and Liam Grimwood. Compound gold medal team: represented Great Britain for 13 years. GB No. 1 1999–2010. 2012 World Indoor team bronze, 2010 Commonwealth Games team gold, European Field Champion, World FITA Field Champion. 12 world records.

How many hours/times do you spend shooting a day/week?

I do two- to three-hour sessions at the club or maybe a maximum of one or two hours at home. It was different in my late teens and early twenties. I seemed to have all the time in the world to practise outside college, living at home with no real responsibilities. At this time I moved from being a good county/national level shooter to knowing I had the potential to be a world-class contender. I put in up to eight or nine hours a day behind the string and it really paid off.

As you get older and take on the responsibility of a career and family, it becomes increasingly harder to maintain a lifestyle that allows you to compete at the level you want or believe you can achieve. Archery doesn't have the funds available to golf, tennis or football and it is so much harder to become and sustain the role of a professional archer. Many try to do this but only a very few really succeed, not owing to a lack of ability but because there is so much competition for the limited opportunities.

I try to balance a lifestyle that allows me to pursue a career away from archery, for a more secure future, while allowing me to compete at the best level I can sustain for the effort I put in. Certainly this is the right approach for me, as it takes the pressure off needing to win to pay the mortgage or put food on the table. It keeps the urge to win in the foreground without any added pressure.

Don't get me wrong, I would love to spend more time practising. I truly believe I have been held back by having to balance my lifestyle, but I have loved shooting and competing the way I have for twenty-seven years and above anything I don't want to lose that.

Do you work? If so, how many hours?

I have a very demanding job that sometimes means working up to 60 hours a weeks. It can be hard to balance my archery, career and family life, but I try to give all three as much time and dedication as possible.

How do you deal with the limited time you can spend with family and friends?

Most of my friends are on the domestic or international archery circuit. As I am shooting many weekends throughout the year, we spend a lot of time together, especially when travelling. The family side can be hard; being away from home most of the year limits the time we spend together. This is one of the reasons I don't shoot as many tournaments as I could, otherwise I would be gone every weekend of the year

Do you see a physiotherapist regularly?

I suffer from lower back pain so I try to see a chiropractor as often as possible. I recommend that everyone should visit a local sports injury clinic or chiropractor at least once because they really understand the muscles we use and know how to get you straightened out, even in areas you don't think need it.

Your upper body especially undertakes a lot of strain throughout the course of a tournament. You are giving your muscles a good workout with little relief. The day after a tournament you can feel fairly bashed, especially after shooting in the wind or walking a challenging field course. It doesn't get any easier as you get older.

Even if you don't think you need to go, a good chiropractor can advise you on exercises that will help keep the movement in your whole body fluid and different core exercises to help with balance and strength while shooting.

Who tunes/looks after your equipment?

Me … I'm the only person I trust to do the job correctly.

Who coaches you and helps you shoot better? Why do you trust them?

I don't have a coach but when I started shooting serious competition archery in 1996 my father used to watch me shoot. He understood my form and would always offer advice or see the small things I was doing wrong. Nowadays I try to learn from my peers. I hear a lot of advice. Some is not asked for, some is useful and some is crazy. I listen to it all, discard the rubbish and work on the rest at my training sessions or keep it in mind for future reference. Even now the simplest words of advice can really help. Anyone who is unwilling to listen to others doesn't really want to win. Until the day there is nowhere to go, no points to improve, no form to better, you can always improve and sometimes you need others to help you do this.

What was your most memorable event and why?

In 1997 I was still a Junior and had scraped the qualifying scores to make the selection shoot for the Senior World Target Championships in Canada. I was probably ranked about eighth in the country and attended the selection shoot as more of a training event and to give myself some head-to-head practice against the best shooters in the country, including World FITA record holder Steve Gooden and British Number 1 Paul Taylor. After the first day of qualifying I was ranked eighth out of nine, about where I expected, and didn't really have much hope of making the team. The next day I had nothing to lose and managed to win the first seven of the eight head-to-heads to get myself back up the board. My last match was against the British No. 1 and I had to win to make the team. I was on such a high that I shot a really good match and made the team by the skin of my teeth. If I had lost or tied a single match I would not have made my first senior team that day. I remember how proud my parents were and how great I felt having achieved my best performance at the time.

Winning the World FITA Field Championships in 2004, having just missed the title in 2002, was also a great feeling, as was winning the team gold medal with Liam Grimwood and Duncan Busby at the Commonwealth Games in 2010.

I also remember winning the senior trophy at an indoor FITA 18m qualifying tournament at Evesham, exactly ten years after my father had won it. To have both our names on the trophy is a special achievement.

What is your advice to archers wanting to get to the top?

Dedication above everything. You need to put in the hours and keep on doing it. Sometimes it isn't fun and you might find it easier to sit at home and miss a session. But you can be sure that someone else around the world isn't … so how bad do you want it?

You need to set yourself achievable goals. It's all very well saying you want to be a World Champion, but you need to get there in a number of stages. Each mile-stone is as important as the next. Be happy that you are achieving your goals. Sometimes they will come quickly, but others will take longer than you wish. Be proud of what you have accomplished, but don't sit back. You need to keep pushing and always believe you can improve.

Always respect the people around you. You may want to beat them into the ground, and they may have more or less ability than you, but everyone around you will play a part in moulding you into the person or archer you are trying to become. If you respect those around you, they will return this honour and it will improve the whole experience. Enjoy what you do and do it with style.

What sayings do you use to help with your archery?

I have a quote from Muhammad Ali on my office wall at home, which I truly believe: 'Champions aren't made in the gyms. Champions are made from something they have deep inside them – a desire, a dream, a vision.'

Deonne Bridger

Club: Kalamunda Governor Stirling Archers
Country: Australia
Bow type: Recurve

How did you start in archery?

My parents loved shooting. I first shot at three years old, so I was kind of born into it.

How many times/years have you represented your country?

I have been competing for Australia for twenty-five years at too many field and target events to count.

Deonne Bridger, with her niece Kailee: 2 times Olympian, Atlanta and Athens. Field team bronze and individual bronze. National Target Champion 1996–2012.

What motivates you to practise?

I practise because I want to be the best. I need to put in a certain amount to shoot at a reasonable level and I shoot more if I want to improve.

How many arrows do you shoot a week?

When training for a big event I shoot 150 arrows five days a week and 200 to 300 on weekends. I like to shoot blank butt to ensure I have enough strength and practise fine tuning my form.

How many hours/times do you spend shooting a day/week?

Fifteen to twenty hours a week depending on time and whether I can get to the club on a weekday.

Do you work? If so, how many hours?

I have always worked full-time, thirty-five hours a week, and tried to fit my training around work.

How do you deal with the limited time you can spend with family and friends?

If you want to be good at something you need to make sacrifices. The end result is worth all the time and effort of not hanging out with friends – especially when you walk into the Olympic opening ceremony.

Do you see a physiotherapist regularly?

When I can afford it. After years of shooting I do have problems with tightness in my back.

Who tunes/looks after your equipment?

I usually get advice from my coaches, but I do most of it myself or my partner Robert Timms does a lot for me nowadays.

Who coaches you and helps you shoot better? Why do you trust them?

My first serious coach is Ki-Sik Lee and I will always trust him as he really taught me how to shoot with better alignment. Keith Gaisford helped me as a junior and spent hours giving me encouragement. My dad John Bridger has been a coach and support all the way. Right now I am my own coach, with input from my partner Rob. He shoots compound but he is an amazing head coach.

What was your most memorable event and why?

I loved shooting the 2002 World Field in Canberra. I shot so well and everything just went right. I think that's why I enjoyed it so much.

What is your advice to archers wanting to get to the top?

Be patient. If you work hard, results will come. Listen and learn. Sometimes you get help from the most unexpected places.

What sayings do you use to help with your archery?

If you remember the process, the outcome is inevitable.

Erika Anear: Australian national indoor, outdoor and field champion.

Erika Anear

Club: Diamond Valley Archery Club, Arrogone Archery Club, Paringa Archery Club
Country: Australia
Bow type: Compound/Recurve – Target

How did you start in archery?

My parents were both archers so I grew up shooting.

How many times/years have you represented your country?

I first represented Australia as a junior at the Trans Tasman Test eighteen years ago. My first senior effort was in 2003 at the World Target in New York.

What motivates you to practise?

I just love shooting. I don't need motivation to shoot. But I do work towards having the best facilities and equipment I can so that I can shoot regardless of hour or weather.

How many arrows do you shoot a week?

I prefer at least 100 arrows a day, and up to 200 a day if I can manage it. Currently work is crimping my life and I just aim to shoot as much and as often as I can.

How many hours/times do you spend shooting a day/week?

Every day I can manage, and preferably for as many hours as I can fit into my schedule.

Do you work? If so, how many hours?

Forty hours a week, not including travel time.

How do you deal with the limited time you can spend with family and friends?

I actually book them into my diary … I did have to book lunch with my mother and sister three months in advance once. Otherwise they're all just used to me being socially useless.

Do you see a physiotherapist regularly?

As often as I can afford for maintenance, if not repair.

Who tunes/looks after your equipment?

I do. No one is on the line with you when things are most likely to go wrong. If you want it done right, you should know how to do it yourself.

Who coaches you and helps you shoot better? Why do you trust them?

My dad James Park, Ki-Sik Lee, my ex-husband Marcus Anear and recently Martin Damsbo have all had great influence on my shooting. As well there's been gold advice from a number of really awesome shooters.

What is your most memorable event and why?

The 2005 Australian National Target, winning my first gold three years ahead of plan.

What is your advice to archers wanting to get to the top?

Have fun. Winning isn't luck, it's hard work. Most folk either learn about losing before they win or when they stop winning. How they deal with it makes the difference.

What sayings do you use to help with your archery?

'Archery is easy. Just shoot the 10s.' 'Everyone's advice is worth hearing, but it doesn't mean you should always take it.'

Fred van Zutphen

Club: De Rozenjagers Eerde
Country: Netherlands
Bow type: Recurve and Compound

How did you start in archery?

My uncle took me to an archery club 100m from my house and since then I have visited the club at least twice a week.

Fred van Zutphen: represented the Netherlands since 1993. Olympian Sydney, bronze World Indoor championships.

How many times/years have you represented your country?

I don't know how many, but I participated at European and World Championships with both compound and recurve from 1992 to 2010.

What motivates you to practise?

The drive to do better. And great colleagues to practise with.

How many arrows do you shoot a week?

When things were going well I have never counted how many arrows a week, but I used to shoot three hours a day in the summer and two hours a day in the winter season.

How many hours/times do you spend shooting a day/week?

Before the 2000 Olympics I did fifteen hours of recurve a week, plus competitions at the weekend. After 2000 this became 10 hours a week of compound, plus competitions at the weekend. Over the last four years this has fallen to nothing in the winter and five hours a week in the summer, plus competitions.

Do you work? If so, how many hours?

Forty hours a week minimum.

How do you deal with the limited time you can spend with family and friends?

My friends were all archers. I have been shooting less since my own family came along.

Do you see a physiotherapist regularly?

Not so much now, but it used to be once a month.

Who tunes/looks after your equipment?

I do.

Who coaches you and helps you shoot better? Why do you trust them?

When I started my uncle Nico van Zutphen and club trainer Antoon Verhagen took care of me and brought me to a national level. I was lucky to have training partners like Erwin Verstegen, Henk Vogels and Marcel van Sleeuwen, and really learned a lot from them. We had one thing in common: we were all shootaholics. The national team coach Reinier Groenedijk taught me interesting things about the recurve and working with Peter Nieuwenhuis in my compound period was a really good time.

What was your most memorable event and why?

The World Championships in Birmingham were very emotional. This was shortly after my good friend Erwin Verstegen died in a car accident. Without him I would never have been where I am now.

What is your advice to archers wanting to get to the top?

Keep practising. Find the right people around you.

What sayings do you use to help with your archery?

'Maybe he is better, but first he has to shoot one point more.'

Göran Bjerendal

Club: Lindome BK
Country: Sweden
Bow type: Recurve

How did you start in archery?

A friend took me and my brother to an archery club.

How many times/years have you represented your country?

For about thirty years, roughly four times a year.

What motivates you to practise?

It still gives me lots of fun and relaxation. Nothing compares with it.

How many arrows do you shoot a week?

During the summer I shoot about 400 arrows a week, and during the winter about 200. I don't know of anything better to do. Since I started archery, 44 years ago, my only major break from archery practice was when I had pneumonia in 1983 and didn't practise for twenty-two days.

How many hours/times do you spend shooting a day/week?

Ten hours a week on average.

Do you work? If so, how many hours?

Forty-five hours a week.

How do you deal with the limited time you can spend with family and friends?

Most of my friends and family shoot.

Do you see a physiotherapist regularly?

No. I have learned a little physiotherapy, enough to help me and my friends through their daily 'problems'.

Göran Bjerendal: European Championships bronze, multiple National Champion.

Who tunes/looks after your equipment?

I don't need any help with this.

Who coaches you and helps you shoot better? Why do you trust them?

As time goes by, I am increasingly my own coach. It used to be my brother and my friends at the club.

What was your most memorable event and why?

There have been so many. I can't pick one in particular.

What is your advice to archers wanting to get to the top?

Pick your own coach. Be very suspicious of those who tell you how many arrows to practise. Listen to your coach but do not 'obey' him/her. Note if he or she listens to you. Never forget how to enjoy archery. Archery is a sport you grow into, not a sport you learn how to do.

What sayings do you use to help with your archery?

The self can sometimes be a better coach … if you pay attention to him.

Jamie Van Natta

Club: Mudjaw Bowhunters
Country: USA
Bow type: Compound Female

How did you start in archery?

My father played golf in the summer but needed something else for the cold months and took up archery. My brother and I wanted to try as well. He enrolled us in an instructional programme and I just took to it immediately. I was twelve and, with very few interruptions, have been shooting ever since.

How many times/years have you represented your country?

A lot. My first World Championships was Junior Worlds in 1996, so that makes it sixteen years. I competed in my first Senior World Championships in 1997 and was World Field Champion in 2008. I have also had the privilege of representing the United States on every World Cup team since it started and been in more than half the World Cup Final events.

What motivates you to practise?

Losing. Just kidding. The love of archery itself is what makes me go practise. It's also sometimes that keeps me from practice because I feel like I have an obligation to accomplish the chores I don't enjoy so much before I go have fun shooting. Since archery is so much fun for me, it's more like a reward if I get everything else done.

How many arrows do you shoot a week?

Not as many as I would like. It really depends on the

Jamie Van Natta: represented USA for 16 years.
DEAN ALBERGA

season and those other obligations. I try to get in two to three practice sessions a week, with at least one of those being on a blank bale. Sessions for me average about sixty to eighty arrows. Usually about an hour is all I can find time for. I try to find more time if I am preparing for a tournament that requires more arrows per day than the usual seventy-two. I think I can get away with less practice in general because I have been shooting for twenty-two years.

Do you work? If so, how many hours?

I have a 'real job' as a computer programmer at the University of Toledo. I work approximately forty hours a week.

How do you deal with the limited time you can spend with family and friends?

Most of my friends are in the archery community, so they understand. My family is very understanding as well because they started me in this sport. My husband is very supportive. We were together for seven years before we got married because I wanted him to know exactly what he was getting himself into. After ten years together, he finally shot his first arrows this March. I hope he enjoys it as much as I do so we can share this, but if not, at least he will understand my need for massages.

Do you see a physiotherapist regularly?

No. I get massages once a month and occasionally see a chiropractor, but that's all.

Who tunes/looks after your equipment?

I do.

Who coaches you and helps you shoot better? Why do you trust them?

I haven't had a formal coaching arrangement in many years. My first real coach was Terry Wunderle, father of Olympian Vic Wunderle. I used to drive seven hours to his house for one day of practice and then come home. He is the reason I have succeeded for so many years. I still listen to every suggestion he has when he sees me, but we haven't had a formal arrangement in many years. I trust him because he has had so many successes, and because what he has taught me has stood the test of time.

What was your most memorable event and why?

I have a lot of excellent memories. I won my first national level event at fourteen and still remember how unbelievable that felt. I think you never forget your first big win. More recently, in 2008, I had two huge come-from-behind victories at the World Cup Final in Switzerland and at the World Field Championships in Wales. Both times I was two points behind going into the last three arrows and both times I was able to focus and shoot three great shots that ultimately won the matches. If I could bottle that focus and feeling I could make a fortune.

What is your advice to archers wanting to get to the top?

First, find a good coach and trust them. In this sport, a strong mental foundation is king and if your coach doesn't address this in the first session, find a new coach.

Second, if it's not fun anymore, try something else. I really think that to excel at this sport you have to love it enough to spend time in the freezing cold, the pouring rain, and the gusting wind voluntarily. I tried the recurve bow once for about a month. I tried everything I could to like it, but I just hated every second. I probably could have been reasonably good at it, but I would have been miserable and I would never have reached where I am now with my compound.

Third, believe in yourself. In a game where mental consistency and fortitude are king, confidence is queen.

Please list your successes.

I don't think it's important to make a list of events and placements and world records. Instead I assert that one of my greatest successes is holding onto my love of the sport in an increasingly money-driven and performance-driven environment. I also consider it a great success that people come to me with questions or in need of advice, and look to me as a role model for themselves and their children. This is the greatest compliment I get by far. Success for me isn't measured in tournament results or world rankings, it's measured in how I feel at the end of the day. Did I shoot strong, confident shots? Did I help someone with an issue? Did I accomplish everything I set out to do? Did I smile just for the fun of it all? This is success for me.

Jay Barrs

Country: USA
Bow type: Recurve/Target, Field, Indoor

Jay Barrs: Olympic gold medallist, Olympic team silver medallist, 2 times World Field Champion, 3 times National Target Champion, 4 times National Indoor Champion, 15 times National Field Champion.

How did you start in archery?

My parents were both archers and got me involved at the age of five or six.

How many times/years have you represented your country?

From 1986 to 2001.

What motivates you to practise?

I really enjoyed shooting and the better I shot the more I liked it. As a kid I really liked winning trophies and medals; as an adult, I really liked winning trophies and medals.

How many arrows do you shoot a week?

For the four or five years leading up to the 1988 Olympics I was shooting at least 300 arrows a day. Most days were between 400 and 500. If I didn't have a tournament I shot seven days a week. My coach, Dick Tone, wanted me shooting that many for several reasons. It gets you in really good shape. It made me stay on the field for five or six hours a day, which is about the amount of time we were on the field at a tournament. This made me concentrate for long periods of time, just like at a tournament. You will understand what happens to your form and mental game as you get more fatigued and this allows you to work through these issues. Shooting that many arrows builds confidence.

How many hours/times do you spend shooting a day/week?

Zero, except when I am getting ready to shoot Las Vegas. Then I start shooting about thirty arrows a day, four days a week. By Vegas I can shoot sixty to ninety a day.

Do you work? If so, how many hours?

When I was training full-time I worked part-time in the evenings for Cavalier equipment assembling arrow rests and plungers. I could do this at my apartment while I watched TV in the evening from about 8:00 pm to 1:00 am.

How do you deal with the limited time you can spend with family and friends?

Because training was my 'job' I still had time to see family and friends. Most of them shot archery, so I'd also see them on the range.

Do you see a physiotherapist regularly?

No.

Who tunes/looks after your equipment?

Me. That is something the archer should do themselves. How else will you know how to fix something if it goes wrong?

Who coaches you and helps you shoot better. Why do you trust them?

Dick Tone. He was a world-class archer in his day so he knew what it was like to perform at that level. His philosophy of keeping the shot simple and to work on focus, rhythm and timing made sense to me.

What was your most memorable event and why?

That would have to be the 1988 Olympic Games, because I won.

What is your advice to archers wanting to get to the top?

There are no short cuts.

What sayings do you use to help with your archery?

No matter what happens, my mother will still love me.

Jon Shales

Club: 'V' Archery Club
Country: Great Britain
Bow type: Recurve, 46–47lb

How did you start in archery?

My parents were archers so it was natural for me to learn to shoot at a young age.

How many times/years have you represented your country?

I don't remember exactly how many times, but I have shot for Great Britain every year from 1989 to 2012 with the exception of 1992 (my final year at school). That makes it twenty-three years.

What motivates you to practise?

Most of the time I just love to shoot. I like to win. Anybody who says 'winning is not important, it is the taking part that counts' probably never won anything. Therefore, I am motivated to train and prepare to the best of my ability so that I can be confident of my ability in tournament.

How many arrows do you shoot a week?

It's difficult to say as it has varied over the years. I work full-time so this limits the time I have for training. I would probably average between 250 and 800 per week, not including weekends. It all depends on how motivated I am, what part of the shooting season it is and what major tournaments I am training for. I think it is probably more important to shoot a few arrows regularly rather than shooting a high number of arrows with long periods of inactivity in between.

How many hours/times do you spend shooting a day/week?

Probably between one and three hours per day, four times per week, not including weekends.

Do you work? If so, how many hours?

Forty hours.

How do you deal with the limited time you can spend with family and friends?

I think I had a different circle of friends to most young people. Instead of good friends nearby from school, I had many archery friends throughout the country. I just met my friends on the shooting line instead of at home. I definitely missed out on some things but they were replaced with fantastic adventures around the world, so I don't really feel I lost out.

I had to sacrifice some family events to be away shooting, but I think my family understood how important archery was to me and how motivated I was. In general my family don't get upset or hold grudges if I am not there for a birthday. I think I probably saw my family more than somebody moving away to university and finding a job in a different part of the country. I still live in the area where I was born.

Do you see a physiotherapist regularly?

No, although I have found a chiropractor to be helpful from time to time. Twenty-eight years of participating in a physically one-sided sport will have very noticeable effects on physique.

Who tunes/looks after your equipment?

I do it myself. I like to be in control and also to be able to solve equipment issues when there is nobody else to help. It is all about being self-reliant. I am slightly obsessive about some details of equipment, form and preparation. I definitely know some top archers are the same and I expect that it would be a common trait amongst top archers.

Who coaches you and helps you shoot better? Why do you trust them?

Several coaches have had great influence over my shooting. Firstly my father taught me the basics of shooting. Then I worked with Barry and June Farndon, Clive Jeacock, Brian Slayford, Steve Hallard and Ian Simpson. If you keep your mind open you do not need to only have one coach. You can learn from anybody if you think what they are doing would improve your own form. We are surrounded by ideas and inspiration, one just needs to be open-minded enough to realize it.

What was your most memorable event and why?

It has to be the 1998 FITA Field World Archery Championships in Austria for the simple reason that I won the individual men's recurve and the team championship. I worked hard for eight years and the sense of achievement was tremendous, but it was also knowing that for the rest of my life I could say 'I am a World

Jon Shales: represented Great Britain since 1990. World Field Champion with 11 World and European medals.

Champion'. Archery has been a huge part of my life for such a long time that I have many great memories of travelling the world on great adventures with fellow archers who have become my best friends.

What is your advice to archers wanting to get to the top?

Work hard and be dedicated. Listen to everybody as you never know who might have something to say that inspires you, but take care to understand what is good advice and what is not. Be honest, truthful and respectful of your fellow archers. Be honest and truthful to yourself. Without the ability to recognize and admit your own mistakes and weaknesses you will never be able to learn from them and correct them. Be positive and don't waste energy being negative or complaining about things that are either not important or that cannot be changed.

What sayings do you use to help with your archery?

My favourite quote is, 'If you don't know where you are going, any road will take you there'. It comes from a book by Al Henderson. To me it means that, without goals to direct you, it does not matter what you do, you will still wander aimlessly and be unable to realize your dreams.

Juan Carlos Holgado

Club: Compagnie des Archers Lausanne
Country: Switzerland
Bow type: Recurve

How did you start in archery?

My father was an archer and I decided to go to the archery club with him when I was nine years old. I became hooked on this sport that has been my life, work and passion.

How many times/years have you represented your country?

I first joined the national team when I was seventeen and stayed on every year as an archer until 1998. From 1996 to 2001 I was the national coach of the Spanish team.

What motivates you to practise?

To improve myself as an athlete and as a person. I love to challenge my limits by working hard to overcome them and become better and better. I enjoy analysing my challenges and find solutions to my problems.

How many arrows do you shoot a week?

When I was a professional archer (1987–95) I spent on average five to eight hours per day on the sport, six days per week. I could practise between 180 and 500 arrows per day, in one or two sessions. The number of arrows was based on the training plan and the stage of the season.

Do you work? If so, how many hours?

When I was a professional archer I was studying physical education at university. After giving up my professional sporting career I worked as an archery coach.

How do you deal with the limited time you can spend with family and friends?

With good organization, planning and a Monthly Agenda. I had to spend my time practising and studying, which didn't leave much for family and friends. The people in the sports centre became my family and friends. Sacrifices are needed to be a top archer and study at the same time. It took eleven years to finish my university degree, when a normal student takes only five.

Do you see a physiotherapist regularly?

When I was professional, once a week, sometimes twice. Each session took fifty minutes.

Who tunes/looks after your equipment?

I do. I always liked to be responsible for my equipment, to tune it myself and make my own arrows and strings.

Who coaches you and helps you shoot better and why do you trust them?

Juan Carlos Holgado: 2 times Olympian. Olympics team gold medallist. FITA event Director.

I had several coaches: Raimundo Holgado, my father (9 to 12 years old); Antonio Bustamante, my club coach (12–17); Eduardo Jimenez, the national (17–19); Mike King (19–20); Victor Sidurok (21–24); Sheri Rhodes (24–26) and Henri Brand (26–27). For the next two years, until I ceased shooting as a professional archer, I coached myself.

What was your most memorable event and why?

The 1992 Olympic Games in Barcelona, because we won the team gold medal and transformed the sport's profile in Spain.

What is your advice to archers wanting to get to the top?

Practise hard and stay focused. Find motivation for your daily practice and be patient. With work, results will come … sooner or later. The Olympic Games do not come every four years, they are here every day.

What sayings do you use to help with your archery?

'I can do it.' 'Focus on the present.' 'Focus on what you can control.'

Keith Hanlon

Country: Ireland
Bow type: Recurve

How did you start in archery?

My girlfriend was going to try it and asked if I would go along. I loved it from the start and knew I wanted to do archery from there on. So I gave up everything else, including the girl.

How many times/years have you represented your country?

Every year since 1989.

What motivates you to practise?

Making my shot better. Preparing for a tournament. Keeping my bow fitness.

How many arrows do you shoot a week?

It depends on the time of year, but on average 1,200 to 2,000 a week. I find that a volume of arrows a week helps to make the shot more consistent and automatic.

How many hours/times do you spend shooting a day/week?

Three to four hours a day, six days a week.

Do you work? If so, how many hours?

I work at my archery shop, so when it's not busy I shoot.

Keith Hanlon: represented Ireland for more than 17 years. Olympian.

How do you deal with the limited time you can spend with family and friends?

I run my business from home, so I can be with them when needed. All my friends are archers.

Do you see a physiotherapist regularly?

Of late, yes.

Who tunes/looks after your equipment?

I do.

Who coaches you and helps you shoot better? Why do you trust them?

Hans Blum and David O'Brien. I trust them because they can explain why they think I should change something. I know they do it for the right reasons.

What was your most memorable event and why?

The 1996 Olympic Games, to date the only one I managed to get to. An amazing experience.

What is your advice to archers wanting to get to the top?

Find a coach you trust and one you know will help you for the right reasons. Shoot lots of arrows.

What sayings do you use to help with your archery?

'Stick to the plan.' 'Smile and be happy.'

Larry Godfrey

Club: Cleve Archers
Country: Great Britain
Bow type: Recurve

How did you start in archery?

My parents introduced me at the age of nine. It was a family sport.

How many times/years have you represented your country?

I have represented Great Britain more than fifty times in about fourteen years, at international Junior and Senior levels.

What motivates you to practise?

The chance to shoot for perfection. I enjoy shooting arrows. And the social side.

How many arrows do you shoot a week?

About 800, depending on my lifestyle and body condition.

How many hours/times do you spend shooting a day/week?

About three hours a day, six days a week.

Do you work? If so, how many hours?

On average twenty hours a week.

How do you deal with the limited time you can spend with family and friends?

I make time and make sure it's productive and quality.

Larry Godfrey: represented Great Britain for more than 12 years. 3 times Olympian. Winner of numerous World and European medals.

Do you see a physiotherapist regularly?

No.

Who tunes/looks after your equipment?

Myself.

Who coaches you and helps you shoot better and why do you trust them?

I discuss coaching techniques with the head coach, Lloyd Brown, to find what works with me. My dad, John Godfrey, because he's my dad.

What was your most memorable event and why?

Olympic place continental shoot 2004. By winning gold for the first time and getting an Olympic place I started living my long-term dream.

What is your advice to archers wanting to get to the top?

Work hard, listen to your body, listen to your mind, get the right advice.

What sayings do you use to help with your archery?

Trust, power, strength.

Liam Grimwood

Club: Blackthorn Bowmen
Country: Great Britain
Bow type: Compound Unlimited

How did you start in archery?

I attended a summer school course and one of the many sports I tried there was archery. I really enjoyed it straight away and I seemed to be the best there. I joined a club shortly after and have not looked back since.

How many times/years have you represented your country?

I have represented the GB team around forty times, competing every year from 2002 to 2012 in one form or another. I have competed in the cadet, junior, senior outdoor, senior indoor and senior field teams. I also represented team England at the 2010 Commonwealth Games in India.

What motivates you to practise?

I have always aspired to be at the absolute top of this sport and there have been moments when I felt very close to this. I believe that hard work and lots of correct practice is what will get me to the top. More recently, since archery became my job, I have also had to be motivated a little by money. At this stage I don't often enjoy practising, but I love the feeling of winning and that's the key thing that motivates me to train every day.

Liam Grimwood: represented Great Britain for 10 years. FITA Outdoor World silver medallist, Commonwealth Games team gold medallist, IFAA World Field Champion.

How many arrows do you shoot a week?

My training is really tailored to what event I am training for. I certainly don't stick to 200 arrows per day, for example. In mid-season, when I am training hard and have a constant string of tournaments, I may shoot as many as 400 arrows in a given day, but some days I may shoot just sixty arrows. I always make sure I set a goal before every practice session and stick to it. I keep a record of what I do every day and this averages out at roughly 1,000 arrows per week.

How many hours/times do you spend shooting a day/week?

I like to split my shooting up into small sessions as this helps keep my focus. My average day's training would be two sessions of two and a half hours. I normally do this six days per week. I always have at least one day off per week where I try to play golf or catch up with friends. I believe shooting every day of the week does not allow your muscles to recover properly and probably would soon get boring.

Do you work? If so, how many hours?

I quit working full-time as an electrician in 2008. Since then shooting has been my main profession. In addition to my shooting I spend around fifteen hours per week on other projects, including coaching, seminars, Grip Archery products, writing articles and taking care of paperwork.

How do you deal with the limited time you can spend with family and friends?

Competing, travelling and training has certainly been a strain at times. I have a very small family, so it's not too difficult to speak to them on the phone once a week while sitting on an airport floor or at the training field waiting for the rain to stop. As for friends, being so busy means I have completely drifted away from my school friends. I only have three friends outside archery, but the sport has given me hundreds of others I share a common interest with. I would now say that I met some of my best and closest friends through archery.

Do you see a physiotherapist regularly?

No. I have only had one injury in my sixteen years of shooting. I had physio repeatedly while that was healing, but other than that, never.

Who tunes/looks after your equipment?

I maintain and tune all my own equipment. Over the past five years I have been learning how to set up and tune bows properly. As well as improving my scores and consistency, it helps to sell myself for prospective coaching work. All my knowledge of tuning and set-up has been acquired by asking people and through trial and error to find out what works and what doesn't.

Who coaches you and helps you shoot better? Why do you trust them?

I have never really worked with a specific coach, mostly because there are no coaches in the UK that I would trust. I think most compounds at the top level tend to bounce ideas off each other or watch videos of themselves. The main influence on my shooting style would be World Champion Dave Cousins. We have spent a lot of time together over the past few years and he has helped develop certain aspects of my form. I think I trust him because we are such good friends off the field and his credentials speak for themselves.

What is your most memorable event and why?

It has to be making the final at the Las Vegas World Archery Festival. Vegas really is the biggest shoot in the world for compounds and it was probably the most excited I have ever felt while shooting. I did not win but it gave me a great experience and my ultimate goal for the rest of my career is to win that tournament.

What is your advice to archers wanting to get to the top?

Train as hard as you can, but make sure it is the right kind of training. There is a huge amount of resources out there to make sure that your form is consistent and your bow set-up is good. Never underestimate the mental side of the sport. The standard at most World Championships is unbelievably high and the only thing that separates the winners and losers is their mental game.

What sayings do you use to help with your archery?

Try your best in everything you do and never, ever give up or stop trying.

Lucy O'Sullivan

Club: Archers of Jersey
Country: Great Britain
Bow type: Compound

How did you start in archery?

I used to watch my dad shoot and always wanted to do it. I started with a recurve in 2000, but did not get on with it as I would have wanted. I moved to compound and progressed from there.

How many times/years have you represented your country?

More than twenty.

What motivates you to practise?

Wanting to progress in the sport, the social aspects, thinking of the end goal (winning).

Lucy O'Sullivan: represented Great Britain for 6 years.
Bronze medal in Senior event aged 15.

How many arrows do you shoot a week?

I shoot twice a week at university and more than four times a week at home, usually two hours a session. I don't count the number of arrows. I think it is quality, not quantity.

Do you work? If so, how many hours?

I am at university full-time. That means twelve hours of lectures, six hours in the gym and more than six hours working on my dissertation and other things.

How do you deal with the limited time you can spend with family and friends?

I don't get to see them as I am at university. It is hard, so when I go home it is nice to go to archery as a family and relax with them at the end of the day.

Do you see a physiotherapist regularly?

Yes. I have had an injury in my shoulders, due to a rising of my front shoulder, and I have to keep a check on them. My form was poor in 2011, so working with a physio and concentrating on technique helped towards the end of the outdoor season.

Who tunes/looks after your equipment?

My dad, John Dudley and Liam Grimwood, or anyone who is available to help me.

Who coaches you and helps you shoot better? Why do you trust them?

John Dudley, but I don't see him often. So it's my dad when I am home or myself most of the year. It is hard to coach yourself as you can't really assess what you are doing without being filmed, but you have to manage with what is available to you.

What is your most memorable event and why?

Winning the Commonwealth Games Test event against an Indian woman on her home soil. The entire crowd was rooting for her, but I kept my cool and shot really well.

What is your advice to archers wanting to get to the top?

Think about technique. I shoot a back tension release aid because I know that I want to have the best technique in the UK. It is hard, but think about the end goal and what you want to achieve from the sport.

What sayings do you use to help with your archery?

Always think positively. Say you will get a ten and generally your mind will only think about the ten. If you are having a bad day, perhaps because it's windy, think that the shoot is good practice for windy days. Come away from any shoot or practice with one positive thing.

Matthew Gray

Club: Sydney Olympic Park Archers
Country: Australia
Bow type: Hoyt Recurve

How did you start in archery?

In 1979 my father purchased an old bow from a local garage sale.

How many times/years have you represented your country?

Since 1988, many times.

What motivates you to practise?

To continually improve on being better than my previous best. The feeling of shooting a perfect shot. The goal of representing my country at the Olympics.

Matt Grey: represented Australia for 24 years. 3 times Olympian, Commonwealth Games team gold medallist. 2 times Bronze World field medallist.

How many arrows do you shoot a week?

When I was at the Australian Institute of Sport I shot about 1,000 per week. Now, with three children and full-time employment, it's about 600 per week. I manage to increase the volume close to an important event to above 750.

How many hours/times do you spend shooting a day/week?

At the Australian Institute of Sport days it was eight hours a day. It's currently about two hours.

Do you work? If so, how many hours?

I'm with the New South Wales Police Force – Marine Area Command and work thirty-eight hours per week.

How do you deal with the limited time you can spend with family and friends?

Time management. I use a timetable to manage my time for family, work, training and social.

Do you see a physiotherapist regularly?

No.

Who tunes/looks after your equipment?

I have complete control of my equipment.

Who coaches you and helps you shoot better? Why do you trust them?

I had Ki-Sik Lee for the preparations for the 2000 Olympics, but our country lacks quality coaches for the elite level, so I coach myself with video.

What is your most memorable event and why?

Making my first Olympic team in 1996. Shooting the Olympic team record of 253.

What is your advice to archers wanting to get to the top?

They need to set clear goals and ask themselves why they want to be a top competitive archer. (Some archers are doing it for the wrong reason.) Then they can achieve goals that are realistic for the time they have to train or their ability to travel.

What sayings do you use to help with your archery?

'What goes around comes around.' 'Be patient.' 'Enjoy the moment.' 'It's not the end of the world.'

Michael Peart

Club: Deben Archers
Country: Great Britain
Bow type: Compound 10 years, recurve 10 years and counting

How did you start in archery?

On a school trip to a YMCA camp in the Lake District.

Michael Peart: represented Great Britain for more than 16 years in both compound and recurve. Former world No. 2 compound archer.

How many times/years have you represented your country?

I have been an international for eighteen years and appeared more than sixty times.

What motivates you to practise?

It's what I do. It's part of my life, like breathing. I want to get better and never give up.

How many arrows do you shoot a week?

About 1,400 seems to help me shoot my best.

How many hours/times do you spend shooting a day/week?

100–150 arrows, twice a day, six days a week.

Do you work? If so, how many hours?

Three hours coaching a week.

How do you deal with the limited time you can spend with family and friends?

I have fewer friends … and I make the most of what time I do have.

Do you see a physiotherapist regularly?

Yes, I get a bad back.

Who tunes/looks after your equipment?

I do.

Who coaches you and helps you shoot better? Why do you trust them?

Lloyd Brown is my coach. He has coached others to Olympic gold, so I think he knows what he is doing.

What was your most memorable event and why?

Winning the Face2Face shoot in the Netherlands in 1996.

What is your advice to archers wanting to get to the top?

I am here because I never give up. I 'should' have quit many times. You have to train or get coaching from someone at the top. Get help from the inside, as it's almost impossible to come in from the outside. The information needed to get to the top is vast and most of it doesn't appear in books or videos.

What sayings do you use to help with your archery?

One of mine is 'A "great" main bow is worth a million "good" spare bows'.

Morten Bøe

Club: Sandefjord Bueskyttere
Country: Norway
Bow type: Compound

How did you start in archery?

My family introduced me to it when I was four or five. I started competing at ten.

How many times/years have you represented your country?

It's been twenty-six years.

What motivates you to practise?

Self-improvement and hunting for that little extra point. And fun, of course.

How many arrows do you shoot a week?

About 500 in training, plus tournaments. I believe in quality, not quantity.

Morten Bøe: represented Norway for more than 14 years. World team gold medallist and individual bronze medallist.

How many hours/times do you spend shooting a day/week?

About ten to twelve hours a week.

Do you work? If so, how many hours?

I am self-employed, so I have no idea … actually it's between thirty and forty hours a week.

How do you deal with the limited time you can spend with family and friends?

It works out. There aren't any children yet, so there's time to spend.

Do you see a physiotherapist regularly?

No, only when in treatment if I'm injured.

Who tunes/looks after your equipment?

That's Morten B.

Who coaches you and helps you shoot better? Why do you trust them?

There's no specific coach, but I use one for working on the mental approach. We share the same thoughts on how an archer should think, so it's easy to believe in the same things.

What was your most memorable event and why?

I have to choose being on the World Team Championship winning team in China in 2001.

What is your advice to archers wanting to get to the top?

Be patient, methodical, believe in yourself. Be in the present time zone when performing.

What sayings do you use to help with your archery?

Said with a half-smile: 'Give me the confidence to be strong'.

Naomi Folkard

Club: Leamington Spa
Country: Great Britain (England)
Bow type: Recurve

How did you start in archery?

I had a go when I was five at a family Scout camp. I didn't like it, but my dad did. He sought out our local club, did the beginners' course and joined up. A year or so later my mum, my brother and I also joined.

How many times/years have you represented your country?

Sixteen years.

What motivates you to practise?

Shooting well, because I enjoy it. Shooting badly, because I want to put things right. Upcoming competitions. Watching other archers and athletes in other sports excel and win.

How many arrows do you shoot a week?

200 to 300 arrows a day, five to six days a week. This is

Naomi Folkard: 3 times Olympian, numerous medals in indoor and outdoor target and field events, both individual and team.

what feels right for me. I have kept logs over the years and looked to see what gives me the best performances.

How many hours/times do you spend shooting a day/week?
I shoot at a rate of about fifty arrows per hour. I like it to be quality practice, so I don't shoot more than nine arrows an end and I take my time between ends.

Do you work? If so, how many hours?
No, I train full-time.

How do you deal with the limited time you can spend with family and friends?
It's OK, I don't have many friends! That's probably because of my archery. I catch up with friends and family when I can, and make the most of the time I have.

Do you see a physiotherapist regularly?
Yes, usually once a week, but more often if my shoulder is tight.

Who tunes/looks after your equipment?
Me. Greg Hill makes my strings, but I do the centre serving and everything else I do myself.

Who coaches you and helps you shoot better? Why do you trust them?
It's Lloyd Brown right now. I have no choice but to trust them. There are others I trust who comment on my shooting occasionally, because I've had conversations with them and what they say is sensible, true and understandable.

What is your most memorable event and why?
The Athens Olympics. It was my first Olympics and walking down the tunnel into the Panathaniko stadium was amazing – I have goosebumps thinking about it.

What is your advice to archers wanting to get to the top?
Work hard. Be focused. Know what you are going to improve each session. Video yourself and strive for a perfect release.

What sayings do you use to help with your archery?
I have many affirmations that I say to myself when I walk back to the target. These keep me happy, enable me to enjoy my competition and give me permission to be safe to shoot how I can.

Neil Wakelin

Club: Stortford Archery Club
Country: Great Britain
Bow type: Compound Unlimited

How did you start in archery?
My younger brother wanted to do it, so we did a beginners' course along with my dad, who became a coach.

How many times/years have you represented your country?
I was with the GBR Team in 1995 and 1996. I then took a break from archery and came back for 2003–8 and 2010–11.

What motivates you to practise?
I just enjoy the feeling of shooting my perfect shot. I often shoot at 2m on miniature scaled faces as I am always able to feel a perfect shot. I am also motivated to practise every day for three weeks before every international or major event that I want to perform well at, as I know that works for me.

How many arrows do you shoot a week?
I used to shoot 60 arrows a day and noticed an improvement over twice a week. In later years I increased this to 100 arrows a day and noticed a further improvement in consistency and fewer poor/unpredictable

Neil Wakelin: represented Great Britain 1995– 2011. European Field Championships silver medallist, FITA Team World Cup silver medallist.

performances. I have never tried more than this as I work for myself and know that I would be unable (or not prepared) to keep it up.

How many hours/times do you spend shooting a day/week?

My 100 arrows take me about one hour a day.

Do you work? If so, how many hours?

I work for myself as a Chartered Building Surveyor, which means I can have flexible hours and fit my archery practice into my life during quiet times. Since most of my work is in the summer, however, this often means I have plenty of time to practise over winter but very little to practise and mentally prepare when the competition season is in full flow. I turned down a GBR trip in 2008 and all trips in 2009 because I was too busy with my work. It's not always as easy as it might seem to others, juggling my business and archery commitments.

How do you deal with the limited time you can spend with family and friends?

I just see them less and spend less time with them than I would like, but most understand my commitment to archery.

Neil Wakelin's 'memorable place' leader board, Jakarta, 1995.

Do you see a physiotherapist regularly?

No, never.

Who tunes/looks after your equipment?

I do. I would never trust anyone else to do it.

Who coaches you and helps you shoot better? Why do you trust them?

I have no formal coach. I seek advice from international archers I respect when required. My wife Melanie is my main coach in the sense that she keeps me focused and encourages me to practise, especially on the days when I don't feel like it.

What was your most memorable event and why?

The 1995 FITA Outdoor World Target Championships in Jakarta, Indonesia. It was my first year representing Great Britain and I found myself in first place on the huge leader board. It was unexpected and only lasted for a short while, but it was definitely memorable. I shot a PB and qualified seventh, which was way above my expectations at the time. I used this event as my 'memorable place' in a self-hypnosis tape made with the team psychologist later that year. I can still visualize myself shooting on the end boss, in my white shorts and T-shirt in a torrential rainstorm, as if it were yesterday.

What is your advice to archers wanting to get to the top?

Decide how near the top you want to get, then estimate how much time, effort and commitment it will take. Then double or even triple it. If you are still prepared to give up the time, friends and be fully committed, and if after considering all this the thought of achieving your goal still gives you a tingling sensation, then go for it.

What sayings do you use to help with your archery?

'It's not over until the fat lady sings.' 'Just stick the sight in the middle and execute my perfect shot.' Then there is also my last affirmation statement. It is dated 10 October 2005 and is as relevant as the day I set it down: 'Like all the top international archers I execute my shot by building back tension. I enjoy the challenge of executing my perfect shot under testing situations.'

Nichola Simpson

Club: Oxford Archers
Country: Great Britain
Bow type: Compound

How did you start in archery?

My husband was shooting, so I thought I would have a go.

Nichola Simpson at GBS Final. Represented Great Britain for 18 years. Commonwealth Games team gold medallist, 1st in Las Vegas (twice) and 1st in Europe in the same year. Holder of 8 World Master records. DEAN ALBERGA

How many times/years have you represented your country?

My first international was the World Indoor Championships in France in 1993.

What motivates you to practise?

To get better, to work on technique, to win competitions.

How many arrows do you shoot a week?

This varies so much. For indoors it's not so many, as it's hard to get the venues. Outdoors I try to shoot six times a week, normally about 200 or 300 arrows.

Do you work? If so, how many hours?

Twenty hours a week, Monday to Friday.

How do you deal with the limited time you can spend with family and friends?

It was hard when I first started, but the family got used to it and they supported me fully.

Do you see a physiotherapist regularly?

No.

Who tunes/looks after your equipment?

My coach, Ian Simpson.

Who coaches you and helps you shoot better? Why do you trust them?

Ian Simpson, he knows how I shoot and think, and can spot the smallest things I'm doing wrong. He hasn't let me down since I started in 1987.

What was your most memorable event and why?

This is a hard one. My first medal, a silver, at the 1994 European outdoor championships was the first time a lady compounder had won a medal. I won the bronze at the 1995 World Indoors in Birmingham on home ground, and my husband and family were there to watch. I can't miss out winning Las Vegas, the most

prestigious indoor tournament going, twice (2008 and 2009). So it is hard to say just one, as they are all special to me in different ways.

What is your advice to archers wanting to get to the top?

Never give up, believe in yourself, and believe you can be the best.

What sayings do you use to help you with your archery?

Anyone can win, nobody is unbeatable

Nicky Hunt

Club: Deben Archery Club
Country: Great Britain
Bow type: Recurve

How did you start in archery?

My brother tried the sport and found a local club. Soon he and my father were away every weekend at shoots. I wanted to join in too, and started at eleven years old.

How many times/years have you represented your country?

I first shot for England Under 18s at the age of twelve and went on to shoot for Great Britain as a junior. I first made the senior GB team in 2007 with my compound,

Nicky Hunt: Former World No. 1. Double Commonwealth Games gold medallist.

and from 2011 with my recurve. To date, I've represented my country around forty times over fifteen years.

What motivates you to practise?

Goals, goals, goals! I need to know what I'm working towards and how I'm going to get there – why are you at the field today?

How many arrows do you shoot a week?

This varies throughout the season. In the winter (my off season) it's up to 300 arrows a day, six days a week. This time is for ingraining (perhaps new) technique and for building muscle strength and endurance. In the summer this may be between 100 and 200 arrows, six days a week. This is the time for quality practice, as the work has been done.

How many hours/times do you spend shooting a day/week?

Again this really depends on the time of the year. If I'm working technically, I may shoot 100 arrows per hour at short-range blank boss, but if I'm working at distance and for quality, then this may take between sixty and ninety minutes to shoot seventy-two arrows.

Do you work? If so, how many hours?

Currently I am very fortunate to be a full-time archer.

How do you deal with the limited time you can spend with family and friends?

It can be difficult, but at the end of the day it's a choice. I have goals I want to achieve and I know what it takes to get there. I talk through my goals with my family so they can understand.

Do you see a physiotherapist regularly?

This varies. I've been very lucky to never have an archery-related injury, but I have seen physios for maintenance, particularly when I'm training at high intensity, for injury prevention.

Who tunes/looks after your equipment?

I'm always involved in this. I often ask people's opinion. There are a million ways to set your bow up. I think it's really important that an archer gets involved in this as it's part of knowing you've ticked every box for the best performance. But also, what if you have a problem when competing away and the person who normally does it for you isn't there?

Who coaches you and helps you shoot better? Why do you trust them?

Michael Peart taught me to shoot compound. He was a hugely successful compound archer, which proved he knew what he was talking about. I'm coached by GB's Head Coach Lloyd Brown, who also has a long list of successful athletes behind him.

What was your most memorable event and why?

Definitely winning the Commonwealth Games. I had set this as my goal four years before and put everything into achieving my dream. To go to Delhi and win individual and team gold was just amazing. The enormity of the event made it special, being part of 'we are England'. I'd won something that most people in the country can actually relate to.

What is your advice to archers wanting to get to the top?

Set goals, talk to as many people as possible, and don't let anyone tell you that you can't do something. If you don't have a goal then how are you going to achieve? If you want it badly enough, you will get there.

What sayings do you use to help with your archery?

Control the controllables!

Richard Priestman

Club: Nethermoss Archers
Country: Great Britain
Bow type: Recurve

How did you start in archery?

I have been in archery all my life; my father was an active archer.

How many times/years have you represented your country?

Too many to count.

What motivates you to practise?

I always struggled to master my own thoughts and body movements and the challenge was to get the shot I was looking for.

How many arrows do you shoot a week?

I used to shoot five times a week.

How many hours/times do you spend shooting a day/week?

Three hours a day, twenty hours a week.

Do you work? If so, how many hours?

I worked 8:30 to 5:30, five days a week.

How do you deal with the limited time you can spend with family and friends?

I just made the sacrifices. Archery was my social life and my 'holidays'.

Do you see a physiotherapist regularly?

Never.

Who tunes/looks after your equipment?

Myself.

Who coaches you and helps you shoot better? Why do you trust them?

I'm self-taught and used other archers and coaches as a mirror to supply me with the information I needed.

What was your most memorable event and why?

Shooting a FITA 25m 589 in the 1991 World Indoor Championships and being in first place.

What is your advice to archers wanting to get to the top?

If I could shoot good, anyone can!

What sayings do you use to help with your archery?

I was once told by the husband of a top archer that 'You will never be any good'.

Roy Nash

Club: Bowmen of Bruntwood
Country: Great Britain
Bow type: Recurve

How did you start in archery?

I started when I was five. My mother initially showed an interest and she could only participate if she took me along with her. The local club was not keen on someone so young starting to learn, but after a little persuasion they eventually relented.

How many times/years have you represented your country?

I started representing Great Britain in 1990 as a junior at fifteen and continued at both junior and senior levels until I went to university at eighteen. I came back to competition in 2000 to make the 2001 World Indoor Championships, and was a regular member of the team until 2007.

What motivates you to practise?

It is a combination of three things:

- Shot perfection: refining the technique to enable good grouping and scoring.
- Fulfilling my potential and living up to my goals: without practice, I'll never get to the heights I desire.
- My need to be the best: I hate losing. I accept being beaten by someone who has shot better than me, but hate it when I lose due to errors I made. The only way to prevent the errors is to practise.

How many arrows do you shoot a week?

I aim to shoot about 700 per week, including competitions. I preferred to concentrate on quality rather than quantity, but would frequently change my training depending on the needs of my training plan.

How many hours/times do you spend shooting a day/week?

Time is not a factor in my shooting. If it takes me eight hours to accomplish my training goal for the day, then eight hours it is. Similarly, if it only takes one hour,

Roy Nash (centre): represented Great Britain Junior 1990–94, Senior 1993–4 and 2001–7. European team silver medallist. Former ranked 10th in the World.

I'll pack up and go home or do something else. I'm a big believer in setting a goal for the day and working towards that rather than setting a time constraint on getting it done and facing that pressure as well as the issue at hand.

Do you work? If so, how many hours?

I work forty hours a week. I have managed to get a shift pattern that allows me to work only Monday to Thursday, but this leads to long days and prevents sustained practice after work through either general fatigue or simply lack of light. On the plus side, I have three whole days of uninterrupted practice/competition.

How do you deal with the limited time you can spend with family and friends?

In my case, it was simple. I was engaged to someone who is just as committed to archery. It is tough, though. Archery is a hobby/sport/lifestyle I have always wanted to do, and I have never seen those commitments as priority above what I wanted to accomplish in the sport, with the exception of my immediate family. Most of my friends are within the sport itself and I meet them frequently at competitions/training. I have never felt that this has been a detriment to my life and wouldn't change it for the world.

Do you see a physiotherapist regularly?

I used to. While on the GB team I needed to visit a physiotherapist on an almost regular basis, mainly due to technique changes that were not properly executed by the head coach at the time. Since leaving the team, I

Roy Nash with Simon Needham.

have never had to see a physiotherapist, but that is not to say that what they do is not valuable. Their knowledge of physiology and muscles can help an archer to develop their technique by training the correct muscle groups and ensure no future problems occur.

Who tunes/looks after your equipment?

Me.

Who coaches you and helps you shoot better? Why do you trust them?

Currently nobody. All my achievements, however, have to be dedicated to a team of four people. Both my mother and my late father were instrumental in my shooting. They coached me, financed me and were the sounding board for many problems and issues that arose as I grew up. My father attended all of my competitions and training sessions. This gave me an incredible advantage in competition. He was not an accredited coach, but I would argue that he knew more about archery than many official coaches. His delivery of real time feedback in a non-judgemental way allowed me to make changes while the impact could still be felt in the competition. I still miss this to this day. The other two people are Barry Farndon and his late wife June, without whose tireless efforts, brilliant coaching and overall support I would have stopped shooting when I was thirteen. They taught me how to be a better archer and more importantly a better human being.

What was your most memorable event and why?

The 2003 Olympic test event in Athens was not my most successful, but the most memorable. After narrowly missing out on an automatic space for the 2004 Athens Olympics, I was chosen to attend the pre-Olympic test tournament. I had the chance to encounter what it is like for an athlete at an Olympic games, the holding camp, the media interest, the standard of the competition to expect. It was memorable because I was shooting well yet I hadn't previously grasped the concept of what was needed to get to the Olympics. With the help of Alison Williamson and Simon Needham, I saw what I needed to do if I too wanted to get to the Olympics. They gave me the drive to make the necessary changes to my lifestyle, training and overall attitude if I were to compete at a Games. It was also enlightening to see that Simon, while giving the impression of being organized, neat and tidy, was living a lie in Athens. On his side of the hotel room everything was neat and in its place and the bed was made. The other side of the bed, however, was another matter: he just dumped his clothes there and hid them from view. I removed that particular task from my 'Must change list'.

What is your advice to archers wanting to get to the top?

Work to a plan. Work out what you think you need to concentrate on within your shooting: fitness, technique, mental, equipment and so on. Decide on the importance of each element and work through them systematically. Keep a record of your progress, good or bad, to enable you to learn from your successes and mistakes. Find someone you trust to advise you. An accredited coach may not necessarily be the best blend with your learning/development style. Sometimes an experienced archer who has already attained the level you aspire to may be better for your progression than someone who has qualified to coach. The most important thing is to find someone who can speak honestly and gives you options rather than instructions.

What sayings do you use to help with your archery?

Always follow the 6 Ps: Proper Preparation Prevents P*ss Poor Performance. A wise man (actually Simon Needham) once told me, 'You can't beat a lucky archer! So never wish a competitor "good luck". Wish them good shooting, but never good luck.' I don't know whether this is true, but why tempt fate?

Sandrine Vandionant

Club: Nîmes
Country: France
Bow type: Compound

How did you start in archery?

My father used to shoot.

Sandrine Vandionant: represented France as Junior and Senior for 15 years at both compound and recurve. Many medals in both target and field.

Sandrine Vandionant with Michele Frangelli.

How many times/years have you represented your country?
I began shooting for the national team as a junior in 1997.

What motivates you to practise?
The pleasure of making progress and the possibility of winning.

How many arrows do you shoot a week?
On average I shoot between 700 and 900 arrows per week, but it can also be more or less. I try to focus on quality. If I'm tired I shoot fewer than 500 arrows per week.

How many hours/times do you spend shooting a day/week?
Between two and four hours a day.

Do you work? If so, how many hours?
I work for an average of fifteen hours a week for the French national federation, principally teaching coaches.

How do you deal with the limited time you can spend with family and friends?
It's not simple, especially as I divide my time between France and Italy. I don't programme a lot in advance and try to enjoy time with friends and family whenever I can.

Do you see a physiotherapist regularly?
I see a physio about every two months, or more if I have a problem.

Who tunes/looks after your equipment?
Me.

What was your most memorable event and why?
The FITA World Championship in New York ... just because it was New York. I was able to shoot in Central Park, which is a magic place, and the atmosphere with my teammates was fantastic.

What is your advice to archers wanting to get to the top?
Be patient and have fun.

What sayings do you use to help with your archery?
It translates as something like: 'Weak people find excuses, strong people find solutions'.

Suvaporn Anutaraporn

Club: Indy Archery Club
Country: Thailand
Bow type: Compound

How did you start in archery?
I started in April 2009.

How many times/years have you represented your country?
In 2010 and 2011.

What motivates you to practise?
Shooting makes me happy.

How many arrows do you shoot a week?
More than 1,000 a week, because I enjoy it.

How many hours/times do you spend shooting a day/week?
Four to six hours a day.

Do you work? If so, how many hours?
No, I don't.

How do you deal with the limited time you can spend with family and friends?
I practise at the national team's field from 10 am to 4 pm. When that's over it's family time.

Do you see a physiotherapist regularly?
No.

Who tunes/looks after your equipment?
My coach in Thailand, Lerdporn Kanchan (we call him Mr Yod).

Who coaches you and helps you shoot better? Why do you trust them?

Mel Nichole and Lerdporn Kanchan.

What was your most memorable event and why?

At the Asian Grand Prix in 2010 I had badly injured my left arm but still won the bronze medal.

What is your advice to archers wanting to get to the top?

Train hard and don't give up.

What sayings do you use to help with your archery?

Fight until the last arrow.

Tapani Kalmaru

Club: Castle Archers
Country: Wales and Great Britain
Bow type: Compound

How did you start in archery?

I first had a go on holiday when I was ten, popping a few balloons. I then nagged my mother for months on end until she decided that it might as well be Castle Archers who looked after me for three hours every Friday night while she attended a university course. I was an archer in no time.

How many times/years have you represented your country?

I have been shooting for Wales since 2004 and for Great Britain since 2005, both at junior and senior level. I first represented GB at the European Field Archery Championships in Rogla, Slovenia, where I won a bronze medal in the junior men's barebow category.

What motivates you to practise?

Money, better contracts, pride, the endless pursuit of

Tapani Kalmaru: represented Great Britain since 2005.

perfection and, above all else, the ambition and dream of being the world's best archer.

How many arrows do you shoot a week?

I'm a firm believer in quality not quantity. I often shoot around 100 arrows blank bale every couple of days with alternate days spent at the range, where I shoot two or three rounds of 70m/50m/18m. If I'm working on my field archery I spend a few hours checking my sight tape at various distances. This way I can make sure my sight tape is spot on. It gives me a range of difficulties when changing target sizes and distances and this in turn prepares me better for a field shoot. In a very good week that would be about 1,000 arrows, but university takes priority. If I can't get down to the range one night because I have some Uni work to do, I'll try to shoot some blank bale, but this doesn't always happen.

How many hours/times do you spend shooting a day/week?

When practising I'm totally invested in that session. I will only go to a session to work on something, otherwise what's the point? This means that I train for roughly three hours a session. If I'm on my own, I tend to shoot at around 100 arrows an hour.

Do you work? If so, how many hours?

University takes up a lot of hours. This year I've had to pay my own way, which means a part-time job. My work hours, including lectures and other studies, can exceed fifty hours a week but they generally average out to around thirty-five to forty hours.

How do you deal with the limited time you can spend with family and friends?

Fortunately I live with my friends. We attend lectures together and make time for a night out every so often, so that hasn't been an issue. Most of my family also go to archery, so I see my mother and father almost every weekend.

Do you see a physiotherapist regularly?

I seem to be very lucky there. My housemate and his partner are both studying sport massage at Uni, so if I need any help with an injury or just a little loosening up they are always there for me. My mother is also studying sport massage on an evening course at Uni. Lucky me.

Who tunes/looks after your equipment?

I tend not to trust anyone with this sort of thing. I often ask people like Liam Grimwood and Chris White for their opinions and take their advice. But as for letting someone else do it for me, I couldn't give anyone that responsibility.

Who coaches you and helps you shoot better? Why do you trust them?

I've had a lot of help over the years and there have been many people I could call my coach. In 2004, when I started representing Wales, I asked Marian Howells to be my coach. Together with Ray Howells, she got me to where I am today by advising, setting training programmes and motivating me to carry on shooting. Since changing to compound in 2007, a lot of my advice has come from fellow archers and my motivation has come more from within. The continuing support of my family has always reassured me that one day I will achieve my goals.

What was your most memorable event and why?

The one that first comes to mind has to be the Commonwealth Games. As well as being the most recognizable competition I have been to, meaning that people outside archery appreciate it, it was also the first time in years I actually achieved my goal. I have always tended to aim above my current level and this seems to drag me up to a higher standard and allows me to better myself. My goal for this tournament was to reach 700, make the top eight and get on television, and I did this with some ease. The reason this sticks out, however, is because on the night before our qualifying round I told my room-mate Geraint Thomas, 'I'm going to shoot 700 tomorrow', and went to sleep.

What is your advice to archers wanting to get to the top?

Constantly set goals. Goals are what define you and guide you to where you want to be. Be smart in your goal approach and plan your way to achieving them, even the little ones.

What sayings do you use to help with your archery?

'Aim for the moon. If you miss you land among the stars.'

Vic Wunderle

Country: USA
Bow type: Recurve

How did you start in archery?

I began shooting archery at the age of five. My first bow was made from a limb off the willow tree in my back yard. My father taped a piece of cloth around the end of an arrow so I couldn't hurt anyone. I would run around the yard all day shooting at trees. A couple of years later my father took me to an archery tournament. I won the under-twelve age category, but I

Vic Wunderle: 3 times Olympian, Sydney 2000 individual silver and team bronze. Numerous medals in target and field around the world since 1991.

was too young to read the scoreboard and my father would not tell me because he was afraid I would be too excited the remainder of the day. At the end of the tournament, the awards were given out. All the kids got participation medals except me. I felt a little sad because I was left out. Then the awards were given for third place, second place, and finally my name was called. I had won my very first tournament. From there I went on to many other local, state sectional, national and finally world titles.

How many times/years have you represented your country?

I have represented the USA in international competitions countless times since 1991 and counting.

What motivates you to practise?

Archery can be fun and enjoyable and it gives my mind a chance to relax and escape. Also the will to win and succeed is motivating.

How many arrows do you shoot a week?

This depends on what I am training for, where I am at in my training cycle, physical limitations and how badly I want to win. The same factors also affect the hours I spend shooting.

Do you work? If so, how many hours?

I work a variety of odd jobs that are all archery-related and the amount varies greatly depending on the season and events that are going on.

How do you deal with the limited time you can spend with family and friends?

Luckily most of my family and friends understand and accept my archery travelling lifestyle. It does, however, make it very difficult to maintain relationships when travelling a lot. Many of my closer friendships have developed through archery because these are the people I see frequently and have lots in common with. I have many great friends around the world but fewer at home than when I began my travelling lifestyle.

Do you see a physiotherapist regularly?

No.

Who tunes/looks after your equipment?

I do.

Who coaches you and helps you shoot better? Why do you trust them?

Currently I am working with Dick Tone as my primary coach. Other great coaches and friends lend help and support when needed. It is easiest to work with someone when you believe they are good at what they do and their goals align with yours. When you know a coach is looking out for your best interests it is easy to trust that person.

What was your most memorable event and why?

The 2000 Olympics, because of its grand scale and level of achievement. In essence, it has defined how many people view my life and archery career. The first Junior World Archery Championships I competed in and won is also very memorable. All of the experiences there were new and exciting. It taught me a lot about competition and about myself.

What is your advice to archers wanting to get to the top?

Enjoy shooting and practising. It is easier to be successful if you love what you are doing. There is no guarantee of success and you may succeed or you may not. If you have enjoyed shooting along the way, it is time well spent. If you succeed in getting to the top, then that is the icing on the cake.

Viktor Ruban

Club: Dinamo
Country: Ukraine
Bow type: Recurve

How did you start in archery?

I was an athlete for two years, but I was not happy and my friends suggested archery.

Viktor Ruban: represented Ukraine for more than 8 years. 3 times Olympian. Olympic gold and bronze medals.

How many times/years have you represented your country?

I took up the sport in 1996 and first represented my country in 2001.

What range of things motivates you to go and practise?

My next training session and to perform well in competition. Also my family, they too want this experience for me.

How many arrows do you shoot a week?

I think that 1,500 arrows a week are enough to get results and maintain the competitive rhythm.

How many hours/times do you spend shooting a day/week?

About five hours a day.

Do you work? If so, how many hours?

No.

How do you deal with the limited time you can spend with family and friends?

I would like to spend more time with my family and friends but my complex schedule makes this very difficult. But every time I go on a trip our team goes together and I am very happy.

Do you see a physiotherapist regularly?

No, but I see a massage therapist when I'm at the main training camp.

Yura Kozhevnikov: represented Russia for 11 years.

Who tunes/looks after your equipment?

I do.

Who coaches you and helps you shoot better? Why do you trust them?

I trust my coach, Lyudmila Prokopenko Tsezarivna, completely. She has had good results with many other sportsmen.

What is your advice to archers wanting to get to the top?

If you know exactly what goal you want to accomplish it can be done.

What sayings do you use to help with your archery?

I tell myself every day that I could win the coming tournament. It helps to overcome the psychological pressure at the competition.

Yura Kozhevnikov

Club: Trans-Baikal Region Archery Federation
Country: Russia
Bow type: Compound

How did you start in archery?

I started shooting while I was at school in 2000.

How many times/years have you represented your country?

Eleven years.

How many arrows do you shoot a week?

3,000 arrows a week.

How many hours/times do you spend shooting a day/week?

Three to four hours a day.

Do you work? If so, how many hours?

I work as a coach when I'm not training.

How do you deal with the limited time you can spend with family and friends?

I spend every evening with my girlfriend.

Do you see a physiotherapist regularly?

No.

Who tunes/looks after your equipment?

I set up all my equipment.

Who coaches you and helps you shoot better? Why do you trust them?

I have been with my coaches for twelve years.

What is your advice to archers wanting to get to the top?

Exercise every day and everything will come.

What sayings do you use to help with your archery?

'Don't be sorry.' 'In the heat of the shot, don't be afraid.'

Ian Simpson [Stumpy]

Club: Oxford Archers
Country: Great Britain

What areas of archery do you coach?

All bow types (including longbow and barebow).

How did you start coaching in archery?

I wanted to help other archers and myself.

How many years have you been coaching?

About twenty-six years.

What helps you motivate archers to practise?

Their goals.

How many arrows do you want you archers to shoot a week?

The target is at least fifty quality arrows per session.

How many hours/times would you expect your archers to spend training a day/week?

You need at least five days per week to be a good archer and seven days a week to be a great archer.

What training do you recommend to get your archers to their best?

Reversals, short distance, blank boss, volume shooting, running, cycling, speed drills, shooting games, blank boss when making changes. Fitness is so important for body and mind. Practising head-to-heads and score rounds.

Do you work? If so, how many hours?

As few hours as possible. Like all humans I am naturally lazy and greedy.

How do you recommend archers deal with the limited time they can spend with family and friends?

Remind them that one day all the competition and fame will go, but their family and friends will always be there.

Do you recommend your archers to visit a physiotherapist regularly?

This is a good idea as it relaxes the mind as well as the muscles.

Who tunes/looks after your archers' equipment?

It's good for them to look after their own, but I do get involved.

Ian Simpson: UK archery coach for both recurve and compound.

What are the main reasons that archers trust their coaches?

Knowledge, experience, friendship, general guidance.

What was the most memorable event with your archers and why?

The 2004 Olympic Games, the ultimate dream of every coach.

What is your advice to archers wanting to get to the top?

I tell them that when Beckham scores a goal he is kissed and hugged by his teammates and thousands cheer. When an archer does well there is nothing. I tell them to praise themselves as this is the only praise they'll get.

What sayings do you use to help archers with their archery?

'Live the lie, because on the day the lie will become the truth.'

Which archers do you particularly admire?

My wife, Richard Priestman, Simon Terry, Rick McKinney, Chris White and Natalia Valeeva.

INDEX